PENGUIN AFRICAN LIBRARY
*Edited by Ronald Segal*

## The Africa

Basil Davidson is a
books and writings                          languages. His
books include *Repor        Southern Africa* (1952), *The
African Awakening* (1955 : dealing mainly with the Belgian
Congo and Angola), *Which Way Africa?* (3rd revised edition
1971 : Penguin African Library), *Old Africa Rediscovered*
(1959), *Black Mother* (1961), *The African Past* (1964 : also
in the Penguin African Library), *Africa in History* (1968),
*The Liberation of Guiné* (1969 : Penguin African
Library), *In the Eye of the Storm : Angola's People* (1972),
and *Black Star : The Life and Times of Kwame Nkrumah*
(1973). He has been visiting professor of African History at
the Universities of Ghana and California, and in 1972 was
visiting professor of International Relations at the University
of Edinburgh.

BASIL DAVIDSON

# The Africans

## An Entry to Cultural History

*Penguin Books*

Penguin Books Ltd, Harmondsworth,
Middlesex, England
Penguin Books Australia Ltd, Ringwood,
Victoria, Australia

First published by Longmans Green & Co. Ltd 1969
Published in Penguin Books 1973
Copyright © Basil Davidson, 1969

Made and printed in Great Britain by
Hazell Watson & Viney Ltd, Aylesbury, Bucks
Set in Linotype Plantin

To
AMILCAR CABRAL
for the past
yet less than
for the future

Civilization is the humanization of man in society

MATTHEW ARNOLD in
*The Oxford English Dictionary*

# Contents

*Contents*

# Illustrations

# Acknowledgements

I wish to record my thanks to the trustees of the William A. Cadbury Trust for crucial help at a time when this book was little more than a programme of research; to Dr J. A. Goody, Mr Thomas Hodgkin, Mr Robin Horton, Mr Raymond Kunene, Dr Godfrey Lienhardt and Professor Roland Oliver for reading my text and giving constructive advice, and similarly to my publishers in London and Boston; to Dr J. S. Spiegler for allowing me to read his valuable thesis on nationalist thought in French-speaking West Africa; to Mr Paul Strand and Mr Werner Forman for their generosity with photographs; to Mrs Caroline Sassoon for her enthusiastic care in illustration; and publicly on this occasion to my wife, because this book's road has been a particularly long and arduous one through years of work and travel, for her unfailing interest and indispensable encouragement.

I am also grateful to the following for permission to reproduce copyright material: author's agents and the Estate of Roy Campbell for an extract from 'Holism' from *Collected Poems* (*Adamastor*) by Roy Campbell; the Clarendon Press for an extract from *Swahili Poetry* trans. by L. Harries, an extract from *Divinity and Experience, The Religion of the Dinka* by Godfrey Lienhardt, an extract from *Karimojong Politics* by Neville Dyson-Hudson, and an extract from *The Heroic Recitations of the Bahima of Ankole* by H. F. Morris; Faber & Faber Ltd for an extract from *Search for Security: An Ethno-psychiatric Study of Rural Ghana* by M. J. Field; International African Institute for extracts from *Africa* magazine, 'The Political Function of the Poro' by K. Little (xxxv.4 1965 and xxxvi.1 1966), 'The Kalahari Ekine Society' by R. Horton (xxxiii.2 1963), 'Ritual Man in Africa' by R. Horton (xxxiv.2 1964), and an extract from *Conversations with Ogotêmmeli* by Marcel Griaule;

author and Longmans Green & Co. Ltd for an extract from 'al-Haji Umar of Kete Krachi' translated by B. G. Martin from *Salaga: The Struggle for Power* by J. Braimah and J. R. Goody; Routledge & Kegan Paul Ltd for an extract from *History of the German People at the Close of the Middle Ages* by J. Janssen; Routledge & Kegan Paul and Frederick A. Praeger Inc. for an extract from *Witchcraft and Sorcery in East Africa* by J. Middleton and E. H. Winter.

All drawings in the text not otherwise acknowledged are by Caroline Sassoon, who made them for this book.

Other drawings in the text: p. 64, from Godfrey Lienhardt, *Divinity and Experience*, Oxford, Clarendon Press, 1961; p. 80, from Neville Dyson-Hudson, *Karimojong Politics*, Oxford, Clarendon Press, 1966; p. 175, redrawn from Marcel Griaule, *Conversations with Ogotêmmeli*, O.U.P. for the International African Institute, 1965; p. 234, from Peter Morton-Williams, 'An Outline of the Cosmology and Cult Organization of the Oyo Yoruba', *Africa*, xxxiv.3, 1964. The map was drawn by John Flower.

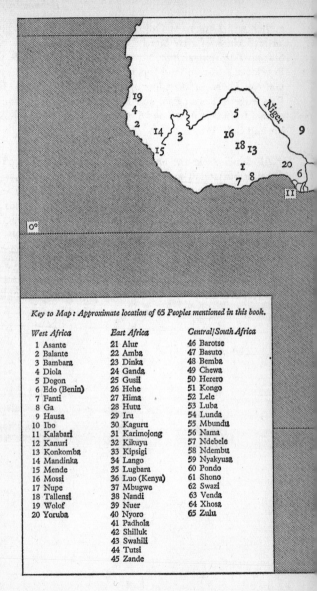

Key to Map : *Approximate location of 65 Peoples mentioned in this book.*

| *West Africa* | *East Africa* | *Central/South Africa* |
|---|---|---|
| 1 Asante | 21 Alur | 46 Barotse |
| 2 Balante | 22 Amba | 47 Basuto |
| 3 Bambara | 23 Dinka | 48 Bemba |
| 4 Diola | 24 Ganda | 49 Chewa |
| 5 Dogon | 25 Gusii | 50 Herero |
| 6 Edo (Benin) | 26 Hehe | 51 Kongo |
| 7 Fanti | 27 Hima | 52 Lele |
| 8 Ga | 28 Hutu | 53 Luba |
| 9 Hausa | 29 Iru | 54 Lunda |
| 10 Ibo | 30 Kaguru | 55 Mbundu |
| 11 Kalabari | 31 Karimojong | 56 Nama |
| 12 Kanuri | 32 Kikuyu | 57 Ndebele |
| 13 Konkomba | 33 Kipsigi | 58 Ndembu |
| 14 Mandinka | 34 Lango | 59 Nyakyusa |
| 15 Mende | 35 Lugbara | 60 Pondo |
| 16 Mossi | 36 Luo (Kenya) | 61 Shono |
| 17 Nupe | 37 Mbugwe | 62 Swazi |
| 18 Tallensi | 38 Nandi | 63 Venda |
| 19 Wolof | 39 Nuer | 64 Xhosa |
| 20 Yoruba | 40 Nyoro | 65 Zulu |
|  | 41 Padhola |  |
|  | 42 Shilluk |  |
|  | 43 Swahili |  |
|  | 44 Tutsi |  |
|  | 45 Zande |  |

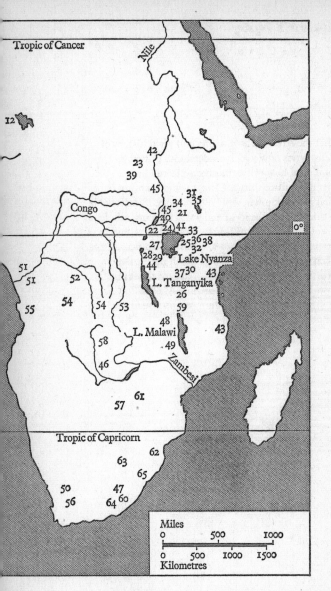

Tropic of Cancer

Nile

12

42

23
39

45

Congo

31
35
34
21
45
40
24 41 33
22
27      25 36 38
28 29      32
44      Lake Nyanza
37 30      43
L. Tanganyika
26
59

51
51
52
55      54      54      53

48
L. Malawi
58      49
46      Zambesi

61
57

Tropic of Capricorn

62
63
65

50      47
56      64 60

Miles
0            500            1000

0      500      1000      1500
Kilometres

0°

13

# Author's Note

That the Africans have a long and vivid history of their own is now widely understood. But what manner of history has this been? Here I have attempted three things. First, to offer a summary of what is now known, or what it now seems reasonable to think, about the ideas and social systems, religions, moral values, magical beliefs, arts and metaphysics of a range of African peoples, chiefly in tropical Africa. Then to consider the ways in which these cultures have grown and changed from distant times until now. Lastly, to fit these aspects of African civilization into their modern perspective as the connected parts of a living whole.

# Prologue: A Scattered Wisdom

Once upon a time Ananse Kokrofu, the great spider of venerable memory, grew bothered about the state of wisdom in the world. People were not looking after it properly. So far as Ananse could tell from his experience of mankind, which was not small, a great deal of wisdom was getting lost. Yet even if living people lacked the wit to respect wisdom as they should there would be future generations, Ananse argued, who would be glad to use every bit they could. So he made up his mind to collect all the wisdom in the world, and store it for safe keeping at the top of a tree.

In due course, the elders say, Ananse did indeed finish collecting the world's wisdom. He packed all this in a gourd and began to climb a tall palm. Halfway to the top he got into difficulties: he had tied on the gourd in front of him, and it hampered his climbing. At this point his son Ntikuma, who was looking up from below, called in a shrill young voice: 'Father, if you really had all the wisdom in the world up there with you, you would have tied that gourd on your back.' This was too much even for Ananse, who was tired from long labour. He untied the gourd in a fit of temper and threw it down. It broke and the wisdom was scattered far and wide. After a while people who had learned their lesson came and gathered in their own gourds whatever each could find; it is this that explains why a few people have much wisdom, some have a little, but many have none at all.

I think that anyone trying to write about the nature and growth of African civilization will quickly come to feel, as I did, that Ntikuma might well have held his peace on that occasion. The gourds of wisdom about the African past are large in number, even multitudinous, but few of them hold very much, while many prove on near inspection to contain little or nothing. But it is also true that the last twenty years or so have proved especially fruitful in the genuine collecting of wisdom about Africa in two great fields of enterprise: those of historical discovery and sociological research. The consequence is that we can be better informed today than any previous generation. If we cannot see the whole truth, we can see much more than before, and with an increasing sense of what is still missing. Ananse, one feels, would not be entirely disappointed with us. After all, he had good cause to understand that nobody can know everything.

Other books have shown the outline of African history as modern research now understands it. In these pages I am concerned almost not at all with questions of chronology. This book is about a new synthesis of cultural patterns and values that has lately begun to emerge from the labour of many workers in several disciplines, and notably in social anthropology. This new understanding of the civilizations of the Africans is exciting for a number of reasons. It points to a totality of experience within the scope of economic and political structure, ideology and religion, witchcraft and the arts of everyday life. It offers an interpretation of Africa that is startlingly different from views about Africa and Africans widely current in the past, and sometimes current still today.

The difficulties in making and presenting any such synthesis are obvious enough. Only a minority of peoples have been adequately studied, perhaps not more than fifty. Much of what is known about them comes from recent or fairly recent work. Inferring a reality more distant in time must be especially tricky when written records are few or unreliable. For a long while it appeared to me that no such project could succeed. Then I chanced in 1962 on the Frankforts' *Intellectual Adventure of Ancient Man* where some vivid contrasts are drawn between the mood and temper of the ancient Egyptian and Mesopotamian civilizations, the one so much a product of 'eternal precedent', the other so greatly a matter of 'imposed control'. These civilizations could, it appeared, be given a character: as for example in Mesopotamian sayings such as 'Workmen without a foreman are waters without a canal inspector', or 'Peasants without a bailiff are a field without a ploughman'. Something of the kind, I began to think, could also be done for Africa.

So in a hopefully Ananse-like way I went on voyaging up and down the continent, asking questions and gathering whatever wisdom I could find in the written word, in travels off the beaten track, in conversations under cottonwoods and various other encounters with the wise of different lands. What manner of civilization was this of the Africans, what were its worth and contribution? What were its dynamics of change, its achievements and its limits? Does its past still tie up closely with its present, and, if so, how and why? The answers, such as I have so far found them, are set forth here.

Supporting notes and references are listed under page numbers at the end of the book. I have also added a short bibliography which includes the writers from whom I have chiefly learned, and to whom my thanks are chiefly due.

# Part One: Africa's World

Behold, I have set the land before you. . . .

*Deuteronomy* 1, 8

And ye shall divide the land . . . for an inheritance
among your families . . . according to the tribes of
your fathers ye shall inherit.

*Numbers* xxxiii, 54

# I  'Just plain nonsense...' and after

At one of their gatherings of 1861 the distinguished Victorians of London's Ethnographical Society found themselves with a delicate problem. They had invited a foreigner, a gentleman from France, to speak on travels through the unexplored forests of equatorial Africa. And why not? They were men who took pride in a liberal breadth of international outlook. Unfortunately this French gentleman, this M. du Chaillu for whom their shocked *Transactions* could afterwards find no Christian name, had not proved satisfactory. In discussing a horde of largely naked savages called the Mpongwe, M. du Chaillu had appeared to suggest that these natives might be other than they seemed. He had gone so far as to argue for certain redeeming features. He had even spoken with some respect of their religion.

It was understandable that the ethnographers should have felt a need to set matters right in the wake of such remarks. They lived in dangerous Darwinian years when the frontiers and even the foundations of proper and accepted belief had begun to take a serious buffeting. There were even moments, if you took a long view, when it seemed as though there were no longer any natural and reliable divide to save the members of the Ethnographical Society from a distant origin in beings so unfortunate as those they called the 'tawny Bosjeman' and the 'leather-skinned Hottentot'. Carried to logical conclusions, such opinions could only be subversive of established law and order. Feeling that something must be done, the ethnographers called in Captain Richard Burton. He, they knew, could be relied upon to use his great authority in the proper way.

Captain Burton did not let them down. This already famous explorer began by offering a redeeming African feature to match M. du Chaillu's. He opined that 'an abnormal development of adhesiveness, in popular language a peculiar power of affection, is the brightest spot in the negro character'. Yet this was about as much as could sensibly be said for the natives *he* had known. M. du Chaillu, they must believe, had been lucky: he had run into a better lot than usual. Compared with them, however, there was the 'superior degeneracy of the eastern tribes', not to mention all the others one could think of. No doubt the Mpongwe might have some sort of religious belief. It might also be true that 'the religion of the Africans is ever interesting to those of a maturer faith, as the study of childhood is pleasing to those of riper years'. But one ought not to go too far.

Not only, in Burton's view, had Africans failed to develop from the primitive to the less primitive: they had also reached a point of helplessness at which, if left to themselves, they would never do any better. In that great schedule of hierarchical progress from savagery to civilization imagined by the more conservative Victorians, with Europe at the peak and zenith of the line, the Africans were simply not in the race. Perhaps they had once set out, though this was more than doubtful: if so, they had long since stopped running. Exactly why was not known. But the reason, whatever it might be, was generally agreed to lie in some fatal deficiency of their nature. Some experts thought it was a matter of the African brain's being too small for civilized development. Others argued that the root of the trouble lay not so much in brain size as in diminished frontal lobes, or an insufficiently reliable 'supragranular layer of cortex'. The results, in any case, were understood to be deplorable. Once an African had become adult, Burton opined in a view widely accepted, 'his mental development is arrested, and thenceforth he grows backwards instead of forwards'.

Defended by their travellers, these Victorians held firm to their hierarchies of racial progress and found plenty of evidence to fortify them. Returning from the upper Nile in 1866 Sir Samuel Baker assured them that the African 'mind is as stagnant as the morass which forms its puny world', and other explorers said much the same. It followed that the evolutionists had clearly got things wrong; and there was quiet satisfaction among the more respectable members of the Ethnographical Society, in that same year of 1866, when the impetuous Dean Farrar proposed once and for all to set the record straight by dividing humanity into three great classes, 'the Savage races, the Semi-civilized races, and finally the two Civilized races' – the latter categories, of course, including none like the Mpongwe.

We are generally a long way from such views. But they are worth recalling if only for their perfectly dramatic contrast with those of modern science. In 1896 a well-known teacher of philosophy at Durham University, F. B. Jevons, published an *Introduction to the History of Religion* which became a standard work. Seventy years later a modern anthropologist of Africa, among the most eminent of his day, could summarize current opinion on Jevons's book by describing it as a 'collection of absurd reconstructions, unsupportable hypotheses and conjectures, wild speculations, suppositions and assumptions, inappropriate analogies, misunderstandings, and misinterpretations, and, especially in what he wrote about totems, just plain nonsense'.

Old views about Africa are worth recalling for another reason. Though vanished from serious discussion, they still retain a kind of underground existence. The stercoraceous sediment of Burton's opinions, and of others such as Burton, has settled like a layer of dust and ashes on the minds of large numbers of otherwise thoughtful people, and is constantly being swirled about. What this leads to, despite all factual evidence to the contrary, are endless suspicions that writers such as Lothrop Stoddard were or are just possibly right when they wrote or write about the 'natural and inherent inferiority' of Africans; that 'in the negro, we are in the presence of a being differing profoundly not merely from the white man but also from [other] human types'; or that 'the negro ... has contributed virtually nothing' to the civilization of the world. However scientifically mistaken, these notions apparently remain part of our culture.

Often it is the aggressive violence of such opinions that most surprises. But perhaps one ought not to be surprised. These notions arose essentially from an identification of categories of 'race' and 'class'. Outside their comfortable windowpanes Victorian men of property saw the hateful devil of a new proletariat, hungry, abused, always liable to strike; and they feared what they saw. At another remove they viewed the Africans in the same obscuring light: as beings of 'the low orders' whom civilization, if it were to survive, must keep sternly 'in their place'. They accordingly tended to think of Africans not only as children incapable of growing up, but as dangerous and potentially criminal children. All but a few agreed that these 'natives' could not safely be admitted to the salons of human equality.

If views like these have managed to remain alive, it is also true that the twentieth century has done something to clear them away. Even during the central colonial period, when inquiry into the nature of African humanity was generally at a low ebb, anthropologists who followed Durkheim and Malinowski played an important part, as St Clair Drake has pointed out, in

helping us to see African societies steadily and to see them whole. They have made clear the meaning and function of cultural elements and institutional arrangements which might otherwise have been dismissed as mere foolish or bizarre custom.

Thanks to them, we have got ourselves clear of much of the racialist mythology of the nineteenth century: whether from pseudo-scientific Burtoniana of the moralizing sort, or from the kind of observation, by no means rare in its connotations of sexual prurience or anxiety, that was offered by an anthropologist of a century ago, in this case a Brazilian, who reassured his learned readers that whereas 'the penis of the African' might be 'large and heavy' under normal circumstances, it 'increases little in size during an orgasm, and never achieves complete rigidity'.

Yet it was still necessary to set African reality within its historical context. The anthropologists of the colonial period did not do this. Largely under Malinowski's severely anti-historical influence, they deliberately looked upon African societies as being timeless entities without past or future. 'It did not occur to us', in the words of one of them, 'to try to relate tribal traditions to a possible actual sequence of historic events in any areas in which we worked.' Nor, with this view, would it have done any good to try. 'We cannot have a history of African institutions', taught the similarly influential Radcliffe-Brown, who for a long time took the same view; there was simply no means of making such a history, and therefore no point in attempting one.

The result of this synchronic approach was greatly to strengthen the impression of a 'complete otherness' of African societies. Presented without history, as living in a perpetual vacuum of experience, these strange peoples came to seem the denizens of a Garden of Eden left over from the remote past. Logically enough, they began to be called 'the undeveloped peoples'. For development supposes history, and they were said to have none.

After the Second World War the historians at last got to work in Africa, and the Garden of Eden rapidly disappeared. Soon they were joined by a new and sometimes brilliant school of anthropologists. African societies began to be studied diachronically, as happening in time; and then it was found that in fact a great deal had happened to them. All this has helped to erase the impression of 'otherness'. It now becomes clear that Africans have developed in ways recognizably the same as other peoples. Individually or collectively, they have arranged their lives on the same basic assumptions, whether of logic or morality, as everyone else. The forms have been as different as Africa is different from Europe, Asia or America: but not the principles of intelligence and apprehension, not the essential content.

What comes out is the picture of a complex and subtle process of growth and change behind and within the technological simplicities of former times. The societies still partially observable yesterday, and even today after the storm-driven erosions of colonial rule, were and are the terminal structures of an ancient evolution. To borrow a phrase applied by Grottanelli to the arts of Africa, they are to be seen not as points of departure but as points of arrival.

In many ways this was a world of its own, a world of country values and beliefs, very much a rural world. Even the large exceptions to this rule, the crowding market cities with their kings and traders, only help to prove it. Much the greatest number of tropical Africans lived in former times, as many live today, in villages or scattered homesteads, having few material possessions, knowing nothing or little of the written word, enjoying the present as a gift from the 'golden age' of remote ancestors, and not much caring for a different future. Yet their technological simplicity was no guide to their social and cultural achievement. In truth they had tamed a continent.

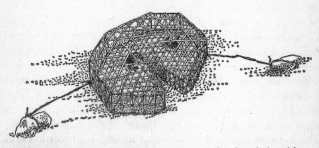

East Coast sea-fishing trap of a type with many local varieties, this one being about 100 cms wide.

# 2 Formative Origins

In setting out to master their own continent, Africans made a first and crucial contribution to the general growth of mankind. Most physical anthropologists seem now to have accepted that vital evolutionary steps which led from near-men towards true men were taken in Africa: in some recent words of Leakey's, that it was 'the African continent which saw the emergence of the basic stock which eventually gave rise to the apes, as well as to man as we know him today', and where 'the main branch which was to end up as man broke away from those leading to the apes'.

Not all the experts would yet agree with Leakey's third claim for Africa's primacy in the production of man: that 'it was also in Africa that true man separated from his manlike (and now extinct) cousins, the australopithecines or "near-men" of two million years ago'. But even if Africa was not in this direct sense the immediate birthplace of *homo sapiens*, there is now a wide consensus for the view, as Posnansky puts it, 'that Africa was in some respects the centre of the Stone Age world'. Though only about 125,000 people may have inhabited the continent a hundred thousand years ago, according to a recent guess, they were probably more numerous than the population of any other continent. They had gone further, in other words, towards conquest of their environment. By the end of the Late Stone Age, they may have multiplied to as many as three or four millions.

They belonged to several indigenous types. Some of their surviving descendants include the Pygmies of the Congo forests and the Bushmen of the south-western deserts. These 'small peoples' were much more widely spread then than now. There may have been as many as a million Bushmen south of the Zambezi at the end of the Late Stone Age, whereas today there are fewer than 50,000. Other but related types included the ancestors of the

Khoi ('Hottentots') of southern Africa; the ancestors of the robust and dark-skinned 'Negroes' of western and central Africa; and those who had descended from a mingling of indigenous peoples with neighbouring Asians, in the north and north-east, that possibly occurred as early as the Middle Stone Age.

These ancestral peoples evolved by intermarriage. They did so to such a point that today it is seldom possible, by blood-group analysis, 'genetically to distinguish very clearly or consistently even among such morphologically diverse groups as Bushmen, Pygmies, and Negroes'. They mingled and moved about their continent, slowly populating it. Of these migrations the most important was that of the 'Negroes', whose Bantu-speaking family of peoples, probably spreading originally from western Africa at least three thousand years ago, have long become dominant south of the Equator.

The linguistic evidence is a little more helpful. African linguistic studies are still immersed in controversy about origins and relationships. But they suggest that all the ancient languages of Africa belonged to a handful of 'founding families' which derived from remote Stone Age progress. As peoples became more numerous and moved about, these mother tongues divided in the course of centuries into a much larger number of 'sub-families'; and these in turn ramified as time went by into the multitude of languages spoken today. The actual numbers need not worry us here; the point is in their ramification. As a rough and ready guide to this process one may take a schematic view, adapting Greenberg's language data:

| Early Stone Age | Late Stone Age | Iron Age |
| --- | --- | --- |
| Up to 50,000 years ago | Up to 2,000 years ago | Spread and multiplication up to A.D. 1900 |
| 4 mother tongues 125,000 people | 37 main languages 3–4 million people | 730 languages 150 million people |

Nothing as statistically neat will have actually occurred, but the development of new ethnic identities may have been broadly along these lines. Very slow in remote Stone Age centuries, the rate of growth and differentiation accelerated in the Late Stone

Age and became comparatively rapid after the onset of the Iron Age some two thousand years ago.

In so far as one can hope to trace the origins of African civilization, it is clearly in this direction one must look: to the formative problems and solutions found by small groups faced with the destiny of peopling one of the world's largest and physically most testing land masses. Here it is that one may light upon crucial keys to questions of mood and temper, or trace the source of attitudes which have stubbornly combined a firm respect for precedent with a restless onward-shifting readiness for experiment; which have instilled a capacity, greater perhaps than that of any other major civilization, for the optimism which comes from living always on a frontier, on the edge of 'somewhere else', on the verge of 'something different', where anything may be possible as long as human courage and endeavour are prepared to make it so: as long, indeed, as a man's inner force or dynamism can avail to drive him forward. It is sometimes argued that the essence of African belief has rested in the notion of 'vital force'. Perhaps it is in this that one may glimpse an old attempt at conceptualizing the challenge of life and survival in a continent of such natural hostility to man.

I do not want to exaggerate. Questions of 'mood' are elusive, fleeting, contradictory. The record of African history is heavy on the side of custom and convention, of 'what our fathers did before us': as a Lozi proverb has it, 'Go the way that many people go; if you go alone you will have reason to lament.' Yet the record is also strong on the side of new initiative. What in any case mattered most – and it will emerge again and again – lay in the creative tension that was quickened and sustained by circumstances which so emphatically required convention and experiment as dual guides to survival. The Luo-speaking peoples offer a striking illustration. To live and multiply in the scorching grasslands of the Bahr-al-Ghazal, far out beyond the dust-harried skylines of the southern Nile, the founding fathers of the Luo had to learn techniques of cattle-raising and millet-farming capable of practice in a land of savagely contrasted seasons. Only rigid conventions could stave off disaster, as anyone may easily conclude who observes the peoples living there today: only strong obedience to the rules which governed their relations with each other and with their tawny land.

Yet the Luo, however custom-bound in the country of their birth, none the less became a people of wanderers who experimented with a copious range of new ideas. They adopted variant forms of religion, helped to found prestigious dynasties of kings, lived repeatedly on the ideological as well as physical frontiers of 'somewhere else' and 'something different'. A maxim of their neighbours the Luyia, another compound of wanderers and sedentaries, sounds the characteristic note. '*Oratseshera akharo khali ebusiba,*' say the Luyia, 'Don't laugh at a distant boat being tossed by the waves [of Lake Nyanza]. Your relative may be in it.' The rules are there, and the rules are good. But the changes and chances of fate may at any moment overturn them. Then a man must be ready to shift for himself by head-on clash or shrewd evasion.

# 3 The Physical Problem

If there were four million Africans two thousand years ago, there were probably as many as 150 million by the eve of the colonial period. They had settled in all but the most arid parts of the continent; even in the deserts they travelled and sometimes lived. When considering how they developed to this remarkable extent one needs to look first of all, even if briefly, at the ecological problems of their environment. These were neither small nor few.

One is helped towards understanding these ecological problems by the fact that Africa's climate seems to have changed little in historical times. Back in the 540s, Julian the missionary to the Nubians used to say that 'from nine o'clock until four in the afternoon he was obliged to take refuge in caves where there was water, and where he sat undressed except for a linen garment such as the people of the country wear'. Anyone travelling in Nubia today will understand why.

It was, as it is now, a continent of startling natural extravagance. Nothing here is done by halves. The dimensions are always big; often they are extreme. There are deserts large enough to swallow half the lands of Europe, where intense heat by day gives place to bitter cold by night, and along whose stony boundaries the grasslands run out and disappear through skylines trembling in a distance eternally flat. There are great forests and woodlands where the sheer abundance of nature is continually overwhelming in tall crops of grass that cut like knives, in thorns which catch and hold like hooks of steel, in a myriad marching ants and flies and creeping beasts that bite and itch and nag, in burning heat which sucks and clogs or rains that fall by slow gigantic torrents out of endless skies, and often in the stumbling miles which lie between your feet and where you need to be. There are fine and temperate uplands, tall mountains, rugged hills, but even these are filled with an extravagance of nature.

If you tramp through the African bush you will soon wonder how anyone could ever impose human settlement on this land, much less keep a footing here and steadily enlarge it. All this wild profusion stands there vast and looming, like a conscious presence waiting to move in again the moment that your back is turned. Give this giant the merest chance, you will feel, and the whole surrounding scenery will again invade these narrow fields and possess the land once more, possess it utterly, as though humanity had never been. Every African culture bears profound witness to this dominating 'spirit of the land'.

Yet the appearance of lush natural wealth is often misleading. Much of Africa is paved with a lateritic soil of low fertility and shallow depth. Much of it is covered and, it seems, was always covered in historical times by fruitless bush and poorly timbered trees. Much of it is pestered by tsetse fly inimical to beast and man. Only the development of an inherent immunity – but this never complete – has enabled Africans to withstand widespread malaria. Other parasites demand their toll, jiggers and locusts, pestilential water-snails, fever-bearing clouds of flying creatures.

Initially, moreover, Africa had few good food plants. Early farming was of dry rice and local yams in western Africa, and of millet and sorghum elsewhere, but of little else until the coming of Indonesian bananas and Asian yams in the fourth or fifth century, and of American cassava, maize, sweet potatoes, paw paw and pineapples in the sixteenth. The position with cattle was somewhat better thanks to the spread of Zebu and Sanga breeds in the first millennium B.C. and later. But even so there were many areas which could raise no cattle because of tsetse.

Poor fertility made it inevitable that this early farming, outside the lower valley of the Nile and some areas of western Africa and the Congo Basin, should always be a matter of frequent shifting from place to place. Settlement for a long time in any one village was difficult or impossible. More often, groups rotated through a series of village sites within the area they claimed as their own. And whenever they moved the wilderness came in behind them and raised its barriers once more.

The crucial inventions in improving this situation, in enabling longer periods of settlement and new processes of growth, seem to have lain in the metallurgy of iron: in identification of the ore, extraction, crushing, smelting, and forging of the metal. Locally evolved or adapted from techniques already known in northern Africa, iron production spread widely in the tropical zones from about two thousand years ago. How greatly its uses were appreciated by Stone Age farmers may be guessed from the mystical rites and beliefs, linking it to an immanent spiritual power, that continued in later times to surround the working of iron and other metals, including copper, gold and tin. Their production was conceived as the fertilization of matter by energy,

A type of African forced-draught furnace for smelting iron ore.
The furnace is filled with alternate layers of ore and charcoal.
This example has a pair of bowl-bellows and twin shafts.
About 100 cms high

the blast furnace of ant-hill earth being the womb with the shaft of the bellows, which were often paired as testicles, as the organ of transmission: a process exercised by specialists under divine protection that was both physical and spiritual, demonstrating man's command of nature as well as nature's command of man, in an idiom perfectly at one with African conceptions.

This metallurgy remained at the handicraft stage. Though practised intensively by many peoples, it was always laborious. Among the Fipa, whose ironsmiths were widely famous, it was observed a few decades ago that a group of men and women, working with a single furnace, could produce no more than two hoe blades and a few smaller tool heads in a day. But this scale of production was enough for an economy largely of subsistence. Once it became possible, the way was open for radical expansion. Archaeologists are generally agreed that this was true for all comparable civilizations. 'It was the adoption of the working of copper and its alloys, and later of iron', in Grahame Clark's words,

that brought about major increases in control over physical environment, not only in working such organic materials as wood and bone, but even more significantly in helping to improve the food-supply through more effective felling and clearance and through the provision of such things as pruning and lopping-knives, plough-shares, coulters and the like.

The more widely such tools were available and the better they became, 'the greater must have been their impact on food-production and so on population'. This completely applies to tropical Africa with the exception of ploughshares and coulters, for which, since the plough appears south of Ethiopia only in recent times – along with the tsetse-immune tractor – we must substitute axe blades and hoe blades.

The process was cumulative. All the evidence for Africa suggests that iron smithing combined creatively with new farming techniques. More food permitted the establishment of stores of food, at any rate from one harvest to the next. Stores of food permitted surpluses, however slender in the beginning; and surpluses could be used to feed a growing number of non-food-producing specialists such as were required for smithing and other early industrial skills. So that 'every increase in the density of population', itself a product of farming settlement,

made possible a finer subdivision of labour, a most essential condition for further technical improvements. The interaction between food-production, population growth, and the ability to use more effective materials for implements and gear was both intimate and continuous.

With this, the processes of Iron Age history were well in motion by about A.D. 500. Groups of iron-working farmers appeared in almost every region between the fringes of the Sahara and the hills and plains of the far south. And so the broad picture is rounded out. The ideological formation of the Africans is framed by the gradual peopling and settling of vast areas occupied previously by a few scattered hunters and plant-gatherers, or not occupied at all. These farmers coexist with the earlier occupants but slowly dispossess them of their traditional feeding grounds, or else absorb them by marriage into a post-Stone Age economy of village settlement and social organization.

One has to think of these pioneering settlers as of small and isolated groups. Alone in their solitudes, pressing onward in their need for new resources to support their growing numbers, they face the wilderness and forge new identities. They link themselves with their forefathers in self-justifying lifelines back to the Life Force, back to their ideas of Origin, back to their spiritual protection in a land that seems boundless and boundary-less, framed only by a few great rivers or the blue lift of hills upon a distant skyline. Here they evolve their own frontiers and frameworks of belief and thought, each group defining itself, enclosing itself, ruling itself, within its own exclusive charter of self-explanation.

# 4 Unity and Variation

It seems to me that this rustic civilization or group of civilizations may be regarded as a large achievement in the annals of mankind. But it is one which has had scant attention from the outside world. By contrast, many writers have celebrated the ancient Greeks for the ways in which they overcame an utter 'lack of precedent', devising and codifying laws 'constitutional, civil, sacral and criminal' with no one to guide or help them – not even, we are told, in the midst of that geophysically so small and helpful Mediterranean world – until they produced what Finley has called a 'situation of compulsive originality'. Yet even while admiring the ancient Greeks, one may perhaps still wonder how far their 'lack of precedent' really existed in the wake of the high civilizations of antiquity which preceded them. Didn't Herodotus, after all, tell us that the names of the gods came to Greece from Egypt?

Without suggesting that the achievements of the ancient Africans were 'the same' as those of the Greeks, it may be reasonable to think that they were in one great aspect superior. They really did evolve much out of little, or out of nothing at all. If one should praise 'the Greek spirit' as splendidly creative and inventive, one may perhaps express some admiration for an 'African spirit' which was far less favourably placed for the elaboration of the arts of life, but none the less made this continent supply the needs of man. Where, after all, lay the precedent for the social and ideological structures built by the Africans, so various and resilient, so intricately held together, so much a skilful interweaving of the possible and the desirable? Where did these systems draw their sap and vigour except from populations who evolved them out of their own creativeness? Even allowing for the distant precedents of Egypt, the peoples who settled Africa had surely less to go upon than the ancestors of Pericles. The balance needs adjusting here.

How great was the African isolation? The evidence that we have, still fragmentary and tentative, points insistently to some kind of 'common fund' of long ago. Peoples separated by vast distances have similar ideas which suggest the same Stone Age source. Creation legends offer a good example.

Among the Dinka of the southern Sudan, latterday descendants of those 'blameless Ethiopians' whom Homer praised, it is held that long ago in a golden age God lived among men and was in no way separate from them. Separation came to this African Eden when a woman with her eagerness or greed for cultivation happened to hit God with a hoe, whereupon God withdrew into the heavens 'and sent a small blue bird to sever a rope which had previously given men access to the sky and to him. Since that time the country has been "spoilt", for men have to labour for the food they need, and are often hungry ...' At which point, for good measure, Death came also into the world.

Several thousand miles away, in the forests of Ghana, the Akan have much the same idea, though there is nothing to suggest that they ever knew any contact with the ancestors of the Dinka or with neighbours of the Dinka who tell the same general story. 'Long long ago', says the Akan legend,

God lived on earth or at least was very near to us. But there was a certain old woman who used to pound her *fufu* [cassava meal], and the pestle used to knock up against God. So God said to the old woman, 'Why do you always do that to me? Because of what you are doing I am going to take myself away up into the sky.' And of a truth he did so.

Such parallels could be multiplied. 'Beast burials' have been found among ancient peoples as far apart as the Nile Valley and southern Africa. Cattle folk as distant from each other as Uganda and Zululand have customarily buried their distinguished dead in shrouds of ox-hide. Rams were the symbol of God in ancient Egypt and Nubian Kush, and have so remained among many West African peoples. The python is a similarly prestigious beast.

Simple diffusion from a 'common fund', or an effect of like

circumstances producing like results? Probably we shall never know. The same basic conceptions of socio-religious belief and organization appear again and again. But so they do throughout the world of antiquity. Anyone who cares to try his luck at tracing everything to Egypt, or Sumeria, or some other single 'fount and source' will find no lack of helpful evidence. The Babylonians, for example, evolved from the Sumerians a 'universe of seven', counting the seven steps of their ziggurats by the names of the seven planets corresponding to seven great gods, seven gates to the underworld, seven winds, seven days of the week. Far away in western Africa, as it happens, there are peoples with a comparable symbolism.

The Dogon of the Middle Niger lands are said to consider that creation began with an egg containing the elemental germs of the world's things: these germs developed 'first in seven segments of increasing length, representing the seven fundamental seeds of cultivation, which are to be found again in the human body, and which ... indicate ... the organization of the cosmos, of man, and of society'. Their near neighbours the Bambara, though of a different history and language grouping, have the same idea. For them 'the earth is divided into seven parts corresponding to seven heavens', and was so arranged by Faro, the agent of creation. Yet it will be a lively step in imaginative speculation that makes the Dogon and Bambara derive these ideas from Babylon.

Whether or not they mean anything in terms of diffusion, there is no end to such parallels. In ways that match with the cosmological symbolism of the Mossi, Fon and other peoples, the Dogon conceive of life's development as 'the perpetual alternation of opposites – right and left, high and low, odd and even, male and female – reflecting a principle of twin-ness, which ideally should direct the proliferation of life'. This dialectical principle is said to be enshrined in another: in a 'conception of the universe that is based, on the one hand, on a principle of vibrations of matter and, on the other, on a general movement of the universe as a whole'. The pairs of opposites 'support each other in an equilibrium which the individual being conserves within itself', while 'the infinite extension of the universe is expressed by the continual progression of matter along this spiral path'.

But there too the diffusionists can have a field day if they wish. For the Mesopotamian origin of the world was likewise 'seen as a prolonged conflict between two principles, the forces making for activity and the forces making for inactivity', a dialectical concept that is likewise found among the ancient Chinese. This strife of opposites, so infinitely more persuasive to modern science than the merely lineal explanations of European tradition, was American as well. Among the Aztecs 'an eternal war was fought symbolically between light and darkness, heat and cold, north and south, rising and setting suns'; and this was the Sacred War that 'permeated the ritual and philosophy of Aztec religion'.

If the comparative study of religion has so far had little to say about the extension of such parallels to Africa, this is chiefly because African religions have often been regarded as no such thing. In forms less crude but remarkably pervasive, the dictum of Sir Samuel Baker has held sway: Africans have been 'without a belief in the Supreme Being'. They have bowed down to wood and stone; and that was that. Yet it has proved to be nothing of the kind. Many studies have subsequently shown Africans to be fully conversant with the notion of a High God who created the world in a time of happiness, before the coming of Death and Work, and with other beliefs common to other branches of mankind. They too, for example, have had the notion of a filial divine saviour such as Nummo, the son of the High God Mawu of the Ewe who was sent down to earth 'to clear the forests and make tools': beliefs, one may add, which have owed nothing to Christian teaching. As elsewhere, monotheism could subsume polytheism in a 'conjunction of the one and the many' so as to allow for varying degrees of cosmological explanation. God might be the remotely theoretical scientist who understood and controlled the total workings of the Universe. But lesser gods and spirits were available as workaday technicians to keep the world in motion.

African writing will tell more about this. Some British anthropologists at present suspect their French colleagues, and notably Griaule, of over-systematizing the cosmological ideas of Africans, and of turning into regular philosophies what may be little more than patterns of symbols. To accusations of this kind the French reply that the British have failed to perceive African ontologies simply because they have failed to look for them; and this particular Anglo-Gallic war, for the moment, robustly continues. But what neither side seems to doubt is the genuine existence, in Goody's words, of 'a rich symbolism and elaborate cosmological ideas of the general variety to which Griaule draws such energetic attention'.

One may reasonably suppose that Africans drew upon a 'common fund' of Stone Age thought that was available to other ancient peoples. Yet it needs to be remembered that most of Africa was in relatively great isolation over a long period, and especially after desiccation of the Sahara had set in seriously around 2000 B.C. This means that the great formative time of Early Iron Age growth and spread occurred when the channels of effective communication with the outside world were long since cut or much reduced. These peoples had therefore to evolve out of their own energy and genius, applying whatever they conserved of the antique fund of Stone Age thought to situations that were new and specific. The manner of their doing so is the cultural history of Africa.

A few other preliminary points should be made. Some reading back into the past from recent or fairly recent evidence will be unavoidable. How great will the distortion be? Less, perhaps, than one might fear. Social anthropologists acknowledge this when they use their 'ethnographic present tense'. With this they describe an observed situation which appears to have been largely the same in the past, and sometimes the remote past. All societies observable today or recently have changed during the past century or less, and often changed greatly. But many of their traditions have held sufficiently firm for the trained observer to spot the important points of transition, and to list to some extent the consequential changes. By taking these into account it is possible to arrive at broadly reliable assumptions about the precolonial situation.

These societies were never static over long periods, and seldom over short ones. They constantly evolved. The base line, then, is necessarily a blurred one. Aside from one or two written accounts with helpful clues, we cannot know except by distant inference what men thought or believed in Early Iron Age times. What can be done is to perceive the nature of the institutional process and to describe systems, symbols, and beliefs which, however modified in detail, have had essentially the same content for a long while. Having got as far as this it may then be possible to understand the reasons why things happened as they did; and why they did not happen, and no doubt could not happen, in some other way.

## Part Two: Social Charters

I ruled with the power that comes from my forefathers, the power without beginning . . .

H. V. CHITEPO, *Soko Risina Musoro*

Lord, thou hast been our dwelling place in all generations

*Psalm* xc, 1

# 5   Founding Ancestors

The implacable parson had not in fact gone there to see for himself, and there was little photography in those days to help the armchair traveller. But Dean Farrar was quite sure that he understood what manner of creatures these Africans were. Their features, he was able to report in 1865, were 'invariable and expressionless', their minds 'characterized by a dead and blank uniformity'. They had 'not originated a single discovery . . . not promulgated a single thought . . . not established a single institution . . . not hit upon a single invention'.

There might be something almost frantic about this piling up of negatives. But Dean Farrar had not written of the woes of little Eric for nothing. Give the Devil an inch, he knew, and the Devil would take a mile. He was not for giving the Devil even half an inch. Among the Africans, he declared at a time when the great majority of African peoples had not so much as been glimpsed by any European eye, 'generation hands on no torch to generation'. Left to themselves, they were beyond salvation.

This was to become the great theme song of colonialist paternalism. Taking material simplicity for proof of primitive savagery, the most commonplace of men, when raised to positions of dominion, became as suddenly convinced of their civilizing mission. 'We have in East Africa,' opined Sir Charles Eliot, Britain's first high commissioner there, 'the rare experience of dealing with a *tabula rasa*, an almost untouched and sparsely inhabited country where we can do as we will.' Elsewhere it was the same. When British pioneers in 1890 rode into the land which became Southern Rhodesia, they could not believe that 'natives' had raised the patterned walls of masonry they found there.

These ideas are among the mysteries of non-African belief that

have somehow survived the colonial period. In the case of
Southern Rhodesia, as it happens, more than half a century later
an ethnologist began asking old men who lived in the rolling
grasslands of the Mount Darwin district, north of modern Salisbury, whether they knew anything of the distant past. They
hesitated and then they began telling him the history of their
people and its kings. They went back to Mutota, the first of their
strong rulers, who was 'still the heart of the nation' and whose
burial ground was the hill of Chitakochangonya. They admitted
that 'we no longer talk about these matters very much, now that
the Europeans have taken the place of Mutota's sons'. But they
remarked that there were elders still alive, even in the 1950s,
'who say that if you listen carefully you can hear the roll of
Kagurukute, the great drum of Mutota, at the time of the new
moon, as you stand looking down upon the river Dande, beside
the lofty grave'. Now Mutota had died in about 1450. The old
men were recalling five centuries of statehood.

In truth the history of the Africans is nothing if not the 'handing on of the torch' from generation to generation. It is quintes-
sentially concerned with the accumulation of ancestral wisdom,
with the demonstration of a *tabula piena* of ancestral knowledge.
For it is the appointed ancestors who have given peoples their
identity and guaranteed the onward movement of life. They may
be private ancestors or public ancestors, 'family' guarantees or
'national' guarantees, but in any case their role is crucial. They
it is who have drawn up and sealed the beliefs and laws by which
men reasonably live.

This statement is of course a simplification. Beliefs and laws
were always subject to change, while the ancestors in their own
time had themselves been men and, as such, subject to the pressures of everyday life. Yet it is a simplification which gets to the
heart of the matter. Leaving aside the religious aspect for a
while, I want here to consider the political and social meaning of
ancestors, and especially of those 'founding ancestors' who, as
Africans say, 'began our life and brought us into the lands
where we live'.

If the everyday thought of Early Iron Age peoples lies beyond
our grasp, we can at least perceive something of their predica-

ment. It is fairly certain, for example, that the remote ancestors of the Shona-speaking peoples, whose descendants appeared so history-less to the British pioneers of the 1890s, settled in the grasslands between the Zambezi and Limpopo more than a thousand years ago. Very typically for African history, they took shape from a mingling and eventual composition between incoming migrants and peoples already living in the land.

These were the early syntheses of cultures that contain the 'beginning' of the story. They must have been many, for the whole of recorded history tells repeatedly the same tale. Historians probing back through oral tradition come again and again upon the evidence for dispersal and migration as these relatively empty lands were gradually settled: dispersal of the Bantu-speaking peoples from a formative homeland that was probably the Congo savanna country; dispersal of the Luo-speaking peoples from a formative homeland in the plains to the west of the southern Nile; dispersal of other Sudanic speakers from this or that 'initial zone' of growth and multiplication.

As early populations grew in size, so did their reasons for dispersal. Political disputes, above all for succession to inherited authority, would cause disappointed leaders to look for a land of their own. These founding heroes would shift away with their followers, few or very few, and find their freedom in another country, by conquest if they must and were able, or else by seeking lands not yet occupied. And as the causes of dispersal became more complex and political, so also did the modes and mechanisms of social change.

But consider the predicament of these early groups in the solitudes of ancient Africa. Each is alone, or feels itself to be so. By moving away from its parent community, each has cut or weakened its ancestral lifeline, and suffers a corresponding sense of anxiety and risk. Often the group is very small, perhaps fifty or a hundred men with a few women and children. Generally it will hope to find wives where it is going; but seldom or never does it know where it is going. Having moved, the migrant group becomes separate, distinct, different from any other. Confronted with an unknown country, it must apply its narrow fund of technical knowledge in new material situations. But it must also do this in new non-material situations: in these, too, the group must invent and adapt.

Above all, each group must relieve its sense of anxiety and risk; it must reach an assurance about its new identity, rules of life, customs and beliefs. As Sangree says of the Tiriki in Kenya, its members must be enabled to supply themselves with answers to the questions: 'Where did I come from? Who cares whether I live or die? Upon whom can I depend for food, land and shelter?' Only a new ancestral lifeline, a new 'system of ancestors' for the group as a whole but also for each evolving segment of the group, can do this. The ordering of a given society into inter-

Ancestral figures in carved basalt, the larger one about 108 cms high, from Ekoi country in south-eastern Nigeria. Drawn in the bush before its removal to the Jos Museum, the larger is from the lands of the Nnam people. Many such shaped and engraved stones exist in this country, but little is known of their origin

locking lineage identities, each with its own forefathers linked in turn to one another, can then supply the necessary 'sense of affiliation and continuity'.

This constant shaping of new identities and separate systems was a worldwide phenomenon, so that early societies in different continents must often have resembled each other in their underlying concepts. This indeed is what modern research affirms for later societies. Every group has needed to define itself in order to believe in itself. So as to enter a firm claim upon the future, every group has had to give itself a name and heritage. But this has supposed agreement on a common group-origin, even if fictional or deliberately contrived. The children of the United States of America derive from many ancestral origins; but they sit in school beneath the daily sign and symbol of the Stars and Stripes, ever visible and reassuring demonstration of their joint identity and common heritage, and hence their common future. The children of Africa have gone through educational academies of a different kind. Yet the 'initiation' courses and ceremonies, seminars and examinations through which they have passed were no less aimed at ensuring joint identity and common heritage as well as common future; and the shrines of the appointed ancestors – the constitutionally crucial ancestors – were there to confirm it.

Constitutionally crucial? Not all ancestors were important, but only those who were recognized as standing in the line of succession back to 'the power without beginning'. These were the appointed ancestors who channelled that power to living men, and who in so doing provided the means of protecting the present, guaranteeing the future, and generally assuaging the doubts and worries of pioneering groups in the wilderness where they wandered and settled. There is thus no true dividing line between founding ancestors and superior spirit guardians. Back beyond Mutota, the founder of their long dynasty of the Mwanamutapas, the Shona think of their great ancestral spirits, their *mhondoro* who, as founding heroes, first taught how to smelt iron from the rocks and how to grow millet and sorghum. 'With this iron the people made hoes, and the *mhondoro* taught them in dreams to till and plant crops.' In that dry country it has always been the rains, rare and irregular, which have made the difference between food and famine: above all, then, the *mhondoro* presided over the giving or withholding of rain, and logically so, for how could the ancestors, in preparing a land for their people, have failed to solve the problem of rain?

It was in these senses that religious needs were seen as lying at the heart of social evolution. Social needs, that is, were conceived in religious terms. 'After settling in an area', Kimambo has noted of the Pare, 'each group established its sacred shrine at which they connected themselves with the ancestors who had founded their group', as well as with any 'local ancestors' whose spiritual powers were important. They did this neither from blind superstition nor from want of a 'sense of reality', but because no group could feel itself secure, settled and at peace with the logic of events until, by setting up the necessary shrines, it had identified itself as a defined community with a 'natural right' to live where it had chosen. Nor did they set up these shrines, generally, in order to worship their ancestors as gods, but to 'connect themselves' with those ancestors to whom suprasensible power had revealed the land and how to prosper in it. The parallel, perhaps, is with saints in the Christian canon. They, too, are forerunners of living men and women. Yet despite their human origins it is through them that many Christians have sought to link themselves with the 'power without beginning', and in ways which have ranged from mere reverence among the sophisticated to outright idolatry among the simple. Just so with the Africans and their appointed – that is, canonized – ancestors.

This bare model may be an abstraction, but it can still convey the essence of the truth. In thinking about it one needs continually to envisage the acute and actual problems of small communities at grips with strange and often hostile circumstances. There are many Biblical parallels. A Kenya historian of the Luo has compared their reactions with those of the wandering tribes of Israel. For the Israelites it was Moses who, as founding hero, brought them out of the sorrows of Egypt to the borders of a land flowing with milk and honey, who spoke with God and knew the ways and wishes of the 'power without beginning', and who defined the laws by which alone the Israelites could prosper. The God they named, however, had not been their own, for he was Jahweh of the Canaanites and lived on Mount Sinai; but they took over God in this Canaanite garb because it was he who had given them a home. Around A.D. 1500 the Padhola Luo came into eastern Uganda from the north-west. They too had wandered far and wide before finding their home. Once installed there they stopped calling God by the name they had used before, Jok, and began calling him Were. For it was God in his local garb as Were who had given them their Canaan, and so deserved their worship.

An interweaving of ideological traditions was obviously a continual process. Many of their early elements have survived in recognizable form. The Yoruba of southern Nigeria show this very well. Few peoples have so elaborate a cosmogony. The Yoruba think of divinity as a family of gods and goddesses who prefigure the social life of man but combine what appear to have been two quite separate traditions: those of the incoming ancestors, arriving in Yorubaland at some time before A.D. 1000, and those of other peoples who were already in the land.

In the Beginning there was Olodumare, God the archetypal Spirit. Having decided to create the world, Olodumare engendered Orishanla and sent him down to do the work. This he rapidly completed with the aid of other 'archangels'. Orishanla then brought mankind out of the sky. They settled at Ife; and from Ife they spread across the Earth and made it fruitful.

But that is only half the story. In another large facet of Yoruba belief it is not Orishanla who created the world at the bidding of Olodumare, but Oduduwa. Coming from somewhere far away in the east – from Arabia according to a later tradition doubtless inspired by Islam – Oduduwa then brought the Yoruba into their land, ruled them from Ife, and begat the men and women who were to rule or provide rulers for other Yoruba communities. 'His eldest daughter, it is said, was the mother of the Olowu of Owu; another was the mother of the Alaketu of Ketu. One son became the Oba of Benin, another the Alake of Ake, another the Onisabe of Sabe, another the Alafin of Oyo.'

How reconcile Oduduwa with Orishanla? In Yoruba traditions

as we have them today, there seems to have been conflation of two initially separate social charters. According to this conflation, 'it was indeed Orishanla who got the commission from Olodumare but, through an accident, he forfeited the privilege to Oduduwa who thus became the actual creator of the solid earth'. The incoming Oduduwa tradition, in short, became woven with another, lying behind the Orishanla tradition, which presumably belonged to the population whom the incomers found and mingled with.

The 'accident' whereby Oduduwa supplanted Orishanla was the fruit of movements made long centuries ago. Yet its enduring sense of spiritual clash and redistribution of power has been so deep as to keep it vigorously alive. Even today,

the priests of Orishanla find it necessary to make a compensatory claim that even though Oduduwa once supplanted Orishanla in the honour of creating the solid earth, and therefore in seniority over all the other divinities, he could not maintain the machinery of the world, and therefore Olodumare had to send Orishanla to go and set things right and maintain order.

The point here lies not in the picturesque details of a legendary compromise between incomers and aboriginals, but in the care that was taken, that *had* to be taken, to legitimize a new arrival and a new synthesis. What right could any people have to come from somewhere else and settle in a new land? The title to any piece of land lay with the Spirit of the Earth. To seal their right to occupy and settle, incomers must make their peace with this Spirit. They could do this only through a process of spiritual reconciliation sanctioned by appropriate rites. Otherwise the Spirit of the Earth would not recognize their legitimate existence in the land. Failing this act of connection, even the appointed ancestors of the incomers would lose their spiritual power, for they would be cut off from its divine source.

This is to some extent translating African concepts into another language of religious thought. God as an entity or being has been usually a distant and even indifferent figure for Africans. What has mattered for them is not the hierarchical father of Mosaic tradition, whom they may think little concerned with the affairs of men, but the ancestral channel of spiritual legitimation through which flows the life-force, or whatever other limping definition one may use, that drives the world and makes it live. In this crucial matter of legitimation, however, 'God' and the 'ancestral channel of the life-force' come to pretty much the same thing. The examples are many.

At some time around A.D. 1350 a people living along the north bank of the Congo river, not far from its junction with the Atlantic Ocean, underwent a familiar split in their ranks. Needing more land, a chief's son decided to leave home. He gathered followers and went south over the wide river near the modern town of Boma. Pushing into what is now northern Angola, they came into the country of the Mbundu and Mbwela peoples. Here, the traditions say, they conquered for themselves a little homeland near their later capital of Mbanza or São Salvador.

Having won this foothold they still had to legitimate their presence; mere conquest was not enough. The traditions are careful to note that Wene, chief of the incomers, thereupon married into one of the clans of the people already settled in the area. But the clan he chose was the one whose ancestors were recognized as holding the spiritual title to the land. Kabunga, the head of this clan in Wene's time, was priest of the shrine of the Spirit of the Earth: the shrine, in other words, at which titular legitimation must be sought through the only ancestors who were valid for the purpose. Marrying into Kabunga's clan, Wene could affiliate himself and his successors to this all-important line of other people's ancestors. He could properly take over Kabunga's title of *mani* and rule henceforth as *Mani-Kongo*, Lord of Kongo, duly accepted by the Spirit of the Earth. Even today, six centuries later, this legitimation is still recalled in annual ceremonies.

Just how strongly such conceptions were rooted in African thought was afterwards shown in the Americas. There, wherever large groups of Africans could escape from slavery and rebuild their lives in freedom, they called at once for guidance from their own cultures. In Brazil the ex-slave *quilombos*, and most notably of all the famous seventeenth-century republics of Palmarès, were founded in laws and customs drawn mainly from the western

Bantu peoples. The *candomble* associations of certain Brazilian cities were, to some extent still are, thoroughly African in content, however exotic in form. Only thirty years ago Herskovits found clear evidence among the so-called 'Bush Negroes' of Surinam – descendants of West Africans taken to this Dutch colony after 1600 who had escaped to the forest and conserved their independence – that the spirits of the Earth were regarded as the possession of the aboriginal inhabitants, of the 'Indians' whose ancestors had first inhabited this land.

The model was obviously subject to much local variation; and the variations became ever more numerous as African lands were filled with the forerunners of their present societies. But essentially it was a model which held good for every situation. It consisted in the framing of a social charter sanctioned by the sense of what was 'right and natural', the sense of walking in the ways of life: confirmed and elaborated, as will be seen, by the most purposive ritual, by a wide range of arts, and sometimes by systematic explanations of the universe. Yet all this structure of sanctioned behaviour had its foundations firmly on the ground. And the ground was that of subsistence economy and family life.

# 6  The Balance with Nature

The formative community of Early Iron Age times, at any rate before about A.D. 500, was typologically a small group of related families established in a homeland they had occupied or inherited. Its immediate boundaries might be no more than a few miles wide; beyond them there might or might not be a handful of neighbours. Always, the lands of the unknown stood menacingly near, and into these a man would venture at his risk and peril. A village or a cattle-camp: one or two other villages or cattle-camps whose evening smoke climbed wispily grey in the middle distance to hills of mystery and danger: such was the outline of the world of long ago.

Within the formative community there was food and friendship, shelter from raiders whether animal or human, a sanctioned law and order. But there was more. There was also a psychological security: personal identification within a system both suprasensible and material in its terms of reference, within a society both 'right and natural' in that it was 'god-made' as well as man-made. Beyond, there stood the void in strong and ever-present contrast. Outside this ancestrally chartered system there lay no possible life, since 'a man without lineage is a man without citizenship': without identity, and therefore without allies. *Ex ecclesia non est vita*; or, as the Kongo put it, a man outside his clan is like 'a grasshopper which has lost its wings'.

This political unit was, even more, an economic one. Having made their homeland, the cluster of families had to survive in it. They could survive only by a process of trial and error as they grappled with its ecology; with its tsetse or floods of rain, its shallow soil or towering forest trees, its slides of hillside pasture or pockets of arable amid lizard-gleaming humps of rock. This was the saving process of invention and adaptation that rounded out the group's charter and gave, to those who were fortunate, the sanction of success.

The result was persistently ambiguous. 'Ideally', in Gluckman's words, 'a tribal situation is stationary ... [and] any change is an injury to the social fabric.' It is an ideal that flows from a pattern laid down by the ancestors, the paradigm of a perfect and unmoving social balance. Yet this is itself the product of experiment and innovation, and, as such, has necessarily remained subject to both. Hence an untiring resistance to disturbance or upheaval has gone hand-in-hand with an absorptive flexibility of adaptation. And hence again there has persisted in African thought an often emphatic cohabitation of the opposed principles of fate and supernatural justice – as Fortes suggests, of Oedipus and Job – arising on one hand from the immovable object of ancestral rules which should not normally be changed, and, on the other, from the irresistible forces of unfolding life and human nature which nonetheless do change these rules.

The economic basis was conceived in family terms, in what Middleton and Tait have called 'a nuclear group'. This is one of those anthropological abstractions which are convenient because they translate the exotic into the familiar, but with little real distortion. The 'nuclear group' – the basic economic unit – may also be called an 'extended family'. As observed in many societies which appear to have changed little in their essential structure for a long time, this 'nuclear group' or 'extended family' consisted usually of a unit of three or four generations from grandparents to grandchildren, and perhaps to great-grandchildren.

At least in principle, this family was or is a self-supporting unit of producers and consumers ideally capable of supplying all its own requirements but, in practice, able to exist only within a community of similar families who help each other in economic and other group-defensive ways. It is under the domestic rule of a single man (or occasionally woman) who may also be the person who represents it in political councils or politico-religious ceremonies affecting several families. It has the use of a specific piece of land. It owns the produce of this land but not the land itself, which symbolically belongs to the appointed ancestors who hold it from the Spirit of the Earth. Ecology fixes an optimum size for the unit. Whenever it prospers in childbirth, and grows 'too big', some of its members have to move elsewhere.

Each such family might be widely separated from its relations in other homesteads or temporary camps. But more often, except in true pastoral societies, homesteads would be close together, or people would live in clusters or hamlets or in large villages or even, as time went by, in farmers' towns such as those of the Yoruba. Yet however much the community might vary in size or in location of its family units, it provided the 'chartered' link between all its members and gave them ideological identity as well as ultimate security. Considered from another angle, people have ordered their affairs inside a 'jural community' composed of a varying number of nuclear groups: inside, that is, 'the widest grouping within which there was a moral obligation and a means ultimately to settle disputes peaceably'. Outside purely family affairs, this was the working organization available for political action.

So it came about that all property and productive relations had to be conceived in terms of kinship relations, since it was the sum of the family groups, combined in a jural community, that was seen as having devised the saving balance with nature. This meant that political action was necessarily kinship action. But this in turn required that every individual must play an expected social role. To the ecological balance, there corresponded another in the field of human relations – an ideal balance of kinship rights and obligations, occasionally quite simple, often very complex, and nearly always structured in terms of countervailing pressures between different sections of society: between, for the most part, different lineages or groups of lineages.

This ideal balance of kinship relations, seen as essential to the ideal balance with nature that was itself the material guarantee of survival, called for specific patterns of conduct. Individuals might have rights, but they had them only by virtue of the obligations they fulfilled to the community. This explains their logic of regarding legality in terms of individual obligations, and not of individual rights. At least in their jural and moral assumptions, these communities lived at an opposite extreme from the 'free-enterprise individualism' which supposes that the community has rights only by virtue of the obligations it fulfils to the individual.

Even the 'simple' forms of this ideal balance call for an imaginative effort of understanding, though they sometimes fall into fairly regular patterns. The chief complicating factor is that a 'nuclear cluster' of related families, enclosing a lineage or descent-line, has seldom formed or forms an isolated community. Its men and women marry the men and women of other 'nuclear clusters'. This produces an ever-changing mobility between each pair of them, and thus between them all. Anthropologists report diverse ways in which such relationships have been expressed, tensions resolved, and the balance held between descent-lines. The Amba of north-western Uganda, for example, are a farming people of about 30,000 souls living between the great Ituri rain forests and the slopes of snow-peaked Ruwenzori. In essence, their system is a simple one. All public affairs are resolved in terms of a balance between descent-lines. Every Amba can expect help from the kinsmen of his own line, but each line (and here I am simplifying) is in principle opposed to every other.

No Amba is allowed to marry within his or her own line. In anthropological terms, 'the maximal lineage about which the [Amba] village is structured is an exogamous unit, and thus the men of the lineage must obtain wives from other lineages'. Among the Amba, as among many other peoples, this arrangement has created a special interdependence. When a woman from Village B bears a son to her husband in Village A, all the men of Village B who belong to her own generation or younger have an obligation to protect, aid and defend their 'sister's son' – although this son now belongs to another and opposed descent-line, the maximal lineage of Village A. In this relationship the kinsmen of Village B are called the 'mother's brothers'. They are expected to act together in affairs concerning their 'sister's sons' in Village A.

These types of cross-relationship varied much in their detail and efficacy and so in their practical results. Generally, they have undergone many modifications over the past hundred years. But in one form or another they are part of the fundamental pattern of social and political growth which governed the peopling of

Africa in remote times, and framed its dominant beliefs and ideologies.

The sequence of what actually happened was not, of course, what this kinship ideology has projected. Characteristically, the ideology has stood things on their head. What actually happened long ago was that the ecology of a given area imposed a process of trial and error which led to an understanding of certain possible forms of livelihood. These saving rules of life, discovered after much adventure, duly shaped an ideal pattern of society. But people have not seen things in this way. What they have seen is that the ideal pattern of society, given by the life-force and the ancestors, produced the possibility of an ideal balance with nature.

Where with an outsider's objectivity we may feel sure that ecology and available techniques were the decisively formative factors in any given culture, peoples living within the ideology of traditional life have traced these factors to the ancestrally-sanctioned community. 'Living and dead of the same lineage are in a permanent relationship with each other ... The living act as temporary caretakers of the prosperity, prestige and general well-being of the lineage, on behalf of the ancestors who did the same during their lives.'

This was the kinship pattern, rather than any particular aspect of farming or other economic action, which came to appear as the essential guarantee of survival. What Middleton observed of the Lugbara was of general acceptance: 'If God made the world ... the hero-ancestors and their descendants, the ancestors, formed Lugbara society.' Hence, in large degree, the apparently 'anti-scientific' mood of yesterday's Africa. Its innovations were many, and were the harvest of a most practical observation that was scientific in its empiricism. But these innovations, in order to become acceptable, had to be absorbed within an ancestral system which, by definition, was itself opposed to experiment or change.

Lienhardt's description of the Dinka has illumined this whole process of desired equilibrium, and its conceptually reversed ideology, with a patient sympathy and brilliant insight. Numbering today about a million souls, the Dinka belong to a Nilotic language group which has lived in the plains around the southern Nile since remote times, although its formation into peoples clearly ancestral to those of today – Dinka, Nuer, Shilluk, Anuak and others – is part of the history of the last thousand years and even of the last five hundred.

A century ago Samuel Baker described them as a crude and feckless crowd with no social or religious notions worth the name. One can see, up to a point, why Baker thought this. 'Apart from imported metal and beads', Lienhardt wrote after living with the Dinka in 1947–50,

there is nothing of importance in Dinka material culture which outlasts a single lifetime. The labours of one generation hence do not lighten or make a foundation for those of the next, which must again fashion by the same technological processes and from the same limited variety of raw materials a cultural environment which seems unchanging, and, until the extensive foreign contacts of modern times, was unchangeable.

Unchangeable: because Dinkaland is an almost unfeatured plain with only occasional trees, and with a rainy season which regularly inundates the land, makes much of it temporarily useless to man or beast, and leaves no more than stray humps above sky-empaled waters where homesteads can be kept and gardens cultivated. In this country of 'general insecurity on the margins of subsistence', the 'only form of wealth which can be inherited is livestock'. It took a man like Baker to feel contempt that the Dinka should lack cathedrals and machinery, or even clothes.

Living where they do, boxed in moreover by other peoples who live in much the same way, the Dinka have evolved both an 'ideal equilibrium' and an explanation, in terms of necessary relationships between the living and the ancestors, of how their equilibrium was formed. The essence of their balance with nature consists in a seasonal system of millet cultivation, stock breeding, and regular retreat to rainy season camps, while its main content rests in the maintenance of more or less numerous herds of cattle. It is not an easy equilibrium, and was perhaps still more difficult in the past when cattle raiding by neighbours could be frequent and material goods were even fewer. It is an equilibrium which could never have resisted any major breaking of the rules.

The rules are deeply engrained in Dinka life. Lienhardt says that most Dinka spend much of the second part of every year, the wet season after August and before December, in cattle-camps 'some two or three hundred yards square, where it has been found that drainage is good'. Such a camp will 'usually consist of a number of slight mounds, built up higher by the accumulation of the ashes of dung smudges and the debris left by generations of herdsmen'. Here the Dinka build low shelters thatched with branches and covered with sods of earth. 'Each shelter is surrounded by cattle-pegs, and while the herdsmen sleep and sit in the protection of the shelters, the cattle are tethered around them.' After the worst of the rains are over, all but the very old people, who have remained in all-season homesteads elsewhere, move out with their cattle across the sodden pastures. There they live in grass shelters until April or May; then they return to permanent homesteads and gardens in places where the floods do not reach. Such is the Dinka year; and it is difficult to see how it could be, or ever could have been, very different. The Dinka have fitted themselves into their land, and the land has given them a living.

This equilibrium imposed by the land emerges, ideologically, as a construct fashioned by kinship relations and attitudes to cattle. Each 'nuclear family' belongs to a larger group by relationship between males. This larger group, *gol*, belongs in turn to a still wider one, again by relationship through males, which is called *wut*. The term *wut* is also synonymous with cattle-camp, so that a Dinka cattle-camp is in some large sense the physical configuration of the Dinka 'jural community', the largest grouping 'within which there are a moral obligation and a means ultimately to settle disputes peaceably'. Over and beyond each *wut* there is also a sense of wider loyalty; this takes visible form when *wuts*, or rather *wut* members, come together in the spring at another sort of camp, a lively *kermesse* of dancing, conversation, and inter-*wut* gossip.

Around this political organization there stands the guardianship of belief and custom. Each *gol* or group of nuclear families unites within itself two broad descent lines which are thought of as opposed and complementary. These are the *bany*, who provide the priests of Dinka shrines to divinity and regulate affairs with the gods and ancestors (themselves to some extent interchangeable); and the *kic*, whom Lienhardt describes as commoners or warriors. In this, again, one may perhaps glimpse the conceptualization of a universe in terms of opposed but complementary forces: those making for conservation, and those that speed the onward movement of life, with both entwined in a single dialectical structure. From another point of view, law and order·are promoted through group relations arranged by patrilineal ties balanced by loyalties through maternal ties.

Ideally, the warleaders and the priests [the *kic* and the *bany*] ... should stand in the relationship of nephew and maternal uncle to each other, thus creating a strong nucleus of two descent-groups related through women, and with different and complementary functions for each political group.

From this there derived a corresponding morality and set of legal norms. No Dinka should get or keep more than enough, because anyone who does so will imperil the precarious balance with nature. Crimes should be settled by acts of compensation so as to conserve, rather than further disturb, the relative strength of *gols* and *wuts*.

None of this should be taken to suggest that Dinka were some kind of moral or legal automata bound blindly to their rules. As in every human community, individuals could exploit or try to bend the rules to personal or joint advantage. This actual variety of choice is reflected in many and perhaps all African societies by the often contradictory advice of proverbial wisdom; and it helps to explain how individual wit or ambition, working within new pressures or conditions, could repeatedly modify these systems. Yet the variety of choice of action had to remain, or at least appear to remain, always within the limits of the ideal equilibrium: outside them, choice could only be antisocial and condemned. Political and religious theory, in short, arose from a specific adaptation to ecology.

But the ideology has seen things the other way round: it has seen the adaptation as a product of the theory. Among the Dinka this comes out emphatically in attitudes to cattle. The cattle are there because of the people. Yet the very predominance of cattle in Dinka life has given them an ideological status which can often appear to suggest the reverse. 'All important relationships between members of different agnatic [father-related] descent groups, and all important acquisitions for any particular group, may be expressed in terms of cattle.' Cattle are the subject of a capacious imagery, often subtle and imaginative, poetic and allusive, which refers to every aspect of Dinka thought about what life is and what life should be.

The Dinka carry this very far, and reveal in doing so how closely their system fits them. Thus the proud owner of a black ox may not be content, in singing with his friends, to be called by the basic name for such a beast, *ma car*,

but will be known by one or more other names, all explained ultimately by deriving from the blackness of his ox when seen in relation to darkness in other things. He may therefore be known as *tim atiep*, 'the shade of a tree'; or *kor acom*, 'seeks for snails', after the black ibis which seeks for snails; or *bun anyeer*, 'thicket of the buffalo', which suggests the darkness of the forest in which the dark buffalo rests; or *akiu yak thok*, 'cries out in the spring drought', after a small black bird which gives its characteristic cry at this time of year; or *arec luk*, 'spoils the meeting', after the dark clouds which accompany a downpour of rain and send the Dinka running for shelter.

Obsessed by cattle? The familiar remark of travellers who have passed this way has substance. But it happens to be a logical obsession. The Dinka have become obsessed by cattle as the 'modern man' by money, and for comparable reasons. The one, like the other, confers status as well as livelihood, and is thought of as unique in doing so. Wander through any modern conurbation, and you will be able to describe the houseowners by income group, or simply by the things that only money can provide. In the case of the Dinka and their cattle, however, a good deal of the 'obsession' is the optical illusion of observer's ignorance. An example from a country further to the south, offering in some ways an environment still more difficult, makes the point.

The Karimojong are a cattle-raising people who live in

northern Uganda. They inhabit about 4,000 square miles of grassland parched by frequent drought, and number some 60,000 souls. Karimojong behaviour, like Dinka behaviour, is closely geared to cattle which form the mainstay of their livelihood. Reputedly a difficult and unpredictable population during colonial times, they have followed rules of their own. Sometimes these rules have seemed perverse or pointless. Imperial authority clashed often with these restless drovers.

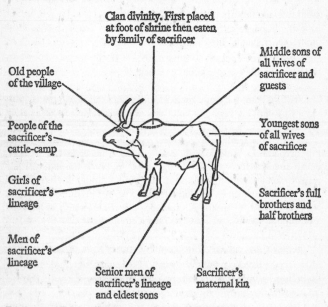

Clan divinity. First placed at foot of shrine then eaten by family of sacrificer

Middle sons of all wives of sacrificer and guests

Old people of the village

People of the sacrificer's cattle-camp

Youngest sons of all wives of sacrificer

Girls of sacrificer's lineage

Sacrificer's full brothers and half brothers

Men of sacrificer's lineage

Senior men of sacrificer's lineage and eldest sons

Sacrificer's maternal kin

Diagram of Dinka distribution of a sacrificial beast

Many of these clashes arose because the Karimojong would insist on moving into a certain area of grazing that lies to the east of their main homeland. There 'they encounter and often fight with other tribes who are exploiting the same general region'. Logically from its own point of view, colonial government wanted the 'cattle obsessed' Karimojong to move not east but west, where they would avoid trouble with neighbours. Just as

logically from theirs, the Karimojong insistently refused. But the logic of their refusal emerged only in 1958 when a government agronomist demonstrated what the Karimojong, it is now accepted, knew already: that 'the grasses of the west are deficient in minerals ... and stock herded there lose condition'.

Often, it is argued, the cattle are too many. But too many for whom? Colonial administration, looking at the problem from outside, saw only that a given square mileage could support a given density of stock. The Karimojong possessed more than this desirable maximum. Some cattle ought therefore to be culled. But the Karimojong looked at the problem from inside, from their own balance with nature, and disagreed. Thus a Karimojong herd large enough to feed a family in the rains may not be adequate in time of drought. 'In the rainy season a cow may give four or five pints of milk a day and still rear a healthy calf; in the dry season it is often possible to take only a quarter of a pint or so a day without risk of losing the calf.' Then the Karimojong, like other pastoral folk, use ox blood as a food. They know that 'a large ox will yield seven pints at a single bleeding in the rains, and five months later will be fit for bleeding again'; yet 'to take a similar amount in the dry season would be to risk losing the animal altogether'. An adequate herd at one season might undoubtedly be more than enough at another. But this, with Karimojong experience of drought, was clearly no reason for culling it.

I make these points only to demonstrate that peoples such as these could have logical and meditated reasons for doing what the uninstructed observer must regard as unnecessary or plain foolish. No doubt, like other peoples, they often behaved foolishly. But judgement should wait upon information. Where the logic seems to fail it may only be because the observer has insufficiently observed. One can make the same kind of point about African farmers who have practised what has been called 'shifting cultivation' or, more contemptuously, 'slash and burn'.

This shifting cultivation has been widely condemned by visitors to Africa, but not always, it would seem, from knowledge of what it was they were condemning. More usually, this was and is in truth 'recurrent cultivation' which had and has a sense and logic of its own. As, for example, with the Bemba. This people began farming in the grasslands of north-eastern Zambia soon after 1650. These grasslands are poor in soil fertility and other resources. Bemba farming equilibrium has required them to move a garden every four to six years at best; even then the yield capacity of the land may support no more than about ten people to a square mile. Another reason why they have had to move their gardens every few years is that they could cultivate successfully only if they fertilized with wood-ash. Their habit, consequently, has been to lop and burn trees around their gardens. Once the trees are cut the possibilities of fertilizer will be exhausted for a decade or more, and the garden must be left fallow.

Apparently very wasteful for the visiting expert: but what else could he have done in Bemba shoes? In contrast to what Polly Hill has called the 'generalized nonsense' that is often written about African economic conditions, there is the judgement of the good Bishop Mackenzie among the Chewa, neighbours of the Bemba, a hundred years ago. 'When telling the people in England,' he wrote, 'what were my objects in going out to Africa, I stated that among other things I meant to teach these people agriculture; but I now see that they know far more about it than I do.'

Those who find shifting cultivation feckless must therefore show what other or different forms of cultivation could have yielded more food. They will not find it easy. Of shifting cultivation in forest areas, the soil scientists Nye and Greenland, who are among the few who have yet devoted serious attention to the matter, reply that 'so far as we know the system is the best that could have been devised'. Even in grassland areas, such as where the Bemba live, Nye and Greenland question how far it really 'squanders the resources of the land'. It certainly 'checks the growth of shrubs and trees and encourages erosion on all but gentle slopes'. Yet 'the systems of cultivation and cropping are in general well adapted to produce the means of subsistence with the minimum of labour'. And the 'minimum of labour', no doubt, is what all peoples have striven towards, but especially the Africans with their ethos of 'enough is enough'.

For the ideal balance always supposed enough but not much

more: enough for a given community in a given place, taking it for granted that whenever the community grew too large for local sustenance, for the achieved balance, some of its members would find new land elsewhere. This attitude may be miles away from the accumulation drive of our own industrial societies with their drumming emphasis on 'more than enough'. But it had its own moral consistency. The puritan fathers of the industrial revolution may have felt that God desired them to burn the candle of labour at both ends: not the Africans. The ideal for them – if with many exceptions, especially in those societies which became more acutely stratified and hierarchical, notably in West Africa – has been 'conformity to the life led by one's fellows, seeking little or no wealth and position' in a carefully egalitarian world where personal gain above the level of the accepted norm would be a source of unhappiness or danger, since exceptional achievement could be only at the expense of one's neighbours.

This is why, as we shall see, exceptional achievement could be interpreted as a sign of social malice: as the workings of destructive witchcraft. 'Among the Bemba,' Gluckman adds, 'to find one beehive is good luck, to find two is very good luck, to find three is witchcraft'; and he recalls knowing a man who had given up living in a fine house he had built 'because he believed that he had become the target of envious witches'. Whoever failed to live the good life according to the ideal balance, or became the recipient of favours beyond the average, might well be thought to have set himself against the norm. And it was the norm of the ideal balance, however battered by individual ambitions or dimmed by social stratification, that shaped morality through the years.

# 7 A Moral Order

Britain lives today, we are told by sociologists, amidst 'a jumble of ethical precepts, now bereft of their significance . . . within a wasteland littered with the debris of broken convictions'. For a world where the ideal is one of personal accumulation, the good of the individual is set in opposition to the good of the community, as witness the consequences of our dominant idols, the motor car and the television set; and the good of the community goes increasingly to the wall. No matter what lip service to the general weal may continue to be paid in Sunday observances or other ritual proclamations, we become communities without any visible means of moral support. Every orthodoxy notwithstanding, we are confronted with an ever more urgent need to find a new morality, a new means of humanizing man in society, a new civilization: or else shake ourselves finally to pieces. So widely accepted are such thoughts that they must sound banal here. They will be excused, perhaps, for the contrast which they offer with the materially simple but morally not defenceless societies we are considering now. With them the situation was evidently different.

Here, of course, I am speaking mainly of those 'stateless tribes' who have seemed most 'primitive', most 'helpless', to observers from outside. Their characteristic ethos was consciously restrictive because it had to be so. It drew its power from a struggle for the mastery of nature formed and then enclosed by the precedents of experience. The result might be technological poverty, material backwardness, a failure to enlarge. These were its negative aspects. But it was not poverty in certain other ways, notably moral and artistic. On the contrary, the very strenuousness of their experience seems often to have given these societies an inner tension and creativeness which emerged in artistic triumphs that were morally inspired. It was as though the awareness of limits on the possible, or rather on the permissible, flowered in a sense of controlled freedom expressed most visibly by their dancing and their experiments in sculptural form: a controlled freedom which we, abandoning a community morality, may find difficult to conceive today.

This is not to say that these societies lacked a dynamism of change or failed to respond to it. But it is to say that the nature of their civilization supposed a notion of community that was restrictive of change in certain decisive ways. With them, the difference between good and bad lay in acceptance and rejection of the mandatory precedents – everyday, practical, all-pervasive – of what had come to seem the 'right and natural'. From this flowed their inhibitive conservatism. The Pondo of south-eastern Africa were typical of many peoples. Those very forces which have made for stability among them, Monica Wilson has observed, also tend to hamper any man who tries to adjust his life to new circumstances, while those traits of character which the modern world admires, such as pushing egotism and the desire for personal wealth or power, are precisely the qualities which used to make a Pondo disliked and even feared among his fellows.

None the less, things obviously did change. Some societies were less successful than others. And wherever the precedents – the rules of everyday life – failed to produce the necessary equilibrium, either the community fell apart or the rules had to be changed. Here there intervened, in ways which are increasingly understood by the study of oral history, a series of multivariant mechanisms of change which have caused the proliferation of a very large number of contrasts and contradictions even between neighbouring peoples.

The Amba mentioned earlier have had two basic rules. Marriages within descent-lines – effectively, within villages – are forbidden. But a man owes help to, and expects help from, his mother's relatives in other villages as well as from his father's relatives in his own village. This particular balance may be seen as having held Amba society together by tying each village to itself and its land, while compensating for the opposition of descent-lines in separate villages by permitting a certain overall cohesion through 'mother's brother: sister's son' relationships. At the same time it also prevented the emergence of any unitary political system.

This was no doubt all right in the old days. But as Amba filled up their land, and found it harder to get more land because neighbours were doing the same, their stubborn dispersal of authority among separate descent-lines led to increasing disputes and appeals to violence.

At the very heart of the system, with its rigid adherence to a lineage ideology, lay a fundamental contradiction which, unless new political principles were introduced, doomed the society to continual internal warfare and bloodshed no matter how much individuals within the society might wish the situation to be otherwise.

It was rather like the modern world and the proliferation of the motor car. The proliferation causes increasing bloodshed and a great many people wish the situation could be otherwise, but it cannot be otherwise because the proliferation lies at the heart of the system.

A great many 'small societies' seem to have found themselves in this growing contradiction between lineage loyalty and the welfare of the community. Many of them began appointing chiefs, with increasing powers, at least ten centuries ago and sometimes more. The history of chiefs is indeed the history of efforts to solve the problem of unity in a continent where disunity within a community with slowly rising populations, and with sharpening competition for good land or trade, was found to pay a continually higher price. Even the staunchly democratic Amba, under pressures of this kind, made some attempt to get themselves a king towards the end of the nineteenth century.

Where chiefs with centralizing powers were not adopted, other techniques of integration were tried. The more numerous Nuer of the southern Sudan have a basic pattern somewhat similar to that of the Amba. But they have contrived to find ways of integrating descent-lines so that relatively large numbers of Nuer can if necessary act together. They have got round the difficulty caused by exogamous marriage rules – which suppose rivalry to the point of warfare between major descent-lines – by mixing up their major lines or 'segments'. A Nuer village or group of villages never contains only one descent-line, as generally with the Amba, but is dominated by a descent-line living in amity with members of other lines. So that while large groupings of Nuer may still be in 'chartered opposition' to each other, the area of peaceful cohabitation has become steadily enlarged.

The point here is that these societies, irrespective of their degree of success or rate of change, always enclosed relations between people within a moral framework of intimately binding force. These relations between people, as Fortes reports of the Tallensi of northern Ghana, were expressed in moral concepts or axioms 'rooted in the direct experience of the inevitability of interdependence between men in society', an intense and daily interdependence that we in our day seldom recognize except in moments of post-prandial afflatus or national catastrophe. The good of the individual was a function of the good of the community, not the reverse. The moral order was robustly collective.

Out of this came its stability, its self-completeness, its self-confidence in face of trials and tribulations. 'These nations,' deplored an Italian description of northern Angola during the 1680s,

with nauseating presumption think themselves the foremost men in the world, and nothing will persuade them to the contrary. They think ... they have not only the biggest country in the world, but also the happiest and most beautiful.

If there were others who thought nothing of the kind, there were still many who agreed. Even when resistance to change had revealed its weakness against an outside world rapidly winning technological power, later missionaries found it hard to persuade them to the contrary.

What Fortes says of the Tallensi was true of most of these societies, perhaps of all of them in varying degree. The 'rights and duties of individuals appear as elements of corporate rights and duties', so that 'the solidarity of the unit is stressed at the expense of the individual's private interests or loyalties'. The Principle of Good was whatever made for community welfare:

when acting as the Principle of Evil, it did whatever was the reverse. And it is in the light of this moral order that one needs to interpret the specific arrangements of structural abstraction – descent-lines, age sets, and the rest – which offer, for us, the only entry to an understanding of societies so different from our own. For the moral order was there even when, to the outside eye, it appeared most absent.

It appeared most absent to many Europeans, as we have seen. Catching a glimpse of what was allowed or disallowed, they found it ludicrous to apply any such term as 'moral order' to peoples who seemed quite without a European sense of shame. Travellers from afar found much to shock them. The Venda of the Transvaal are only one among many peoples, for example, who have considered that premarital sexual experience was morally, because socially, valuable and even necessary, provided always that it should not lead to pregnancy. Premarital pregnancy was severely discouraged because the children of unmarried parents represented an immediate problem for the community, posing the question : to whom should they belong? ; so that, at least among the Southern Bantu, the stigma of illegitimacy attached to the parents and not to the offspring. Otherwise the Venda saw to it that youths and maidens after the age of puberty should be carefully instructed in the 'facts of life', so as to have a limited form of sexual outlet before marriage.

Among these people there was a deliberate and prophylactic use of frankness, even a forthright grasping of the nettle of maturity, and no evasion by means of that characteristically nineteenth-century construct, 'adolescence', which supposes capacity without expression. According to Venda accounts of traditional life collected in the 1920s, a sexually mature girl who continually 'stays with her mother' was 'contemptuously called "Afraid-of-men", "Waddle-about" ... They do not consider her a normal human being, they call her a procrastinator.' When a girl is grown up, she ought to have a *mudavdu* (a sweetheart), and she ought, but within strictly understood limits, to make love with him. This partial intercourse was called *davhalu* among the Venda. 'When a man *davhalu*'s in the old proper way,' Venda elders were recalling some fifty years ago, long before mechanical forms of contraception were available, 'the girl keeps her legs together, he does not touch the pudendum, the penis being merely passed through between the legs', while the girls were subjected to a monthly examination to make sure their 'play' really was according to the 'old proper way'. If a girl allowed herself to be deflowered she was punished by a public scolding, thought to be a shameful thing; and the family of a deflowered bride would have to pay a fine in marriage compensation.

More than compensation was involved. The Zulu are another people who have believed that 'failure to observe moral rules connected with sex' would 'cause evil to befall the community', and have evolved corresponding customs. Their *ukusoma*, like the *davhalu* of the Venda, was aimed at combining 'delayed marriage with a strong emphasis on virginity before marriage'. Involving muscular control on the girl's part, *ukusoma* was thought to produce firm thighs and buttocks, features that were therefore taken as a sign of innocence, so that a Zulu girl was 'proud to display her body as a proof of her moral uprightness'. Krige records a ceremony where girls who had clothed themselves were even criticized with the implication that they had led a loose sexual life. Nudity could thus be the reverse of obscene. So could the frankness in girls' puberty songs, combining moral with sex instruction. 'He mounted me on the *mons veneris*,' primly sang the wise Zulu virgin, 'because he knows very well': respects, that is, the rules of right behaviour.

Sexual morality, like any other, was deliberately selective: it mirrored, that is, specific kinship arrangements. Among the Nyakyusa of northern Malawi, another case in point, these arrangements seem to have been keyed to an emphasis on the fear of incest within groups far wider than the nuclear family. Otherwise, Monica Wilson tells us, the Nyakyusa are very tolerant in matters of sex, even regarding homosexuality as a venial sin if committed by youths, or else as a misfortune occasioned by witchcraft. The Tallensi consider it reasonable for an impotent or sterile husband to call in a friend who acts in his stead, once again in terms of a kinship structure which has placed a prime value on succession and family alliance.

The actual rules have been as various as the kinship structures.

Much is now understood about the latter, though much else remains to be explained. One chief division has been observed: into those societies which reckon descent through mothers, when mothers' brothers become more important in matters of office and succession than fathers; and those which reckon descent through fathers and fathers' brothers. An earlier generation of anthropologists tried to explain these matrilineal and patrilineal divisions by supposing they reflected different stages of ancient society. When early peoples were in the 'hunting and gathering' stage, it was argued, fathers took the lead because theirs was the crucial economic activity; but the introduction of agriculture restored authority to mothers because it was women who weeded and hoed.

This explanation has the virtue of neatness, and there may be something in it; but closer observation has shown a far more complex truth. All the Bantu-speaking peoples who inhabit the greater part of central and southern Africa are farming peoples. They hunt and keep cattle, but much of their food comes from cultivation. Yet the central Bantu peoples reckon descent matrilineally, and so confirm the old explanation, while southern Bantu peoples often refute it by doing the reverse.

Laying such obscurities aside, one is left with kinship structures which form a unity of basic pattern diversified by local variation. The interest lies in the arrangement. Thus the Tallensi jural community was a clan which consisted of two or more maximal lineages. A maximal lineage is defined as 'the most extensive grouping of people of both sexes all of whom are related to one another by common patrilineal descent' – a descent which is 'traced from one known (or accepted) founding ancestor through known agnatic [father-related] antecedents'. In this society it followed that men were supreme. Women were obliged by the moral order to marry outside their own lineages, and normally lived away from their relatives.

This balance between clan ties and maximal lineage ties formed the central feature of the Tallensi political system, and promoted its stability. Invisible to early observers, it worked by a subtle conjunction of checks and balances. Not seeing it, these observers reasonably concluded that Tallensi had no government at all, since they had no chiefs with central authority nor any other palpable means of keeping law and order, or of administering rewards and punishments. In fact, however, Tallensi were and in some measure still are greatly concerned with the uses and abuses of political power. They have carefully allowed for the exercise of the first and the discouragement of the second.

Like the Amba, this people of about half a million souls have lived in villages, but, unlike the Amba, they have tied their villages intimately together. Tallensi clans and lineages have been composed of men living in different villages, the disintegrating force of geographical separation being balanced by the integrating force of kinship. Their social charter has thus had a two-way pattern of pressures. At any given moment, there is in Taleland

a system of mutually balancing segments in which are vested the rights and duties through which the structural equilibrium is sustained. This tendency towards an equilibrium is characteristic of every phase of the social structure ... Loyalty to the local clan is balanced by a contrary loyalty to a component unit or a neighbouring clan.

The balance, of course, was imperfect. The ideal was not achieved by Tallensi any more than by others. The very conditions of fixed village settlement in this ecologically hazardous savanna made stability repeatedly difficult. Droughts, swarms of locusts or other pests, the constant need for fission or fusion among village units faced with populations which varied in size according to the fortunes of the day: all such trials were factors of upheaval. Yet the pressures of Tallensi moral order worked steadily for resolution. Quarrels were many, but fights apparently few. And they were few precisely because the Tallensi were much of Lord Acton's opinion on the corrupting influence of power. They regarded power, and therefore the effort to obtain it, with profound distrust.

Others thought the same. A majority of African societies have been like the Lozi of western Zambia who are 'apparently terrified of giving away power, even power to protect, for once a man is elevated it is feared he will stand against those he ought to care for'. Even societies with chiefs and kings seldom deprived themselves of the right of deposition, at least up to the nineteenth century; and the founding notion of England's Magna Carta, that you could justly act against an unjust ruler, was deeply rooted here. Since offensive warfare is nothing if not a violent exercise of power, the Tallensi were against it. They stressed peace and non-provocation 'as the ideal relationships between neighbours'.

Clasped in their community structure of morally sanctioned checks and balances, the Tallensi thought it sinful to instigate warfare, since warfare could gravely damage their equilibrium. Warfare might be unavoidable now and then, but they deplored it as exchanging a possible immediate gain for a probable later loss. 'War occurred when members of one clan committed a grave injury (e.g. murder) against members of another, from which theirs was divided by social barriers more powerful than any ties uniting them.' Within a given grouping, an act of violence could be settled by compensation according to the rules. Outside the grouping, it would call for remedial action beyond the rules. So warfare was not 'an instrument of policy, but an act of reprisal. Punishment, not conquest, was its purpose. Territorial annexation was incompatible with the social structure' – would upset, that is, the intervillage equilibrium – 'nor could captives or booty be taken. It was a stern taboo to retain any of the foodstuffs or livestock pillaged in war. All had to be destroyed or immediately consumed.' In other words, to take cattle from neighbours and graze them would call for more land, and thus disturb the pattern of community settlement.

But this concept of community was more than a political device limited to relationships between people living at any given time. Had it been only that, it could scarcely have survived the human appetite for power and privilege. Far more, it was rooted in Tallensi notions about how their society had come into existence, and by what right it could continue to exist. Here we are back to the legitimating relationship between ancestors and living men, and between ancestors and land. What advantaged living men was whatever lay along the grain of ancestral precedent, and this was conceived ideally: as flowing from the 'bargain' which the ancestors had struck with the Spirit of the Earth. Unless living men kept to the bargain, the ancestors would not do so either. Then chaos would come.

It is of course doubtful whether Tallensi ever thought of all this in abstract terms of clans and lineages. For them, the kinship structure was self-evident from earliest childhood. But they took good care that people should remember its crucial loyalties. They celebrated annual festivals designed to perpetuate these loyalties, festivals that were both a confirmation of the existing order and a reaffirmation of its supreme validity.

For these and similar constitutional purposes they had two contrapuntal sets of functionaries, chiefs and Earth-priests, neither of whom had any directly political powers. The chiefs were thought of as representing the ancestors who had 'come into the land', while the Earth-priests spoke for those already settled there. As with other examples, a compact had been established between the two groups, immigrant and already-settled, so that both should live 'for ever in amity side by side'. Tallensi therefore 'believe that the common good of the whole tribe depends on the faithful ritual collaboration of chiefs and Earth-priests, after the fashion, as they put it, of husband and wife. If this breaks down, famine, war, disease or some other catastrophe will descend upon them.' Again one sees the deliberate emphasis on the ideal dual balance: of men in community, and of men with nature.

It followed that the office was carefully distinguished from the person who occupied it. For the person had power only by virtue of the office, since it was the office alone which conveyed the saving power of conservation. This distinction between the person and the office, the profane and the sacred, defines a central aspect of belief and action. Little can be understood without keeping it in mind.

The Zande cult of ancestors is centred round shrines erected in the middle of their courtyards, and offerings are placed in these shrines on ceremonial, and sometimes other, occasions; but when not in ritual use, so to speak, Azande use them as convenient props to rest their spears against, and pay no attention to them whatsoever.

The casual construction and everyday insignificance of African shrines make repeatedly the same point. What is important is not the contingent object but the immanent power which will be vested in the object on ritual occasions.

Clearly, then, these peoples were not astray in a mystical fog. On the contrary, they had a farmer's hard-headedness about life and the world. Tallensi ideas of right and wrong derived from their convictions about the constitutional relationships which bound them together; and in this respect they were as logical and realistic as British constitutional lawyers who speak of 'the Crown' as the supreme arbiter of British right and wrong. However mystical 'the Crown' might sound to an uninstructed Tallensi visitor – he would find that he could easily see the Crown jewels, but never 'the Crown' – quite a few British natives would be able to tell him that its powers were drawn from precedents subject to logical explanation. The validity of the logic in terms of commonsense behaviour might be questioned, but not the logic itself.

Some near neighbours of the Tallensi, the Konkomba who number about 80,000 and farm ·a reach of land about seventy miles wide that is 'alternatively a swamp and a dust bowl', can be called in here to illustrate the chain of logical legitimation. The Konkomba do not know when they first came to their land, though it was probably in the sixteenth century. They have no consciousness of history as a sequence of experiential cause and effect that goes beyond the naming of ancestors for half a dozen generations. If they live according to a strictly defined pattern of behaviour and belief, this is because the pattern is built into a daily fabric of their lives, and corresponds to a balance conceived by ancestral wisdom in 'a time that has no time'.

This does not mean that the Konkomba have not innovated or changed. They have done both. But they have done so by modifications of a pattern seen as mandatory in its underlying principles. These principles are governed by their habitat. Like Dinkaland, their country is flooded for several months every year; but the Konkomba use their land differently from the Dinka. They are primarily cultivators, their crops today consisting chiefly of yams, rice, millet and sorghum. These they farm in ways that can admit of few experiments within a pre-industrial economy. Yet the Konkomba do not think of their pattern as being shaped by ecological necessity and the range of available tools. Of course they see both these conditions, not being farmers for nothing, but they see them in terms of a timeless contract between their founding ancestors and the Spirits of the Earth. This contract between the living and the dead represents their social charter, their unwritten constitution.

Any alteration within the structure of Konkomba society requires, accordingly, to be fitted into the total structure by appropriate rituals. Otherwise there is bound to be trouble with the authorities – with the Spirits of the Earth and their attendant ancestors who guard the ideal balance. Kinsmen who want to shift their homesteads have to be sure of ancestral approval. 'When a man or group of men wish to move and settle in a stretch of unoccupied bush, they consult a diviner who discovers from them whether it is advisable to move and, if the answer be positive, the location of the shrines, commonly groves of trees, in the new area they propose to occupy. Thus a new relationship is established from the beginning between a group of kinsmen and the territory they occupy', and between this new group and the rest of Konkomba society. With this, they have 'connected themselves with their ancestors' and adjusted their new settlement to the ideal balance. Now they can face life safely on their own.

In any familiar sense of the word this manner of explaining life is not scientific. Although the outcome of practical observation and of trial and error over many years, it is in large part seen as 'given' and not open to question. It continues, however, to be very directly concerned with effects which flow from causes: in its farming context, much more often than not with material effects which flow from material causes. This is where descriptions go wrong whenever they suggest that these societies were dominated by a preoccupation with spiritual or mystical effects and causes. It is indeed very doubtful how any farming community could survive if that were the case. The 'fetish-ridden superstition' of the Africans is an illusion raised by the difficulty of understanding these beliefs and actions without inquiring into what they actually mean and do.

All the modern evidence shows that these societies were and are minutely aware of their natural and material environment, and insistently concerned with it. Flora, fauna, soil properties, water and mineral resources, climatic regularities: these are the things that have chiefly occupied their attention. All observers who have made lengthy firsthand studies of these peoples are agreed, writes Evans-Pritchard, that 'they are for the most part interested in practical affairs, which they conduct in an empirical manner, either without the least reference to suprasensible forces, influences, and actions, or in a way in which these have a subordinate and auxiliary role'.

The truth appears to be that they have thought and acted

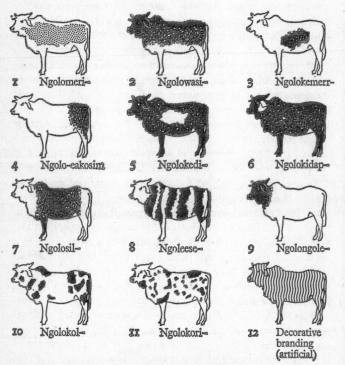

1  Ngolomeri-  2  Ngolowasi-  3  Ngolokemerr-

4  Ngolo-eakosim  5  Ngolokedi-  6  Ngolokidap-

7  Ngolosil-  8  Ngoleese-  9  Ngolongole-

10  Ngolokol-  11  Ngolokori-  12  Decorative branding (artificial)

Karimojong cattle classification by hide markings

on two different but related levels. It is the second level, concerning suprasensible effects and causes, which has proved the stumbling block to seeing them as rational and logical. Without the key to understanding, their beliefs and actions must often seem perversely irrational and ghost-ridden. Between old and new views of the Africans the real difference is that the key is now available in a number of cases sufficient to portray the whole, at least in general outline. This key rests in a comprehension of their moral order.

# 8  Elaborations I: Age Sets

When does a community become a 'state', or a 'tribe' turn into a 'nation'? Little can be gained from arguing such matters of nomenclature, much of which is still befogged by old misunderstandings. It is more useful to see how the actual structures evolved, as it were, on the ground.

Anthropologists have drawn a broad working distinction between 'societies with governments' and 'societies without governments'. By this they mean, essentially, distinction between systems which contained a central authority of some recognized sort and others which did not. Thus the aristocratic governments of the Wolof of Senegal or the Yoruba of Nigeria were clearly very different in their structure, and therefore in their mood and ethos, from the egalitarian systems of the Tallensi or Konkomba.

Seen historically, however, the range of Africa's political systems much more resembles a continuum between extremes. At one end there were societies which stayed close to the 'ideal formative community' of founding ancestors during remote times: the community of pioneers consisting of a handful of nuclear families bound together by common experience, and governing themselves, while they settled and slowly grew in numbers, by more or less simple forms of gerontocracy. Developing from this there came structures of kinship whose organization, as time went by, evolved complex and contrapuntal balances and checks upon the use and abuse of power.

Tallensi self-rule lay towards this end of the continuum. Their government embodied no king or other person with political authority, no executive service, no capital or central place of assembly, but lay in a series of arrangements deploying a pervasive influence at three levels. First, there were guiding precedents for the practical questions of everyday life. Do we hoe today, and if so whose garden? Next, at a level removed somewhat from everyday affairs, Tallensi self-rule took effect in ties within clans and between maximal lineages, imposing and defining wider obligations. Do we exact compensation from those people over there, or owe them any, and if so how much? At a third remove, Tallensi government assured a larger concept of unity and mutual obligation: the concept of a moral order upon which 'everything' was immanently built according to a social charter within which all Tallensi, in varying depths of awareness, always dwelt, enabling them at any time to say: This is the country we belong to, and this is why.

At the other end of the continuum there were states with very obvious and puissant forms of central government, having emperors and kings, hierarchies of wealth, executive services, administrative capitals, formidable armies. 'We entered Kumasi at two o'clock', a British envoy wrote of the Asante capital in 1817, where

upwards of five thousand people, the greater part warriors, met us with awful bursts of martial music ... an area of nearly a mile in circumference was crowded with magnificence and novelty. The king, his tributaries, and captains, were resplendent in the distance, surrounded by attendants of every description ... More than a hundred bands burst out on our arrival ... at least a hundred large umbrellas or canopies, which could shelter thirty persons, were sprung up and down by the bearers with brilliant effect.

Yet even in such states as this the old authority of kinship remained of critical influence in deciding what was politically done or not done. With important exceptions to be discussed later, men acquired office by virtue of their positions in the kinship structure, and exercised power by sanctions whose ultimate creation depended not on any royal will, but on ancestral mandate.

After 1720 the kings and chiefs of Asante brought within their power a territory somewhat larger than Ghana. But even later, when men began to be appointed to office by merit, chiefs were seldom allowed to forget that they drew their authority from their representative status. Within the metropolitan part of the empire this status was conferred by ritual acts carrying a legal force because they emerged from the Asante social order. The culmination of these rites was the seating of the new chief upon his seat of office, his *akonnua* or stool. With that, a double function was fulfilled. The *akonnua* stood to the chief as a throne to a European king, but it also stood to chiefship as the European crown to kingship: it was a physical thing to be used on appropriate occasions, but also a supreme symbol of constituted authority.

Seated on his *akonnua*, the chief is considered to be absorbed by his office.

Appearing then before his people, he swears fidelity to them and is admonished by his senior councillors to remember, among other things, that he may never act without their advice, and must rule with justice and impartiality. It is impressed on him that he belongs to the whole chiefdom in his capacity of chief, and not to his own lineage.

He must forget his own position in the kinship structure, must rise above family considerations, and must enlarge his boundaries of thought and judgement to include the whole complex of descent-groups over which he is called to rule. When he fails, those who have elected and installed him possess the constitutional means to depose him, and they have often used it.

Thus there is no point along the kinship continuum at which a true dividing line may be drawn between centrally rural societies on the one hand, and 'governmentless' or 'stateless' societies on the other. It is rather that the web of kinship was spun in varying patterns and appearances. Here it might glimmer in the open sunlight of village life, or there be veiled in the awesome shades of chiefly pomp and paraphernalia. But the web of kinship was present in all these societies, the necessary underfabric of their structures.

Its influence or resilience differed greatly from people to people, and was increasingly submerged or limited wherever society became deeply stratified, or kings and nobles reinforced their power. Yet even where this happened it did so as a partial process, hesitant and still profoundly moulded by the past. The influence of the kinship structure remained powerful even in defeat.

The source of this endurance lay in the power to resolve conflict or promote common action. How much any given structure did this clearly varied, since the kinship continuum ranged from very simple forms of self-rule for very small groups, such as the thirty- or forty-member Bushman 'extended family', to structures which enclosed large numbers of people. Obviously, too, some peoples governed themselves better than others, were luckier or more inventive. Outside influences such as Islam also played their part. But the efficacy of kinship was realized repeatedly, and above all in the ability to conserve social unity: in the capacity, that is, to counterpoise the competing claims of lineages, clans, or other segments of any given people.

It is difficult to grasp this efficacy from outside. People in modern societies think of their problems in quite other terms. Yet the difference may still be one of degree, a matter of interpretation at varying levels. Caught in litigation with a neighbour, a 'modern' man will think first of the immediate and practical evidence: whose trespass, whose tort? A little later he may ask other questions: how do he and I stand in relation to society? How much weight can each of us pull? And then thirdly, at another level of judgement: what kind of dispute is this, how will it be judged in relation to the moral order? These might be called the personal, corporate, and socio-moral levels. But it is only in so far as the third level, the socio-moral level, may appear of small or no real relevance in our present 'jumble of ethical precepts' that there exists an essential difference between present and past. Otherwise a man conflicting with his neighbour in a kinship system asks the same three types of question. What is the immediate evidence in dispute? What corporate allies can each side depend on? What are the moral issues at stake? In either case the relative efficacy of the two systems, as ways of humanizing man in society, is realized at successive levels of influence on behaviour: in the nature of significant evidence, in the operation of corporate alliances, and in the persuasion of the socio-moral order.

Here I want to look at a few examples on the second level, that of corporate alliances and arrangements. They illustrate some characteristic elaborations that appeared among many peoples, though by no means among all. Age sets or age grades form one of them.

The Tiriki are a people, numbering today about 40,000, whose 'incoming ancestors' arrived in north-western Kenya four or five centuries ago, migrating probably from Uganda. Their community embraces groups of descent-lines owing allegiance to common ancestors. These groups live in villages or related clusters of villages near the head of Lake Nyanza. But their corporate unity, as a people, has rested chiefly on their dividing of all Tiriki males into regular sets by age. Applying the 'ethnographic present' for the sake of convenience, although the position today is no longer what it used to be, the Tiriki have seven of these age sets.

Suppose you are Daudi Imbadu of the Tiriki. Until you are ten or so you are counted as a 'small boy' with minimal social duties such as the herding of cattle. Then you will expect, with some trepidation, to undergo initiation to manhood by a process of schooling which lasts about six months and is punctuated by ritual 'examinations'. Selected groups of boys are entered for this schooling once every four or five years. 'Life during the six months' seclusion period', Sangree found, 'is characterized by strict regimentation and a focus on group activities to the exclusion of all private or individual undertakings. All the initiates of a hut eat, sleep, sing, dance, bathe, do handicrafts etc. . . . [but] only when commanded to do so by their counsellor', who will be a man under about twenty-five.

The accent, one sees, is on social transformation. Circumcision gives it a ritual embodiment within the first month or so, after which social training continues as before until the schooling period is complete. Then come ceremonies at which elders teach and exhort, the accent now being on obedience to rules which have been learned. The Tiriki social charter is thus explained and then enshrined at the centre of a man's life.

'During the many evenings in the seclusion hut and at the special ceremonial meetings in the circumcision grove [the aspirant to manhood] is taught by his counsellor and by the initiation elders the host of duties, responsibilities and privileges that accompany age-group membership.' There is inculcated a sense of respect for elders, of brotherhood among members of the age set in question, and of skill in practical matters such as the use of arms. The parellel may be wildly remote in context and content, but one is irresistibly reminded of the English public schools. Even visiting Tiriki mums are said to be like their English counterparts, alarmed for their offspring but jealously proud of their progress.

Early in his teens Daudi Imbadu has completed this initial training in behaviour, although further training for a widened scope will continue throughout his life. Now he is judged not as an adolescent but as a young adult capable of assuming some responsibility in community affairs. How much he assumes will depend on character or circumstance. But generally it will grow with time until, some fifteen years later, Daudi and his brethren are elevated to a new set, that of warriors. This is the most admired status that any man can have in Tirikiland where, as it used to be, people have been constantly preoccupied with small-scale raiding or defence against it. These are the fifteen years during which Daudi can make his name by deeds of prowess. These will mark him out for leadership when, in the next move upwards, he moves around the age of forty into the set of elder warriors.

The elder warriors are the men who really govern Tirikiland in so far as any corporate government exists there. By this time the brethren in this set have been able to show their worth. Some take the lead; others merely enjoy the title. All are in any case expected to retire from what may be called 'executive duties' around fifty-five; then they become eligible for initiation into the next set, that of judicial elders ripe and wise enough to preside over courts of law. This age set of fifty-five to seventy may also be regarded as in some sense executive, since it is the next one upwards again which presides over the shrines where Tiriki laws are sanctioned and, at need, made or modified by ancestral order or advice. From about seventy to eighty-five, if he lives that long and is recognized as having the requisite qualities of character and intelligence, Daudi belongs to the chosen few whose experience and wisdom give them the final and legislative say in major Tiriki affairs. At last, near eighty-six or so, Daudi will be elevated to the ranks of very old men no longer fit for active life.

Theoretically these seven periods mark a revolving cycle of 105 years. If Daudi should survive to that age, unlikely but possible, he will have completed all stages from small-boyhood to retired eldership. In practice, of course, these arrangements have been geared to the easy-going habits of rural life, and each grade has overlapped to some extent with the grade above and the grade below. 'This does not mean, however, that every Tiriki [has not had] a clear picture of the sorts of activities commonly regarded as *most suitable* for each age group during its occupancy of any given age grade.' Even today 'the concept of fixed progression by the age groups through successive social statuses is an openly expressed part of the way the Tiriki conceptualize their own society both past and present'.

Other peoples near and far – the neighbouring Kipsigi and Nandi of Kenya, the Bantu of southern Africa, many in western Africa – have comparable age systems. They vary in detail, as one would expect, for each is the product of local evolution. The Karimojong of Uganda think of their history in terms of four age groups, each consisting of a generation reckoned as about twenty-five years. These have 'always' succeeded each other in time, and are named respectively after the zebra, mountains, the gazelle and the lion. But at any given moment only two of these generation sets are recognized as being in active existence: a senior one, which is closed to recruitment, and a junior one which is still acquiring its full complement of men. Each of these Karimojong generation sets consists in turn of five serially recruited age-groups with different statuses and obligations.

As a whole, the active male population of the Karimojong, reckoned as lying between about ten years old and sixty, are thus divided into two sorts of people, 'those in authority and those in obedience, the leaders and the led', and then again subdivided into groups with varying rights and duties. What this really means needs to be looked at in the light of Karimojong realities. A large part of any man's life is passed in isolated cattle-camps far from home, in driving cattle from one reach of pastures to another, or in small home-hamlets scattered through the bush. It is age set training which gives these people their structure of behaviour. Only this can overcome the social isolation of long and difficult seasons when a man may never see more than a dozen or so of his neighbours. Otherwise 'there is often no tie of kinship or neighbourhood or even [descent-line] section between the groups of herders who meet, mingle for a while, and then disperse to reform in other fortuitous combinations', as they shift with their beasts across the land.

This extreme disaggregation, ever renewed with every season, means that each small group is at the mercy of internal quarrels brought about by rivalry for scarce pasture and water, or of raids by similarly hard-pressed neighbours along the borders of Karimoja.

It is here that age-set affiliation has its greatest utility, for it immediately allocates to any individual in any collection of persons, however transient, a niche in a universal ranking system. Every individual has, accordingly, a pattern of response already roughly created, and needing only application to the context in which he finds himself ... Provided only that a man is both Karimojong and adult then he can be automatically grouped and ranked by age, whatever his company or whatever the circumstances. By these means, any aggregate of Karimojong in any place at any time can be structured to take common action.

But it is the 'third level' of awareness which makes this system work by providing the guides and sanctions of a universally acepted moral order. Like other 'stateless societies', the Karimojong have no police force or body of men with physical authority to act against offenders. Their age-group training would go for little, either in emergencies or the common run of daily life, were it not for moral assumptions – the psychosocial formation – on which it rests and which frame and fortify its rules.

Ultimately, it is the elders who guard and impose these rules. 'Whether individually or collectively, Karimojong consider obedience and respect for elders to bring good fortune through their beneficence; and equally, disobedience and disrespect to bring individual punishment and suffering, or collective calamity.' The attributed ability of elders 'to intercede with deity on the community's (or individual's) behalf, or to refuse to do so in time of need, or positively to curse, provides a graduated range of supernatural sanctions with which to back their decisions'.

Cursing by elders is the major punitive sanction, applied in varying degrees of doom, just as good behaviour is rewarded by appropriate blessings. Mild cursing may cause barrenness in wives or cattle, failure of crops, early death. More serious forms of curse, collectively expressed, may drastically generalize such woes. Offending Karimojong are, it appears, deeply and immediately concerned to avert the wrath of retribution. They must plead or pray for remission in words which Dyson-Hudson, who records them, found were no less binding for being stylized in form:

OFFENDER: Father, father, let me be. Help me. Leave me alone. I will not do these things again, truly. I will not repeat them.
ELDER: Very well. Have you believed?
OFFENDER: I have.
ELDER: Do you still argue?
OFFENDER: No, I have believed.

The moral basis is repeatedly emphasized by the meaning which Karimojong attach to this pleading before elders. Every form of pleading takes place within the structure of Karimojong belief, and 'connotes someone struggling with a force greater than himself that may only be removed at its behest rather than his own'. So an offender's remission depends upon forgiveness by the powers that underpin society. But this comes only when the forces of good are enabled by appropriate individual action and voluntary acceptance to overcome the forces of evil. Then the offender can not only be relieved of further accusation but can also shed his own sense of guilt – and in this pattern of consciousness, as we shall see, there lies much of the value of traditional psychotherapy, especially in cases of mental depression.

Other forms of 'separation by age' suggest a resolution of specific problems, as with the Nyakyusa. They carry separation to an extreme. They divide their male population not only socially into age sets which cut across descent-line loyalties, but geographically into age villages as well. In its actual place of dwelling each male generation is physically separated from others, so that 'the local unit consists not of a group of kinsmen ... but of a group of age-mates with their wives and young children'. Boys beyond infancy must form generation villages in the same way as men.

Why should the Nyakyusa do this? For themselves it is 'right and natural' and requires no validation other than in terms of what is 'right and natural', a circular explanation which gets us nowhere. But Monica Wilson, who has studied their system of life, suggests that Nyakyusa patterns of sexual morality may lie at its base. She notes that Nyakyusa have no ceremonies to mark the threshold of maturity and circumscribe behaviour: 'Therefore any young man past puberty is a potential mate for a woman of his own age.' This might not matter very much if it were not that Nyakyusa men customarily marry late while girls marry early, with the result that there are 'many bachelors and very few girls available to them', a shortage rendered the more acute by Nyakyusa attitudes which favour a man's marrying as many wives as he can afford. Moreover, Nyakusa social rules also suppose the inheritance of a father's widow by his son, except for his own mother or her kinswomen. 'So it is scarcely surprising that the seduction of the young wives of an ageing father is a common theme for scandal, and that a father's jealous fears are matched by those of his son.' Out of all this, Wilson argues, there has come a social anxiety about incest between step-son and step-mother on the one hand, and between father-in-law and daughter-in-law on the other; and Nyakyusa accordingly separate sons from fathers by making them live in different villages.

But with active males thus divided, physically and emotionally, how does Nyakyusa society hold together? The answer lies in a range of values likewise inherent to the system. Nyakyusa have evolved a compensatory mechanism by stressing what they call *ukwangela*, 'the enjoyment of good company and, by extension, the mutual aid and sympathy which spring from personal friendship'. This 'implies urbane manners and a friendliness which expresses itself in eating and drinking together; not only merry conversation, but also discussion between equals which the Nyakyusa regard as the principal form of education', an attitude which modern educationists, one feels, may incidentally well approve. They place, it seems, a tremendous emphasis on the good fellowship of *ukwangela* within a given village and across the whole network of kinship relations.

These attitudes are more than platonic. Like other Africans – like all predominantly rural people? – Nyakyusa are down-to-earth about the frailties of human nature. They may think that a man should have *ukwangela* out of sheer good will. But they do not count upon it. They expect him to have it out of self-interest, failure to have it being the path to ruin by witchcraft. It is fear of this retribution by witchcraft that 'compels generosity and conformity with public opinion in the village and thus creates a sense of mutual dependence between neighbours', while by the same token 'the disapproval of neighbours spells ill-health'.

As so often, that part of the moral order which has been conceived in terms of witchcraft is thus to be seen in a dual light. Witchchaft stands for Evil in the sense that it strikes at men and women who fail in their social duties and who, in so doing, open the gate to Evil. In another light it operates as a belief restraining Evil, or punishing anyone who harbours Evil, with troubles that we should usually regard as mere misfortune. Either way, to see witchcraft belief as an extraneous and arbitrary element is to misread the nature of this civilization. Having supposed Good in the form of a given moral order, Africans have been obliged to suppose Evil in whatever undermines it. God without the Devil is what no people have yet been able to imagine.

# 9 Elaborations II: Secret Societies

If democracy means participation, these societies were democratic, even extremely so. Ingeniously, coherently, they resisted the alienation of the individual from the springs of community action. Their very patterns of self-rule supposed an ever-present awareness of exactly where the power lines ran, and through whose hands and precisely for what purposes. Their politics were intimate, immediate, always close at hand, not faceless or remote. Much more than with the exercise of power these systems were concerned with its everyday control. Even the label sometimes given them by modern research, 'segmentary societies', speaks loud in this sense. Essentially they were composed of counterpoised 'segments' or lineage groupings of a given whole, each contained within itself but dependent on the others.

This kind of government was possible for small or fairly small communities. One may even regard it as the major political instrument evolved by Africans for populating their continent with its sparse ancestral communities. Even when small communities became transformed into large ones, minor governments into major governments, village states into farspread empires, these foundations in segmentary self-rule were never entirely lost.

Today they may perhaps be seen in the 'purest' condition among peoples who have remained numerically few in lands beyond the skyline of the beaten track. Yet it would be a mistake to think that only numerically small peoples continued to practise segmentary self-rule, or those who least felt the influence of change. Nobody has shown this better than the Ibo. They live in fertile and densely populated country east of the lower Niger, and must have numbered several millions long before the general explosion of population which has occurred in modern times.

These peoples have always enjoyed a reputation for restless enterprise in trade. They have combined a positively Athenian eagerness for any new thing with a corresponding distrust of
authority; and their many village governments have reflected
this.

In a typical Ibo forest village, deep in the tall timber east of
Onitsha, there would be fifteen or twenty 'extended' or 'nuclear'
families. Government was by council of elders, the *ama-ala*, whose
permanent members were the fifteen or twenty recognized family
heads. 'However, any adult male held the right to sit on the
council. Normally this right was not exercised, but if a decision
was to be taken which vitally affected an individual he could insist
on his right ... an important check upon elders who inclined to
take decisions without proper consideration.' In everyday affairs
it was customary for the council of elders to rule by decree and
proclamation. 'But where decisions likely to produce disputes
were to be taken the *ama-ala* could order the town crier to an-
nounce a village assembly.'

All men could attend assembly and discuss contentious matters.

Every man had a right to speak, the people applauding popular
proposals and shouting down unpopular ones. Decisions had to be
unanimous and it was here that young or wealthy men with records
of service or dedication to the village could influence policy. If the
elders tried to enforce an unpopular decision the young men could
prevent any decisions through the operation of the unanimity rule. If
the *ama-ala* acted arbitrarily and refused to call the assembly the
people could demand it by completely ignoring them and bringing
town life to a halt. The village assembly was considered the Ibo man's
birth right, the guarantee of his rights, his shield against oppression,
the expression of his individualism and the means whereby the young
and progressive impressed their views upon the old and conservative.

Flexibility was the keynote of the Ibo system. They seem to
have played with a relaxed and easy skill on all the possible chords
and rhythms of segmentary organization, using age sets, lineage
loyalties, cross-cutting kinship relationships, ancestral cults and
other such techniques whenever it happened to suit them. Their
judicial system had the same mood of experiment.

A man might attempt to settle with the individual who had aggrieved him. If this failed he could appeal to a respected elder to intervene or call members of the two families together. He could also appeal to the ward or village elders. There were no set rules as to where he should begin his appeal for redress but he could appeal against the decision of the families to the ward elders and finally to the *ama-ala* of the village.

This flexibility was perhaps a function of the natural fertility and farming wealth of Iboland. Density of population could blur the rigidities of precedent. So could variety of occupation. By the sixteenth century, and probably much earlier, simple forms of subsistence economy flanked by a minimal exchange of manufactures, locally produced, had given way to more complex economies in which a division of labour was able to support markets every four days or eight days. Though these were not fully-fledged money economies, they permitted an intensive commercial life in which currencies such as the cowrie shell were increasingly used. In this respect it appears probable that the peoples of western Africa were economically in advance of most other African populations except along the northern and eastern seaboards. Here the mechanisms of change springing from labour specialization and trading opportunity had long ago their deep effect.

The earliest written account of Ibo life, that of Olaudah Equiano in 1789, makes this clear. Taken in slavery to North America, the enterprising Equiano regained his freedom and went to England, where he became active in the anti-slavery campaign of those years. His book is full of useful detail. He stressed the farming base of Ibo society, praising the natural richness of his country and pointing out that 'agriculture is our chief employment, and everyone, even the children and women, are engaged in it', but adding a good deal about craft industry and trade. He said that 'our women of distinction wear golden ornaments which they dispose with some profusion on their arms and legs', although there is no gold-bearing ore in Iboland. 'When our women are not employed with the men in tillage, their usual occupation is spinning and weaving cotton, which they afterwards dye, and make into garments', a craft which certainly goes back to a remote past in these regions. Writing for an English audience very conscious of the processes of manufacture, he agreed that the Ibo manufactured little: still, apart from their cottons, they made 'earthenware, ornaments, and instruments of war and husbandry' – and, he might have added, much excellent sculpture.

Specialist communities served a demand, developing from centuries before Equiano's time, for various goods and skills. Ibo of Nri near the Niger became noted for their priests and diviners; those of Awka for their herbal doctors, metalsmiths and carvers; those of Nembe for their salt production; those of Ilelima for their potting skills; those of Nkwerri for their commercial ventures; those of Abiriba for their mercenary soldiers; and others for different goods or services.

Long-distance trade was another factor in political development. It was certainly of great age in this region by the time that Europeans came on the scene. There is for example no copper or tin ore in Iboland, yet Igbo-Ukwu near Awka, an Ibo site where a cache of fine objects in bronze was unearthed some years ago, has yielded two radio-carbon datings which point to probable medians around A.D. 850 and 840. These are much earlier than historians had expected. Even if they may still prove too early for association with the bronze objects, there is much evidence to show that long-distance trade was active in the region at least six centuries ago. European traders arriving on these coasts after about 1500 found peoples, such as the Ijaw, who were well equipped for commerce. Later, the ocean trade in slaves brought its powerfully twisting stimulus, and a string of little monarchies and republics emerged in the delta of the Niger.

Like some other 'segmentaries' who have lain in the path of strong outside influence through trade, these peoples evolved a culture which has emphasized personal competition. Uncommonly among Africans, they have been markedly 'success orientated'. Egalitarian but individualistic, they have thought it an essential aspect of the 'right and natural' that talent should lead to enterprise, and enterprise to promotion, and promotion to privilege. They have insistently stressed social mobility. In this they have been poles apart from their neighbours across the Niger, the aristocratically governed Yoruba, whose hierarchies were laid down in heaven and have ever since persisted in supremely complacent assurance of their worth and value. Encased in such hierarchies the Yoruba built urban states of imposing rank and ceremony, and an empire that was at one time among the largest of its kind. But not the Ibo: their clamorous and personal democracy was based on dispersal of authority.

They could of course combine for practical purposes at the village level. Age sets among men or women gave them one means of doing this. Mutual aid was recognized as a moral obligation. Councils of elders decided seasonal questions of planting and harvesting, market regulation, self-defence. All this, if you like, belonged to the common sense of everyday life. But in certain parts of Iboland, chiefly where long-distance trade had influence, the system went further. It evolved a technique for limited solidarity of a kind which, like the age set, was used in one form or other by many systems. This elaboration of the segmentary kinship structure was the corporate association or society.

It took different forms even within Iboland. Where regular Ibo kingships developed, as they did in western Iboland, possibly by borrowing from the Yoruba-Benin range of hierarchical structures, they were buttressed but also balanced by groups of officials ranked on varying levels of authority. Accession to these offices – at the head of which stood the king, still no more than *primus inter pares* – was decided by individual wealth and enterprise rather than by birth. In states such as these the officials formed a more or less exclusive club, a 'titled society'. Members had titles to positions of public value, and drew their influence from these ranked positions in the socio-moral order as well as from the secular arm of the law.

Other forms evolved in the Niger delta, where from about 1650 onwards there reigned a mood of go-getting 'frontierism' thanks largely to the pressures and opportunities of the ocean trade. Here it was, along these Atlantic creeks and seaways, that ingenuity hit repeatedly on fresh elaborations of political and commercial practice. In these restlessly profiteering little city-states there were corporate societies of quite extraordinary interest. Best known among them, perhaps, was the Ekpe or Leopard

Society of the eastern Ibo and other ethnic groups in the trading towns of the Cross river.

Ekpe may be compared to a marriage between Freemasonry and a tightly organized municipal corporation, with now and then a dash of Tammany Hall thrown in for human interest. It was in one respect an open society. All men in these Cross river towns were eligible for membership no matter whether they were Ibo or Efik, Ibibio, Oron, or anything else – even occasionally European. In other respects Ekpe was a closed society in that membership was by subscription, and rank within Epke was carefully graded according to a member's seniority and wealth. The result was a combination of limited democracy and rule by rich

Mask in wood of the Ekpe Society, region of Benin, about 25 cms high. The masker wears it on his head, his own face and head being veiled in grass and his body in a suit of knitted string. He is shown here emerging from a sacred grove

men: democratic but not egalitarian, competitive but also restrictive. As such it proved a successful means of uniting peoples of different ethnic origin, and of exploiting this unity to win advantage from the European monopoly at sea. If the European seatraders acted together for their own interest, so also, with Ekpe, did the Cross river land-traders.

Under the control of its senior members, who were also its wealthiest, Ekpe 'promulgated and enforced laws, judged important cases, recovered debts, protected the property of members, and constituted the actual executive government'. Lively details of how Ekpe worked in practice are happily to hand in a manuscript diary, written in the 'trade English' of the delta by one of its leading members in Old Calabar. Its narrative is vivid, as almost any part of it can show. After the local king's death in 1787 Antera Duke, as he wrote his name, noted,

At 12 clock time wee have Willy Honesty call all genllmen for meet in Egbo Cobham Cobin for know who wee will giv King of Old Calabar and after 8 clock night wee have all us town genllmen meet for Coffee Cobin to settle everry Bad bob we was mak sinc wee father Dead so wee kild 2 goat.

Translated, this comes out as:

At twelve o'clock Willy Honesty called all the gentlemen to meet in Egbo [i.e. Ekpe] Cobham's cabin to decide whom we will make King of Old Calabar, and after eight o'clock at night all of us town gentlemen met at Coffee's cabin to settle every bad quarrel we had had since our father [the late king] died. So we killed two goats.

Called to existence by Cross river participation in the long-distance trade that was always the chief *raison d'être* of these towns, Ekpe could prove a formidable partner. Not only did it punish crime or misdemeanour by Africans, it disciplined the European traders as well, declaring boycotts when it found or suspected European fraud, 'closing the river' by common consent to all European shipping, and generally exercising an authority so determined that European dealers sometimes thought it worth while buying their way into its membership. Intense in its accent on competition and personal initiative, Ekpe none the less succeeded in providing these turbulent communities with 'an over-riding common interest in preserving the stability of the society and the social order of which it formed a part'.

Ekpe was able to buttress this sense of common interest by coercive sanctions, applied when necessary through a police force consisting of young men of one of the society's junior grades; and these sanctions could go as far as execution in serious cases. But the power to apply coercion and to get it accepted by the public rested on more than wealth and local prestige. Like all other such societies, Ekpe had evolved from the kinship structures of earlier times, in this case mainly from those of the Efik people, and its elaboration carried with it the persuasiveness of old ancestral charters. In another aspect it was therefore a religious society. Its ceremonies and equipment were of a sacral nature. Accordingly they were barred to the knowledge of non-members. This is why such societies of Ekpe have been called 'secret'. Although their existence and social impact were in no sense secret – on the contrary, they were necessarily public – their rites and meetings were surrounded by a host of taboos intended to promote awe and respect, and quite evidently capable of doing so.

Trade was their life blood. By 1700 the great affair of the Cross river towns and their neighbours westward in the delta was the sale of inland captives to European slavers. These captives were occasionally taken by force. Delta merchants raided inland in cannon-mounted canoes able to seat a hundred men or more. But new techniques of peaceful slaving were now evolved for this Afro-European commercial partnership. Ekpe members found a counterpart to their European seaward partnership in a landward combinatioin with the old market networks of Iboland. Long a central part of Ibo life, these networks were modified and extended so as to serve the ocean trades. Prominent among them was that of the traders of Arochuku. With these traders, commerce and religion once again marched together as in other times and continents.

They did so by an elaboration of oracular belief. The men of Arochuku, a ridge of country running southeastward from the central Ibo uplands, had become famous for their services of a

revered Ibo oracle, the Ebinokpapi. This was their chief specialization. They used it as a means of founding and cementing an
itinerant trading corporation whose colonies were established,
during the seventeenth century, in almost every part of Iboland.
One authority lists no fewer than ninety-eight Arochuku trading
colonies clustered along the main trade routes before and after
1700. Through these corporate Aro colonies there was channelled
the growing trade of Iboland. House-to-house buying and selling gave way to regular marketing at two great four-day fairs,
opened by Arochuku men at twenty-four day intervals, that were
attended by 'thousands of traders from all over the surrounding
countryside'.

After 1700, when slaving became the central part of this commerce, religion was once again there to help. It became conven-
tional that captives, whether taken by force or condemned to
enslavement for major criminal offences, could be offered to the
Ebinokpapi oracle in appeasement of the powerful spirit which
it spoke for, a spirit whose displeasure was believed to bring
general disasters in its train, and whose 'interests' were energetically furthered by the oracle's trading agents. Once offered to the
oracle, captives were taken over by the Aro men and marched
briskly to the slaving ports.

All this belonged to those mechanisms of change, including the
import of guns and gunpowder which 'enabled the rich and
efficient to fight their way to the top of the trade', and which the
European trading connection so greatly helped to drive and
quicken. Yet 'secret societies' for the purposes of government
were far older than the European trade. There is the striking case
of the Poro among the Mende and others of Sierra Leone.

Valentim Fernandes wrote about this before 1510. From information probably gathered between 1497 and 1507, his memoir
offers a picture of political and religious customs which manifestly refer to the Poro, most powerful of Sierra Leonian 'secret
societies', whose influence was recognized as paramount by later
observers. 'If the king wants to go to war', Fernandes explains,

he gathers the elders and holds his council. And if it appears to them
that the war is unjust, or that the enemy is very strong, they tell the

king that they cannot help him, and give orders for peace despite the king. All the villages of Sierra Leone have the same religion, and they believe the idols can help them, and succour them in difficulties.

The 'idols' – or what the Portuguese called *fetiçiãos*, 'fetishes' – were in fact no more such than were the painted saints and golden altars of Portugal itself: the confusion of image with spirit may indeed have been made less often in Africa than in Europe. But the religious connection was a real one. Authority functioned in these villages at two levels which were mutually complementary: the profane or political, and the sacred or religious. Neither was thinkable without the other.

As an instrument of government the councils of the Poro were concerned with most aspects of public life. They took decisions affecting the whole community, which in each case might number several thousands of people. They presided over matters of peace or war, the exercise of justice, the enforcement of penalties, the market price of yams and other goods, or the organization of dances and other public fun. Where chiefs or kings were also part of the political structure the Poro councils acted as a check and balance on their powers. They were themselves balanced by the powers of the chiefs or kings, but generally, it would seem, the councils were stronger than the chiefs or kings. In any case these councils were the main organ for investigation of crimes, anti-social behaviour such as malignant witchcraft, the regulation of affairs with neighbouring communities and other social business. A fairly typical conclusion by a European observer who travelled through Sierra Leone in the 1820s was that the Poro could be said 'to possess the general government of the country'. This is confirmed by most of what is known about the history of these peoples.

There seems to have been somewhat less of the spirit of competition in Poro than in Ekpe or comparable societies elsewhere. But competition was actively present in its grading of membership. Material success as well as seniority were the keys to power; and these aspects of promotion within Poro were steadily enlarged by the pressures of the ocean trade.

Membership was indispensable to self-respecting adulthood.

Lengthy periods of training at the age of puberty were obligatory on boys and girls–the latter being organized in a parallel women's society, the Sande, with social but not political powers – when pains were taken, and inflicted, to ensure that men and women should understand and heed the rules of law and custom. Writing chiefly of the past, Little says that

pain is inflicted deliberately upon them to instil habits of self-discipline, and they are taught to obey the elders without question. In the old days training lasted for two or three years, and sometimes longer; and throughout the whole of this period of schooling the Poro had complete control over virtually every youth in the country.

Thus trained and indoctrinated, young men could become members of Poro, though at first as juniors who were bound to carry out Poro commands but had no voice in Poro councils. 'Poro in the political sense', again according to Little,

consisted solely of the higher grades of the society. These comprised men who in some cases had risen to a position of seniority by further and more extensive periods of instruction, and men who through membership of certain descent-groups had an hereditary right to high positions in the society. In addition to the taking of an oath of greater and greater solemnity, each upward step involved payment of fees, and so only a very wealthy man of advanced years could hope to pass initiation into these higher degrees.

Among some of the inland peoples of Liberia, where Poro also functioned, there are said to have been as many as ninety-nine degrees, while only a few descent-lines were eligible for initiation into the 'final secrets'.

The principal 'chartered sanction' behind this system was a conviction that certain spirits could bring sickness or death. According to convention – and for many ordinary people, no doubt, according to belief as well – these spirits inhabited a sacred area of bush, quite small but exactly defined, whence they could and did emerge to exact punishment upon offenders. Whenever they wished to do this they became embodied in Poro officials whose heads were adorned by wooden masks fringed with capes of raffia, and who wore various other symbols of spiritual authority. Thus projected, the spirits 'descended with irresistible force upon any community rash enough to ignore the society's dictates', so that the 'Poro bush' became in social terms a 'veritable power house of supernatural force'.

It would be wrong to see only a means of disciplinary coercion in these beliefs. They contained as well an element of physical and psychological healing, whether through the administration of herbal medicines or parapsychical diagnosis and treatment of a kind to be discussed later. These techniques were an integral part of Poro schooling. Much value was attached to the quality of this schooling because the nature of healing materials and techniques was believed to vary, for better or worse, according to when and how they were used.

Poro authority thus combined spiritual power with specialized knowledge, two conditions which enabled it 'to perform a role analogous to that of the medieval church in Europe'. Like that church, 'Poro was also in a position to indoctrinate the "laity" with its own particular beliefs and practices, and could use its professed knowledge of supernatural matters to control most of the general life of the community', rewarding the 'good' with its blessings and punishing the 'bad' by excommunication from its ranks, and thus, for all practical purposes, from the community itself. A report of 1861 noted that 'the placing of the society's sign in a person's compound signified that he had incurred the society's displeasure, and was a warning that he must not move outside his farm or have anything to do with his neighbours until the bad was removed': until, that is, the offender had duly come to heel or made amends.

Small wonder, then, that Sierra Leonean society remained structurally static over so many years. Once in place, and then buttressed by the opportunities of an ocean trade controlled by Poro in the persons of its senior and most successful merchants, the system was well equipped to defend itself. Many an enterprising or luckless youth must secretly have cursed his elders while hoping to be able one day to do as they did.

This counterpoise between seniority by age and promotion by individual enterprise has regulated many African societies. Basically identical in their dual nature, sacred and profane, these systems have obviously differed in their details. Their influence was much diminished during the colonial period but seldom altogether destroyed, so that within limits it is right enough to speak today of Poro, and of some other 'secret societies', as continuing to function beneath the surface of parliamentary and other modern forms of political life. Their survival forms part of the problem of transition from the past to a different future.

Some of these societies are so deeply rooted in history as to have become barely separable from otherwise new structures of daily life, even in the second half of the twentieth century. Such is the venerable Ogboni Society of the Yoruba, founded in an Earth cult of great antiquity, held firmly in the intricate balance of Yoruba life, and of continuing significance to the life of millions of people. Although superficially deprived of political authority by structures of parliamentary self-rule of European type, the Ogboni Society has remained a powerful nexus of influence within Yoruba political allegiances, especially those of the Action Group which spoke for most Yoruba before and after the independence of 1960.

Other societies, some of them neither respectable nor respected outside their own ranks, have sprung from the distortion of traditional ideas and beliefs operating within a new and alien political context. They are even more a problem of transition. Anticipating that subject, one may glance here at the startling example of the Owegbe Cult, a new society which disturbed the electoral procedure and eventually the peace of Nigeria's Mid-West Region early in the 1960s. In Owegbe one hears the authentic voice of the past as well as the ardent clamourings of human frailty, and in ways which curiously dramatize the present African dilemma.

It all began, so far as such things ever have a true beginning, when an ambitious nobleman of seventy, Chief Omo-Osagie of Benin, a most religious city if ever there was one, fell into difficulties over a libel action. That was in 1944. He called in 'a consortium of native doctors' who were to help him to win this action by obtaining supernatural aid. These doctors duly collected their 'medicines' and established their shrine. Eventually the medicines consisted of oddments such as the heads of a swallow, a squirrel and snake, together with a human skull and various other things which were pounded together and placed in pots at shrines dedicated to Owegbe. Little images of more or less human shape were placed on the altars, and various rites prescribed.

From the libel action of 1944 the Owegbe Cult turned to bigger things. With political rivalry increasingly to the fore as independence drew nearer, Owegbe became a weapon used by local members of the non-Yoruba N.C.N.C. party against the Yoruba Action Group which, on its side, had the backing of the Ogboni Society to ensure the loyalty of voters. After independence the party clash became tougher still as leaders competed for jobs and patronage. The Owegbe Cult developed means of 'encouraging' or 'discouraging' voters in the interests of certain of these leaders, notably the aforesaid Chief Omo-Osagie.

Members of Owegbe claimed supernatural powers which evidently carried some credit. At the official inquiry these powers were duly rehearsed in court to the enjoyment of the audience. One colourful witness – and the whole report makes a remarkable portrayal of Benin politics – assured the commission of inquiry that he could 'render himself invisible and cause painful reactions to be felt by anyone beating him, while he enjoyed immunity to any pain himself'. The witness went on to say 'amidst much laughter, that when the Police beat him with their batons in trying to quell some disorder in which he was involved, it was the Police who felt the blows, not himself'.

Then came the turn of another veteran, Prince Shaka Momodu the Lion of Ishan, formerly a Mid-West Minister of Internal Affairs. He denied Owegbe membership but 'claimed that the Ishan militant youth who fought as his supporters in the Ishan riots possessed a brand of invulnerability superior to that of Owegbe. He himself claimed that he is gunshot-proof and matchet-cut proof . . . and that he was not only the Lion of Ishan but of the Mid-West. When I pointed out,' observed the learned judge who presided over the inquiry, 'that even lions were not gunshot-proof, he claimed to be a special lion and offered to give a demonstration of his invulnerability, but,' adds the judge with a tactful respect for local susceptibilities, 'the matter was not pursued since I believed that the Prince must be bluffing.'

Another witness declared in relation to a certain electoral fracas,

we were fully prepared for that battle ... Although we were un-
armed we used some native herbs and all the rest of it, washed ourselves fully all right, and even if you used a double-barrelled gun on
me that day it would not penetrate. I can assure you that it is through
the help of that preparation, otherwise I would have been a dead
person today.

And then there was the energetic Chief Omo-Osagie, eager to
become Premier of the Mid-West 'by virtue of being head of a
new regional party, which would make him the *fons et origo* for
the distribution of patronage among his trusted lieutenants and
supporters'. Seniority plus wealth, backed by supernatural power,
was to rule as it should; and the Chief, duly promoting himself
to a new kind of grade according to the times, flourished the
number plate of his car. This could not be B1 – Benin 1 – because
B1 was the possession of the Oba of Benin, descendant of a line of
rulers already six centuries old. So the Chief took B2. In this, at
least, he was very up-to-date.

Before being brought under control the Owegbe Cult had
assembled enough anti-Yoruba support to raise in the political
division of Benin no fewer than 251 shrines, each with its attendant 'party branch'. Its purpose 'was to gain control of the
Regional Government' for Chief Omo-Osagie and other local
leaders of the N.C.N.C. To do this it married old attitudes and
beliefs to new ones. However distorted by the confusion of the
times, behind it lay the old acceptance of an inseparable com-
panionship between the profane and the sacred: between 'this
world and the next', between political power and appropriate
religious manipulation.

Is it possible to go further and to analyse the religious structures which could hold such beliefs together, fertilize them
through the centuries by one elaboration or another, and give
them mandatory force? To questions like these the sociologists
have begun to offer new if still tentative answers.

# Part Three: Structures of Belief

Cradle of the world's systems and philosophies,
and the nursing mother of its religions.

J. E. G. CASELY HAYFORD, *Ethiopia Unbound*

Let us not run the world hastily;
Let us not grasp at the rope of wealth impatiently;
What should be treated with mature judgement
Let us not treat in a fit of temper.

Yoruba maxims (trans. E. B. Idowu)

# 10 A Science of Social Control

The study of religion, we are told, remains even today 'an enormous and untilled field for research'. And it is understandably one that scientists have seldom cared to enter, at any rate since Bruno was burned at the stake and Galileo bullied into saying that the Earth was flat. Even when they have entered this field, they have generally done so with the suspicion of being sadly, even rather shamefully, out of place. To many anthropologists of the nineteenth century, Professor Evans-Pritchard has lately written, 'religious belief was ... absurd, and it is so to most anthropologists of yesterday and today'.

Yet it is now perfectly evident that scientific elucidation of all those systems of thought and belief which have passed in Africa under the catch-all label of 'religion' – and I use this often misleading word only for want of a better – is vital to any genuine social analysis. We cannot begin to understand the drift and logic of African apprehension of reality unless, for example, we have grasped the reasons why appointed ancestors should have become 'the jealous guardians of the highest moral values ... the axiomatic values from which all ideal conduct (has been) deemed to flow'. In this large sense the study of religion is the study of social fact.

When the lords of the Karanga carved their empire from the lands between Zambezi and Limpopo long ago, and built their stone dwellings at Zimbabwe, they set up a shrine to *hungwe*, the fish-eagle, and erected soapstone effigies to the power they also called *Shirichena*, the Bird of Bright Plumage, or *Shiri ya Mwari*, the Bird of God. Attending this shrine the priest or medium of the most powerful of the appointed ancestors, Chaminuka the great *mhondoro*, was required to interpret the meaning of the cries of *hungwe*, and crucial decisions of state were influenced by what he said. For more than three centuries before 1830 it was to the spirit of Chaminuka, and its oracle the Bird of Bright Plumage, that the kings of the Karanga appear to have turned for guidance in their testing problems of state.

Carving in soapstone of *Shiri ya Mwari*, the Bird of God, from Great Zimbabwe. A number of such figures, the bird in this one being about 37 cms high, stood upon the walls until found by white explorers who removed them

Now the old European explanations could see in this behaviour only quaint foolishness engendered by the fogs of superstition, or else, yielding somewhat later to the facts, an in-built but arbitrary social mechanism. This has led to misunderstandings: to the point, continues Evans-Pritchard, where 'most of what has been written in the past, and with some assurance, and is still trotted out in colleges and universities, about animism, totemism, magic, etc., has been shown to be erroneous or at least dubious' by investigators working from another standpoint and in greater possession of the facts.

Modern anthropologists have had to rethink what they mean by religion. For it has become clear that religion was, or is, much more than a mere 'comfort' or useful function in traditional structures based on ancestral charters fashioned by the imperatives of daily life, and fastened by a corresponding moral order. We are really faced here with structures of belief which were not only mandatory in a social sense but also explanatory in a material one, and, as such, were the basis for rational thought.

When the priest of *hungwe* interpreted the cries of *Shirichena*, the 'messages' he gave to the king of the Karanga were not accordingly a farrago of savage fancies. They were advice – obviously of a value depending on the wisdom of the priest in question – that was drawn from a particular study of reality: in this case, from a logically elaborated series of explanations about the way the world of the Karanga worked. However picturesque and peculiar his methods of conceiving such advice might be, the effective task of this religious leader was to safeguard community welfare and survival. His advice was therefore framed to ensure that behaviour stayed in line with the 'ideal equilibrium' of the ancestors: of those who had 'shown men how to live' in this land. That the advice might be couched in esoteric explanations of a bird's cries did not mean that it was any the less concerned, in practice, with the social or cultural problems of the day. Just how practical such advice could be, and how closely the product of a judging of realities, was shown with startling clarity in 1896 when the priests of the Karanga advised revolt against European invaders, with whom, as they concluded, no peaceful action would any longer carry weight.

Seen in this way, 'religion' in this context stands for an apprehension of reality across the whole field of life. This was the explanatory apprehension that produced its mandatory force. Out of it, in one way or another, there emerged what may reasonably be called a science of social control.

One may boggle at use of the word 'science' in these societies. Certainly they were 'pre-scientific' in that, generally, their thought had 'no developed awareness of alternatives to the established body of tenets', and thus no urge towards systematic search for such alternatives. But at the same time there was also a developed awareness of the practical possibilities of prediction based upon observation: of what Lévi-Strauss has called 'the science of the concrete'. In fact, traditional thought was copiously empirical in its approach to natural phenomena. Experiment, after all, had been its saving virtue from early times. Nothing else can explain the Africans' intense attention to the detailed knowledge of environment.

Their persistent classifying and naming of phenomena, whether known by observation or inferred by intuition, needs perhaps a little emphasis. The Dogon of the Western Sudan – to confine examples to the peoples mentioned in these pages – classify the plants they know in twenty-two chief families of which some are divided into as many as eleven sub-families, though according to criteria which might have surprised Linnaeus. The Karimojong can distinguish, 'as precisely as any outside professional observer, what the topographic features are that bear on a predictable water-supply'. They name these features accordingly; and 'for any herder, it is this "grid" applied to known stretches of territory with named pastures, that in part determines his movement plans over the year, and from one year to another'. Lévi-Strauss remarks that the many known classifications such as these 'are not only methodical and based on carefully built-up theoretical knowledge. They are also at times comparable, from a formal point of view, to those still in use in zoology and botany.'

Transposed to the field of social relations, comprehending natural relations, the same remark continues to hold good: thought remains concerned with prediction based on observation. The 'primary intention of much African thought,' Horton has argued,

seems to be just that mapping of connections between space-time phenomena which modern Christian thought feels is beyond its proper domain. Though, by the standards of the more advanced contemporary sciences, these religions could seldom provide value explanations or make completely successful prediction, there is a very real sense in which they are just as concerned with explanation and prediction as the sciences are.

So that

the really significant aspiration behind a great deal of African religious thought is the most obvious one: i.e. the attempt to explain and influence the workings of one's everyday world by discovering constant principles that underlie the apparent chaos and flux of sensory experience.

In so far as we make 'this aspiration central to our analysis, we shall find ourselves searching for translation instruments not so much in the realm of Christian discourse as in that of the sciences and their theoretical concepts'.

Horton goes on to urge, and I think that many anthropologists would now agree with him, that traditional thought 'can be seen as the outcome of a model-making process which is found alike in the thought of science and in that of pre-science' – taking 'pre-science' to mean the forms of empirical inquiry into the workings of the world that preceded any theoretical analysis of inherent physical structure and process.

In order to understand traditional politics one must, accordingly, first understand traditional religion. Only in this way can the categories of description be grasped. Horton offers a parallel. 'A chemist, asked to give a thorough description of some substance in his laboratory, can hardly avoid mentioning such characteristics as a molecular weight and formula, which refer implicitly to a massive body of chemical theory' taken for granted. 'In the same way, an African villager, who is trying to describe what his community is, can hardly avoid implicit reference to religious concepts', likewise taken for granted.

Enough is understood about a number of African societies to demonstrate this in practice. Horton takes the case of a people among whom he has lived, the Kalabari of the Niger delta, a fishing and trading community who have dwelt along the Atlantic creeks of southern Nigeria since unrecorded time, and certainly for many centuries.

Kalabari apprehension of reality posits three kinds of spirits. First of all, there are the spirits of the 'founding heroes' who first settled in Kalabari country and fathered their remote ancestors. These spirits are considered to be 'instruments of collective village welfare', since it is they who first framed the Kalabari way of life; and it is to them that one turns in all matters which affect the whole community. Secondly, there are the ancestors of different Kalabari lineage segments, 'considered as instruments of collective descent-group welfare'. These are capable of being opposed to one another in defence of their respective living descendants, so that conflicts at this level may have to be referred to the spirits of the founding heroes. Thirdly, and in a way that the modern world may find attractively subtle and realistic, there are 'freelance spirits' – 'water-people' who are thought to live at the bottom of the Kalabari creeks and who 'cater for individualistic competitive aspirations'. The water-people are ready to confer their benefits on all comers according to the offerings made to them. They are not associated with any of the permanent social groupings in the community.

Though with many cults and much individualism, the Kalabari system is neither arbitrary nor chaotic. It consists in a triangle of forces: with the spirits of the lineage ancestors 'underpinning the life and strength of the lineages, bringing misfortune to those who betray lineage values and fortune to those who promote them'; secondly, with the spirits of the founding heroes 'underpinning the life and strength of the community and its various institutions'; and, thirdly, with the spirits of the water-people as 'patrons of human individualism', as 'the forces underpinning all that lies beyond the confines of the established social order'.

Thus the Kalabari apprehension of reality – their religion and what has followed from it – has composed a theoretical model of the workings of their world according to observed and meditated experience. A given people, that is, entered a given environment – the founding heroes of the Kalabari settling in the delta – and there adjusted themselves to the needs of social growth. These needs they have codified in terms we call religious. And if we ask just *why* Kalabari thought should have taken a religious form we are simply confused by the terms of our modern dichotomy: science–supernatural, reality–religion.

In traditional thought the dichotomy was not there because the apprehension was a total one. It was concerned not only with what was, but also with what ought to be and with why it ought to be. It was mandatory as well as explanatory. Things being as they were, such and such actions or ambitions were permissible, while others were not. As organic aspects of the same necessary truth, means and ends were indivisibly conceived. Today in modern societies we have torn means and ends apart; and the price of our progress has become a split consciousness. Science tells us what can be done but not what ought to be done or why it ought to be done. The mandatory moral issues are necessarily eluded, and scientists who raise them are likely to be chided for speaking out of turn. Otherwise the mandatory issues, the moral issues of choice that govern behaviour, are left to the promptings of whatever feeble residue of our own traditional morality may still exist, or else to sectional decisions about the 'national good'. And so we have a situation in which science predicts disaster with the continued spread of nuclear weapons, but the spread continues despite all lamentations because the mandatory moral force to stop it is no longer there. Whereas in African apprehension, persistently, the explanatory-mandatory duality of thought possessed its ultimate satisfaction in what was also its ultimate sanction. Conformity to prescribed behaviour became the only way of doing what was 'right and natural', of belonging to the 'community of the blessed', of flowering from the isolation of the one into the communion of the many.

If these ideologies are looked at in this way they will not present a paradise. Reality was often tough and tortuous. Many individuals will have fallen by the wayside; and whole communities engulfed themselves in ruin. Even where such ideologies were most successful in achieving social harmony, a heavy price was paid in conservative conformism.

There is no case for gilding the past. But there is a case for understanding it. This approach will at least begin to make sense of what men actually thought or did, and why. Patiently pursued, it will elucidate all that enormously diverse range of 'founding myths' preserved by African peoples, such as the Lozi belief that they descend from Mbuya whom God begot upon God's daughter Mwamba. It will open those 'social archives', as Lebeuf has called them, composed by the Dogon in the carving of sculptured masks at conscious intervals in time, or by the Sao and

Kotoko in piles of polished stones which symbolized the vanished generations, or by others in still other ways.

Then much becomes clear. It becomes clear, for example, why these 'archives' were not conceived as records for the satisfaction of historical curiosity. Or why luckless kings could be omitted from remembered lists because they had failed in battle, or had otherwise upset the ancestral scheme of what should be and should not be. Or why new dynasties, fitting themselves into the charters of the dispossessed, were careful to 'rewrite' the past or else suppress it; and why, with the recent intrusion of a world of new ideas, the traditions often change again. D'Hertefelt mentions an illuminating case from modern Ruanda. There the ancestral charter of the Tutsi kingdom had long supposed strict hierarchical inequalities, but the ideas of national independence now spoke a different language. So the founding myths were re-interpreted during the 1950s in order to buttress with their force a premise, quite new for that stratified kingdom, according to which 'all Ruanda people are equal' – or, if they are not, then the fault lay with colonial rule. What had been in line with the 'right and natural' of the past was no longer so today, and the symbols accordingly required adjustment in their meaning.

Yet the underlying significance of all such ideological data did not change, at least until very recent times. They remained the embodiment of a specific world view, of an all-round apprehension of how things were and ought to be. Where circumstances changed the symbols were adjusted, diminished or extended – but to reaffirm the past and not to deny it. Just because they were total systems, their predictive capacities had to be hedged around with devices for explaining or ignoring failure, because their mandatory aspects depended on their explanatory – that is, predictive – claims; and these claims could not, in the nature of the systems, be 'wrong'.

This takes us into the field of 'totems' and 'taboos'. These manifold differentiations and prohibitions were long regarded as mystical projections of the 'primitive mind', as phantoms deriving from aboriginal fears and fancies. Or else they were explained as more or less mystical aids to solving material problems: such as, in the matter of sharing out food, that one clan ate eland but not buffalo while its neighbour ate buffalo but not eland.

Yet totems and taboos can now be seen to display their true function as symbols deriving from a theory of social control. This theory was perfectly non-mystical in that it rested upon the observation of real phenomena; but it was couched in mandatory-moral terms. Within it, totems and taboos may be said to have played the part of markers – symbolically embodied markers – along the boundaries of the 'right and natural', defining the theory and its system of control but also protecting these from the assaults of contrary phenomena. They may perhaps be seen as the selective and contingent 'programme data' of a given social computation. Selective and contingent because they were designed to exclude events or actions which would threaten the system, and had otherwise no meaning 'of their own': programmatic because they aimed at the achievement of a desired ideal.

Modern research is getting us nearer to an understanding of all this. The Ndembu of north-western Zambia are undoubtedly among those who would have once been said to 'bow down to wood and stone', or at any rate to wood, and generally to suffer from a great deal of self-mystification. They attach a complex symbolism to three of their trees, the *mudyi*, the *muyumbu* and the *mukala*. The *mudyi* and *muyumbu*, which yield a milky latex when their bark is cut, are respectively associated with maternity and womanhood, and with the virtues of the ancestors: goodness and strength, generosity, long life and fertility. They also have to do with social harmony. While the *mudyi* stands for the segmental unity of lineage or village, the *muyumbu* 'represents a general unity – the unity of the moral order recognized by all Ndembu and sanctioned by the ancestor spirits'. The *mukala* tree, on the other hand, secretes a reddish gum. Ndembu associate it with blood and the properties of blood: with manhood and adult responsibility in society as a whole.

So long as the key of the moral order was missing, these ideas looked like wild superstition or 'primitive customs' of merely arbitrary choice. In fact, Ndembu see them as a code which can guarantee – the phrase is that of Lévi-Strauss – 'the convertibility of ideas between different levels of social reality'. They even say as much. When Ndembu explain that the red gum of the *mukala* tree stands for blood, they call this symbol by a term in their language which means 'to blaze a trail'; so that a symbol is conceived as a tree-blaze or landmark, as 'something which connects the known with the unknown', and thus links one level of apprehension with another. But it is social reality with which this linking process is connected. The symbols are social symbols. They are intimately part of a determined socio-moral order.

What merely happens at such 'rites of passage', or is seen to happen by the uninitiated observer, cannot therefore give any real description of them. Patient learning can alone do that; and it is only in recent years that any such insights have become available. As Ndembu see these rites, crude and simple though they may appear, 'each boy is sacramentally imbued with the whole Ndembu moral order, which is immanent in but also transcends the social order' – since by ancestral sanction it controls the social order – 'when he is circumcised under the *mudyi* tree of his mothers, passed over the tree of the ancestors (symbolized by a log of *muyumbu*), and lodged finally on the tree of maturity (placed to rest and recover on a freshly cut branch of *mukala*)'.

Given the key of the moral order, other 'primitive customs' can be heard to speak the same clear language. They too emerge as media 'for giving tangible substance to moral obligations'; reflect 'a conviction that there is a moral order in the universe, and that man's wellbeing depends upon obedience to that order as men see it'; and appear as links in a chain of equilibrated relationships.

A number of African peoples have believed that their kings or ritual leaders must never 'die', and have gone to great lengths from time to time (it is difficult to know how often) to deal with the indisputable fact that they did die. Lienhardt tells how the Dinka have traditionally buried alive their chief ritual priests, their 'Masters of the Fishing Spear', whenever these dignitaries were approaching natural death. On these solemn occasions, the Dinka say, they would dig a pit and place the dying master in it on a comfortable bed. Then they would make a platform over this, using strips of hide, and finally cover it with cattle dung.

Yet the dying Master of the Fishing Spear 'will not be afraid of death; he will be put in the earth while singing his songs. Nobody among his people will rail or cry because their man has died. They will be joyful because their Master of the Fishing Spear will give them life, so that they shall live untroubled by any evil.' So long as the Master still spoke, they would not bury him. Only when he no longer replied to their words would they heap the dung upon his grave. 'And nobody will say "Alas, he is dead." They will say, "It is very good." '

Now the inwardness of this rite was that the Masters of the Fishing Spear were concerned with the condition and movement of the rivers which control men's lives in Dinkaland, and so were believed, in line with Dinka apprehension of reality, 'to carry the life' of their people. This being so, a Master's natural death would symbolize death for his clan by means of one disaster or another.

What [the Dinka] represent in contriving the death which they give him is the conservation of the 'life' which they themselves think that they receive from him, and not the conservation of his own personal life. The latter, indeed, is finally taken away from him by his people so that they may seem to divide it from the public 'life' which is in his keeping, and which must not depart from them with his death.

So the ritual burial is 'associated by a wide range of associations with a social triumph over death and the factors which bring death in Dinkaland'. It is to be seen, in other words, as a conscious effort at control deriving from a given ideology, an ideology evolved in turn from ecological necessity and from Dinka means of meeting that necessity.

Purposes varied. Other rituals belonged to those aspects of this 'pre-scientific' science of social control that were concerned with the endowment of authority. Whenever the emperor of Oyo died in old Yorubaland, appointed officials are said to have cut off his head, cleaned his skull, and taken out his heart. During installation rites the next emperor was obliged to sacrifice to Shango, a senior god, 'and was given a dish containing the heart of his predecessor which he had to eat'. A little later he was called on to swallow a potion of corn gruel from his predecessor's skull. These dramatic rites were occasioned by the need 'to open his ears to distinguish truth from falsehood', to give 'his words compelling power', and to assign 'to him alone the authority to execute criminals and his enemies at home, and to make war on enemies abroad'. The point lay not in the gruesomeness, but in the mobilizing of chartered powers behind the granting of a solemn office, thus guaranteeing legitimacy, as Fortes says, and imposing accountability on its proper exercise.

From this standpoint one may grasp why these societies needed many more rituals than ours. In our societies most individuals 'know their place': they feel themselves to be clearly and even self-evidently differentiated by class, accent, education, income, or professional affiliation. Rituals may survive in affectionate gestures to an irrelevant past, as when budding lawyers in London have to 'eat their dinners' at an 'inn' which is no longer anything of the kind. But with these societies the situation was otherwise. They were faced with the task of creating a differentiation of roles and statuses from a more or less undifferentiated community of social equals; and then with the task of safeguarding these offices from disorderly infringement by persons who might otherwise live in much the same way, or exactly the same way, as the office-holders.

Summing up, religion appears in all its varied African garb as the projection and affirmation of certain norms which govern the evolution of society. It is the selective codification, for its impact on everyday life, of a 'two-way' network of moral pressure: of the workings of the principle of Good in its positive sense, on behalf of whatever supports or guards a specific social system; and of the workings of the same principle in its negative sense – the sense of Evil which promotes or provokes, chiefly as one form or other of punishment or deterrent, whatever may go against that system. Hence Africa's multiplicity of religions: each system has required its own matrix and interpretation. And hence, too, a further elaboration into processes of what Turner has called 'social analysis': the application of oracles and the varied testing of reality in magical ways. This is where we arrive at systems of moral or metaphysical explanation embodied in 'wizardry', in beliefs about witchcraft and sorcery that are likewise central to these systems of social control and their parent ideologies.

# 11   Of Witches and Sorcerers

Fifteen Africans – twelve men and three women – have been gaoled after being found Guilty at Fort Victoria of having eaten the body of an African baby after opening up his grave . . . In statements said to have been made to the police the accused said: 'We are witches and this is the food of witches.' *The Times*, 19 January 1968.

Confessions such as these, admitting one or other gravely anti-social horror, are no rarity in the courts of Africa. While they by no means prove that the actions confessed were actually committed, they certainly point to vivid and profound beliefs in witchcraft. So do many newspaper reports. Only a few days before the above incident President Kenyatta had 'urged a crowd of 40,000 Kenyans . . . to give up witchcraft'. All over Africa there appear to be people who think they are witches, and who sometimes claim guilt for the crimes of witchcraft. And there appear to be far more people, even countless people, who believe in the power of wizardry, whether for good or evil; who are encouraged or dismayed by a host of signs and omens; and who lay out cash they can ill afford on spells and counterspells.

It is all very disconcerting. Only think what Dean Farrar would have made of it: surely here, if anywhere, is the daily documentation of those African features 'darker and deadlier' than baseness or brutality or a fatal shortage in the frontal lobes? A great many followers of the Dean have certainly said so and not a few others, one imagines, continue to think so. Even if they are wrong, the awkward question still remains: how can magical beliefs, and confessions of doing things such as eating dead baby, remain possible within a moral order which is derived from the empirical observation of real phenomena?

A sociological answer calls first of all for seeing these beliefs in a general perspective. They have been common to all pre-scientific societies. Every old civilization contained them and more or less violently wrestled with them. A fairly early but characteristic European example occurred in A.D. 1080 when King Harald of Denmark was told by Pope Gregory VII that 'he must no longer tolerate among his people the gruesome superstition according to which Christian priests or wicked women are held answerable for bad weather, storms, unfruitful years, or outbreaks of plague'. But King Harald had to tolerate it, for this was what a great many people continued to believe for centuries.

So long as the Age of Faith held firm, superstitions of this sort seldom much bothered the Church in Europe. Beliefs in wizards and their powers were generally treated in the ecclesiastical courts as more or less harmless forms of heresy, inseparable from peasant ignorance, and were punished as such. Although persons found guilty of witchcraft in thirteenth-century Germany were sometimes burned to death by the civil authorities, the Church itself approved 'only of disciplinary punishments against these offences and expulsion of the offenders from the communion of the Church', and refrained in this early period from calling in the 'arm of secular justice for the bodily chastisement of those accused of sorcery'. Even for a later Scotland, severe on such heresies, there is the record of a wayward Celtic parson who was allowed to keep his benefice even though he was believed to have danced his flock around the phallic figure of a god.

Things grew harsher when the supremacy of the Church began to be seriously challenged as the unique explainer of the world, and thus the necessary upholder of its social order. Early in the thirteenth century the great heresy of the Albigenses in southern France required a holy war to put it down. Other challenges followed: soon there were new signals of alarm. In 1310 the Synod of Trèves found it wise to renew 'with increasing severity the old Church decree: "No woman shall give out that she rides about at night with the goddess Diana, or with Herodias and an innumerable company of other women, for it is diabolical imposture." '

Throughout the fourteenth century the Age of Faith was increasingly threatened, while men sought explanations of the world in terms which conflicted ever more sharply with the teachings of the Church. As this continued, the condemnation of witchcraft or what was considered to be witchcraft or confessed to be witchcraft, flowed into and filled the minds of men. The fifteenth and sixteenth centuries presided over a tidal wave of witchcraft superstition and repression; and it is not difficult to see in this a consequence of profound cultural and social tensions.

Janssen, a careful if Catholic historian, has put the matter in terms that are very suggestive for the later African context. 'Things assumed a different shape' from the relative tolerance of earlier times, he writes, 'after the belief in demons and in witchcraft was strengthened by the appearance of gnostic-Manichaean sects which taught that there were two conflicting equally powerful principles co-existing from eternity, a good principle and a bad principle, and that the bad principle was lord and ruler of the material world.' Whatever the social influence of such sects might really be, heretics began to be regarded as allies of the bad principle and were accused of terrible crimes: the devil, adjured with certain formulae of prayer, visited them during their assemblies and led them into every imaginable vice.

'The Black Death, which in the fourteenth century carried off almost a quarter of the population of Europe, was largely regarded as the work of diabolical powers: the general consternation rose in countless cases to frenzy.' Thus a report of 1484 by a Rhineland clergyman claimed that 'magic potions for protection against the Black Death were brewed at secret, nocturnal gatherings, dissolute banqueting was carried on, and the old heathen belief in manifold, occult, magic arts and the flights of witches gained increased strength'.

After 1500 these frenzies carried all before them. In 1532 an imperial decree made sorcery a serious crime throughout the Holy Roman Empire. In the 1570s the Elector of Saxony went so far as to decree that fortune-telling was to be punished by death. An English law of 1563 condemned to death all who were found guilty of 'invocations of evil spirits, and of sorceries, enchantments, charms and witchcrafts ... whereby any person shall happen to be killed or destroyed', a draconian act which spoke volumes not only for the existence of these beliefs among ordinary people, but also among the potentates who made the laws. Elizabeth's successor James (1603–25) went further still by unleashing a plague of witch-burnings, especially in Scotland.

Janssen has summed it up.

After the outbreak [of the Great Schism] belief in the power and the arts of the devil became universally widespread, and the demoralization resulting everywhere from the religious, social and political movements and struggles, especially favourable to the development of the witch-superstition, procured for it an extension undreamt of before, and led to the most barbarous procedure.

The words are not too strong. Hailed as the 'dawn of modern reason', which in some respects it certainly was, the sixteenth century also became the great epoch of magical superstition. Large quantities of 'magic books' were published. Vast numbers of magicians trod the countryside as 'wondermen, ring-slippers, mist-makers, illusionists, mandrake-hawkers, quacks, howlers, spider-eaters, conjurors, benison-healers, hare-catchers, bullet-stoppers, sure-shots, stab-proofs, sword-dancers, love-compellers, mice-drivers or rat-leaders, spear and sword doctors'.

The records make all this sound like mass hysteria. Countless women, mostly of advanced years, confessed to being witches and to having committed fearful crimes. They were burned without mercy, however obviously impossible their 'crimes' must now seem. 'A midwife confessed that she had killed as many as 170 children, twenty-two of whom were related to her. An old man confessed to having said that if he had not been arrested three days before he would have destroyed everything for twenty-five leagues round with hail and gravel-stones ... The seventy-five-year-old woman, Anna Ottlin of Zeilitzheim, confessed that she had committed over one hundred murders, and begged that, as she was old and feeble, she might be allowed three days' respite, when she would tax her memory and tell of each separate crime in detail.'

Where voluntary confessions were not available, appalling tortures were applied with racks, thumbscrews and the Boot, an iron frame screwed ever more tightly to the accused's foot. 'Another witch, who had been several times tortured but had always recanted everything after being set free, was finally, after still severer torture, brought to confess that she had dug up the bodies of sixteen children, boiled them and made witch salve out of them.'

To the stake went numberless people with bodies so broken or torn that they could no longer stand upon their legs. Typical was the fate of the landlady of the Crown Inn at Nordlingen, Marian Hollin, who was tortured no fewer than fifty-six times in the most agonizing way; or the little girl of Ratisbon who confessed to lawyers and clergy that 'the devil entered her in the shape of a fly, and that she had often been in and out of hell with the devil', whereupon two jurists 'were of the opinion that she should not be punished by death by fire, but only stretched [on the rack] a few times by way of warning, then be put in a pillory, have her cheeks burned through and sent into perpetual exile'; or the dozen witches of Spalt who were burned in a single day; or the fifteen hundred of Ellingen who were burned in a single year; or the thousands of others, bemused, bitterly tortured and finally burned, who died in holocausts during those mysterious times.

It is obvious, then, that pre-scientific Africa need make no apologies to pre-scientific Europe. Beliefs in magic, moreover, were a long time a-dying in Europe even among men of science: Sir Isaac Newton, Fortes has remarked, 'held beliefs about occult powers that would seem thoroughly sensible to a modern Melanesian or pagan African'. Even in 1967–8 the European Christian community in Rhodesia was exhorted by its leaders to pray for rain. Over and beyond such points, however, there are difficulties in making Afro-European parallels: we need, in fact, a general sociology of witchcraft that has yet to be attempted.

Most observers seem agreed that witchcraft fears have much increased in Africa over the past fifty or a hundred years, and also that these fears are less controlled than they used to be by social restraints or other in-built protective mechanisms. As will be seen later, the reason appears to lie in the disintegration of traditional structures and systems since the 1880s: in the passing of Africa's age of faith, and consequently in a growth of personal anxiety and alienation. No longer checked by the dykes of traditional precedent, witchcraft fears have fed on new or greatly increased mental and social strains. If this view is right, and it seems to be, then there may be some relevant parallels between transitional Europe in the sixteenth and seventeenth centuries and transitional Africa today.

What appears certain is that the understanding of witchcraft beliefs in historical Europe can be illuminated by the study of witchcraft beliefs in contemporary Africa. Here the parallels are often close. Like those of Europe, African witches are thought to fly through the air at night, consort in gruesome covens such as Macbeth encountered, and share unpleasant habits. Among the Ga of Ghana, not particularly exceptional in this respect, the spirits of witches have been said to leave their bodies during sleep, glide through the air on the back of an owl or some other creature, often accompanied by brilliant balls of fire, and cluster in a warlock's meeting where the 'personalities' of chosen victims are ritually eaten, after which these victims die.

The worst of these Ga witches are believed to have hooks or spurs growing on their heels: a 'fact', of course, which cannot be disproved, any more than the 'evidence' of European or African witch-persecuting courts could or can be denied, since only accredited 'witch-finders' can know about witches. 'This woman', a Ga traditional doctor diagnosed in one case, 'is the chief witch of your town. She has killed more than sixty people and is doing all sorts of other mischief. She has hooks on her heels, and when she sleeps with her husband they torment him.'

Voluntary confessions have been common, just as in Europe; again, more often than not by worried women. A Fanti witch explained on examination that she kept a snake in her vagina that was powerful in witchcraft. 'If I want to go out to a witch meeting at night,' she explained, 'I leave it behind to make my husband sleep soundly till I return. When my husband wants to have sexual intercourse with me I take the snake out of my vagina and hide it and return it when my husband has finished.'

The psychology of these confessions must also have parallels in other lands.

'One witch, asked by a witch-doctor [during the 1950s] if all her own children were alive, said: "Seven are dead. One remains alive."'

Why had these children died?

' "The members of our company [of witches] have to make contributions in turn. When my turn came round from time to time I brought them to be killed by my company." '

'Another said: "I have killed Adwina Obroyni and I killed my five children . . ." '

Ordeals in witch-finding continue the parallels. The commonest European ordeal was dousing in a bath or pool of water. 'Even as late as 1436 the council at Hanover decided to submit an accused person to trial by water. Floating on the surface was a sign of guilt, sinking to the bottom that of innocence', the rationale behind this being that the devil dwelling in witches 'makes them much lighter, although other people do not notice this; and whether they will or not they are obliged to swim on the top of the water'.

David Livingstone has a wry comment on this in his memoirs of 1857. He describes the common African ordeal of causing a suspected witch to eat an emetic substance, those who vomited being considered innocent, while those purged were thought guilty and sometimes killed. 'I happened to mention to my own men the water-test for witches formerly in use in Scotland: the supposed witch, being bound hand and foot, was thrown into a pond; if she floated, she was considered guilty, taken out, and burned; but if she sank and was drowned, she was pronounced innocent. The wisdom of my ancestors excited as much wonder in their minds, as their custom did in mine.'

The practical elucidation of these beliefs and practices in Africa owes much to Evans-Pritchard's classic study of 1937, *Witchcraft, Oracles and Magic among the Azande* who live along the Congo-Sudan divide. Seven years later an American anthropologist, Clyde Kluckhohn, published a similarly important analysis of Navajo witchcraft. Since then we have had perhaps thirty detailed studies of African occult beliefs, chiefly by British researchers working in the Evans-Pritchard–Kluckhohn tradition. These explorations offer new views of African culture as dramatically enlightening, in their way, as the contemporary work of historians and archaeologists. For it is now seen that ideas about the occult were not gratuitous superstition, but an integral part of cultures which could not be upheld without them.

Leaving aside for a while the psychology of witchcraft, two substantial points appear from the evidence. The first is that these beliefs occurred in Europe, and have continued to occur in Africa, despite the fact that there cannot be such persons as witches. The second is that a great number of real persons, whether in Europe or Africa, have applied to a vast range of spells, charms and rituals so as to call the occult to their aid, or defend themselves against it. One imagined activity, then, and another that is real. Though facets of the same spectrum of ideas, these two activities, the imagined and the real, are generally though not always distinct in the thought of African societies. To maintain this distinction, which is often an important one, the imagined activity may conveniently be called *witchcraft*, and the real one *sorcery*.

Witchcraft has been widely believed in, but nobody can ever have seen a witch. Sorcery and sorcerers, on the other hand, are no such mystical beings. There are few Africans for whom they have not formed a normal part of daily life.

Not all African societies have been equally concerned about witches. Some have bothered very little, others have seemed obsessed by them. In general, however, witchcraft is believed to be the 'natural exercise of evil' by persons who are possessed by a malevolent but innate power which can be used to hurt other people. Witches exercise this power automatically, as it were: merely by feeling anger or annoyance, or even without being conscious of the harm they do. 'True witchcraft', in short, 'is part of an individual's being, a part of his [or her] innermost self.' What is 'known' about witches can only be what is believed about them. But what is believed about them is that they embody the workings of evil.

Sorcery, by contrast, is the 'unnatural exercise of evil' by anyone who may wish to draw upon the power of evil, through the use of appropriate instruments and processes, so as to damage an enemy or rival. You practise sorcery as an ordinary person and not as a witch. You do not yourself possess malevolent power: you have to acquire it. This you achieve by applying to a specialist in the casting of spells, or else by casting spells yourself. In either case you employ sacrificial goats or hens, charms, bits of flesh whether animal or human, fragments of excreta or other *disjecta membra* of your intended victim's; and you pay a fee to your specialist if you do not cast the spell yourself. There is no particular mystery about ensorcelment.

Linked with these beliefs there is defence against witchcraft and sorcery; and about this there is no mystery at all. More often than not it is conducted by respected practitioners, qualified in their art, who have served a long apprenticeship and live by skills which may include divination and herbal medicine. Such practitioners may nowadays be called traditional healers or native doctors; Europeans used to call them witch-doctors. Sometimes, on the side, they may be sorcerers as well. If so, they are understandably discreet about it, just as a modern doctor is who prescribes or operates against the law.

Clearly, the root of the matter lies in witchcraft, since ensorcelment and anti-ensorcelment are only its everyday and willed derivatives. Now an earlier view was inclined to hold that the existence of witchcraft belief must prove the absence of a moral order. What can be seen today is that the reverse was true. For the witch within the ancestrally sanctioned charter stands for the subversive norms, the impulse to disorder: in short, for the antimoral which supposes the moral.

One is irresistibly reminded of those gnostic-Manichaean sects of sixteenth-century Europe, and their two opposing principles. However different the context, they apply remarkably well to the evidence of skilled observers who have lived in African societies. One should note, of course, that in contrast to the gnostic idea of Good and Evil as two entirely separate forces, African religion has generally supposed only one force which is capable of acting, according to the circumstances, either for man's welfare or man's woe. But this difference apart, the evidence shows repeatedly that the ideological ground of witchcraft and sorcery in traditional Africa is indeed the battlefield on which the Principle of Good meets the Principle of Evil, or, as Christians would say from an ideology otherwise very different, where God confronts the Devil.

# 12  Upside-down People

Long ago when God lived among men before the coming of
Work and Death, things were not as they afterwards became.
Evil may always have existed. Yet in the days before the Fall, the
Akan of Ghana say, 'its eyes were not yet open' and there was
nothing for it to do. The trouble began when God separated himself from men. As soon as Eve listened to the temptings of the
serpent, and Adam in turn to Eve – most African versions of the
Fall are variants on the same cautionary theme – Evil was
awakened and made free to stalk the world, 'seeking whom it may
devour' and finding many.

So for African religion, as for Christianity, Evil has appeared
as an inherently *necessary* part of the world of men. If Evil has
become a natural part of this world, the fault lies not with Good
– with God – but with men's frailty and failure. This being so,
there is always the millennial hope of paradise regained, of a
world expunged of Evil, of progress unalloyed. It seems that
every great culture has shared this hope in one way or another,
and indeed, in the nature of human apprehension of reality, must
share it: not least perhaps, though in secular terms, the conscious anti-religious humanism which has inspired the social
revolutions of the twentieth century.

Africans have also longed for a world without Evil, or, as they
would put it, without witchcraft. Some of them have expressed
strong ideas upon the subject. Mary Douglas tells us that the
Lele of the Kasai region in the south-western Congo basin 'can
clearly visualize what reality would be like without sorcery' –
meaning all forms of wizardry – 'and they continually strive to
achieve it by eliminating sorcerers'. Like Christian revivalists,
they try 'to push evil out of the world of reality'. Normally, it
seems, their culture offers a balanced acceptance of reality, of

things as they actually and irremediably are. But every now and then the Lele are consumed with a burning revivalism. This takes the form of anti-witchcraft movements that are 'nothing less than an attempt to introduce the millennium at once'.

So 'we have to reckon with two tendencies in Lele religion: one ready to tear away even the veils imposed by the necessities of thought and to look at reality direct: the other a denial of necessity, a denial of the place of pain and even of death in reality'. Much the same could be said of other African cultures. They accept and allow for the facts of 'disturbance and disorder' – for the negating consequences of psychological resistance to a given moral order – but they believe at the same time that these facts can and should be opposed by appropriate counteraction. In practice, this can only mean anti-witchcraft action. 'Zande morality', notes Evans-Pritchard, 'is so closely related to their notions of witchcraft that it may be said to embrace them. The Zande phrase "It is witchcraft" may often be translated simply as "It is bad".' Get rid of the witches, and Evil will once more be put to sleep or expelled. Man, with the Fallen Angels, will be able to climb back to Heaven.

But it is also true that Evil has been a long time in the world, and has become a natural part of it. For most African peoples who have been studied, its position appears thoroughly systematized. Often this comes out in ways which are dramatically vivid, as with Middleton's investigations among the Lugbara.

The Lugbara number about 200,000 farming people who have long inhabited a fertile country in north-western Uganda and the adjacent Congo. Middleton lived among them between 1949 and 1953, and wrote a book about them that is one of the crucial works of modern anthropological analysis. He found their socio-moral order at first sight an improbable one, and in some respects perfectly impossible. 'Every family cluster' of fifteen or thirty persons in its scatter of homesteads 'sees itself and its neighbouring lineages as surrounded by a circle of people whose territories are filled with sorcery and magic, and who are evilly disposed towards them, even though they live in lineage-groups and are descended from the same hero-ancestors as their own kin.'

But the farther away people live, the worse they become. Near strangers may be witches and sorcerers: far strangers are altogether horrible. Of the most distant strangers who live beyond the bounds of Lugbara society, 'beyond the magicians and sorcerers', the Lugbara say desperately hard things. They hold that these creatures are barely human in appearance, habitually walk on their heads, eat each other, and generally live in ways which men – that is, Lugbara – cannot hope to understand, much less approve.

Now what the Lugbara are really saying, Middleton points out, is that they conceive of difference as being measured not in miles or years, but in socio-moral distance. 'It does not matter', in other words, 'that for one group [of Lugbara] the beings with superhuman powers or inverted attributes', such as habitually walking on their heads, 'live ten miles away and for another group they live twenty or fifty miles away. Only the external observer realizes the contradictions of this situation, in which groups only a few miles apart point to one another and make almost identical accusations of sorcery and inhuman attributes and behaviour'. For the essential distinction to a Lugbara farmer lies between his own group – normal people because they live within, and thus are validated by, his own ancestral charter – and all others who live outside this charter, and who are consequently abnormal in deepening degree according to their socio-moral distance from him.

These ideas, in short, are not 'mere fairy stories told for amusement'. On the contrary, they are a systematic *positioning* of Evil. They are statements about the Lugbara moral universe and its negation. Those who live outside that universe are more or less completely opposed to it, 'upside down', reversed in their attitudes and understanding. They are asocial and amoral according to everything that Lugbara believe about right behaviour; and the degree of their inversion grows with distance.

But Evil is not the attribute only of strangers. Lugbara remain consistent with themselves in going on to believe that in some sense it is also present in their own midst. Here too there are upside-down people; and these are witches. Rather untypically for African societies, they are always men; and they are men who open the gate to Evil by harbouring *ole*, 'indignation', and so committing *ezata*, which Middleton translates as 'sins'. Spite, jealousy, disappointed ambition, undue greed, aggressiveness: all these are the fruits of *ole* and lead to socially destructive acts or wishes. And whenever a man gives way to *ole*, witchcraft is bound to be the outcome. He will not 'do anything', he will cast no spells and call up no spirits; but any trouble that follows will none the less be his fault – the workings of the *ole* to which he has given way. His 'sins' will then be seen as destroying ties of kinship and neighbourhood, 'the ties that are necessary for the existence of any kind of orderly social life'.

But the concept of *ole* has to be seen in a dual light: one man's Evil is another man's Good. Being the channel to a supernatural force, *ole* can also be used as an instrument of just retribution, somewhat in the same way as the concept of Hell for traditional Christians. A man who believes himself sinned against by a kinsman can invoke the spirits of the ancestors who will then act on his behalf. Disobedient 'sons' (they may be his sister's children, according to classification, as well as his wife's) tend to upset the ancestral order; and then, in a Lugbara statement quoted by Middleton,

... It is good that an elder invokes his ghosts against his disobedient 'sons' ... A man stands in place of his (dead) father, and if a wife or child does him ill he will cry to [the spirit of] that father and trouble will seize the child. This is good. This is what we call *ole*. *Ole* does not destroy the land. It is bad for a man to strike with his hand, or with his spear; now the [spirits] strike on his behalf.

Thus Good-and-Evil, Janus-headed force of the ancestors, is able both to guard and disturb, to cause sin and make amends, to lead to trouble and yet supply the remedy.

Other studies have reinforced such findings. Among the Nupe, a numerous and enterprising people of Nigeria, Nadel found that 'the witch is identified with the person openly and successfully setting aside the social values and thus denying the state of society desired and thought "good"; attacks against witches are thus attacks upon the successful enemies of the ideal society'.

Anti-social happenings are accordingly traced to someone's

anti-social attitude. Being so traced by appropriate divination –
by invocation of the protective spirits of the ancestors, themselves
the spokesmen of all supernatural power – they will be found to
have come from someone's fecklessness or forgetfulness, in which
case this someone must make amends. Or else they will have
come from someone's deliberate malevolence by recourse to
sorcery, in which case anti-ensorcelment action will be required.
Or worst of all – and closer, here, to the gnostic idea of Evil as a
force existing in its own right – they will have come from someone's witchcraft through involuntary possession by Evil, in which
case this someone may have to be killed. For it has been generally
thought that the presence of Evil, in known shape, could not
sensibly be tolerated. 'Suffer ye not a witch to live', the Children
of Israel were told in Exodus; and all pre-scientific societies have
often agreed, though seldom with the panic of sixteenth-century
Europe.

We come back to the 'ideal equilibrium' and its protection. In
their functional aspect, beliefs about witchcraft appear repeatedly
as the protectors of the 'right and natural', the major instruments of conservation against everything that could make or seem
to make for social upheaval. They it is who have discouraged
dangerous thoughts about new technology and organization. In
the moral framework, then, these beliefs have the same dual force
as what we call religion, being explanatory and mandatory at one
and the same time. And this is why the two concepts, witchcraft belief and religious belief, cannot meaningfully be separated.
They are part of the same matrix. The good life called for the
conservation, so far as possible, of a divinely given balance with
nature, of an ideal community of equals or near-equals, but
found its chief safeguards in beliefs about witchcraft. If there
were many sceptics, they were only the exceptions which proved
the rule.

There is much supporting evidence. Though usually reported
in the present tense, most of it refers to situations which are passing away but which certainly held firm until fairly recent times.
Thus Brown and Hutt, discussing in 1935 the difficulties of getting the Hehe of central Tanganyika (now Tanzania) to adapt to

new techniques, remarked that this once powerful people were made suspicious of 'development' by their witchcraft beliefs. 'No man', according to Hehe morality,

must be too much in advance of his neighbours, or there is a danger that a jealous warlock will kill him by witchcraft. Thus a man must not wear clothes which differ too markedly from those of his neighbours, nor must he seek methods of gaining wealth or social superiority which involve too great a departure from traditional tribal life.

The notion that Evil will attack those who stray from the path of righteousness, or that Good may use Evil to straighten or punish sinners, is strikingly confirmed by Marwick's studies of the Chewa of Malawi. They too have possessed the concept of an ideal socio-moral order laid down with divine force in the distant past, and stayed in being by the watchful guard of appointed ancestors. Those who deliberately oppose this conservation are persons possessed by Evil – and the capital letter is again justified in that we are concerned here not with some vague notion of badness, but with a very precise concept of mystical power – while those who suffer misfortune are the victims, more often than not, of their own sinfulness: of their failure, that is, to obey the rules. Those who go against whatever is 'right and natural' are accordingly attacked by what is 'wrong' but what, in its existence since the Fall of Man, is also 'natural'. This 'wrong and natural' is the force of witchcraft, whether exercised by those who cannot help it because they are seized by Evil for reasons of their own nature that they do not comprehend, and cannot remedy, or by those who call in Evil by way of the material techniques of sorcery.

Marwick lived among the Chewa for prolonged periods between 1946 and 1953. As part of his field work he collected details of 194 cases of misfortune of one sort or another, ranging from an individual's loss of property to marital upset, disease or death. He found that

in eighty-three cases the victim of the misfortune had, in terms of Chewa social norms, been at fault; and, in a further thirty-four, someone closely associated with the victim, such as a kinsman or friend, had been at fault. Of these 117 cases with moral implications, seventy-one were ones involving beliefs in sorcery; and forty-six did not involve such beliefs.

Of the seventy-one cases where misfortune was attributed to sorcery (or to wizardry in its wider sense of including both sorcery and witchcraft proper), sixteen were to do with a failure to discharge personal obligations, twelve with being conspicuously successful in everyday life, nine with being quarrelsome or aggressive, seven with sexual misdemeanours or sexual jealousy, and five with being mean or avaricious. To us these misfortunes, in so far as we should recognize them as such, would be the mere fruits of accident or character. To the Chewa they demonstrate the workings of Evil, set in motion by wrong behaviour.

Chewa have also believed that people can and do use Evil deliberately. But they are not necessarily at fault in doing so. You may or may not be justified in calling in the services of Evil: it all depends on the circumstances. Marwick collected evidence about 101 persons who were named as sorcerers. He found that fifty-two of these alleged sorcerers had acted for reasons which Chewa accept as justifiable in terms of their social norms. Such was the case of a newly married woman who 'killed' her husband by sorcery because 'he had angered her by spending a longer time with his first wife than with her'. Now if this punishment seems unreasonably drastic it must also be remembered that Chewa, while they have fully recognized the immediate physical reasons for death, have seen its actual incidence as the common work of witchcraft. 'Killing' by sorcery could therefore be accepted, though not necessarily approved, as a common event.

It might not be approved at all. The other forty-nine sorcerers in Marwick's records, or nearly half the total, had acted for unacceptable reasons. Seventeen were said to be habitual sorcerers. They were hopelessly 'devoured by the Devil', as older generations of Christians might have said, and had become regular channels for the workings of Evil. The rest were instruments of Evil in lesser and not hopeless ways. Nine were deplored as being jealous or greedy; seven as quarrelsome or threatening; five as involved in sinister activities such as incest; four as impotent or sterile; and seven for other socially disapproved characteristics.

'In general', Marwick concluded,

my case material confirms that beliefs in sorcery provide a medium for dramatization of social norms. Although about half of the sorcerers in the sample were believed to have no anti-social traits before becoming involved in the cases recorded, they were nevertheless now sorcerers, serving as symbols of social evil.

Initially guiltless, they had fallen by the wayside. But as to the victims of sorcery,

two-thirds of the 118 cases involving beliefs in sorcery (including seventeen concerned with vengeance on sorcerers) were ones in which anti-social or socially inadequate behaviour was attributed either to the victim, or to someone closely associated with him.

They had invited the attentions of Evil, and Evil had not failed in its Good-given duties.

But what about accidental misfortune? If all interruptions in the ideal order of everyday life are to be attributed to mystical intervention, benevolently motivated or otherwise, where is the place for mere bad luck? Logically, Africans have provided no such place in their systems of thought. Nothing, in their philosophy, is without an ultimate cause beyond its immediate cause. In this *science du concret*, this restless probing into causes and motivations, so stubbornly optimistic in its reliance on the interior logic of all things and all behaviour, no one need remain the victim of hazard. In all situations your actions and reactions can be purposive – if only you will take the right advice, and so select the proper course of action among the alternatives that are open to you.

# 13 Explanation and Prediction

When you walk along a bush path and are bitten by a snake or twist your ankle on a root, you will not fail to know the immediate reason for your pain. Disbelieving in coincidence, however, you will want to know more than this. Why was it in *your* path that the snake or root happened to be lying? Why *this* particular conjunction of cause and effect?

These are the questions that may worry you, for they clearly point to the witchcraft that interrupts the ideal flow of daily life. You will proceed for advice to a diviner: prudently, since if someone's witchcraft has caused you to be bitten by a snake today, what still more dangerous hurt may not await you tomorrow? Consulting his oracle, the diviner will explain that you are the victim of witchcraft either because you have sinned – gone against the rules – or because, though innocent yourself, you have attracted the malice of someone else who has sinned. In either case he will tell you what to do, so as to avert a worse misfortune in the future.

If worse misfortune still befalls you, it will not follow that the diviner was wrong in his prescriptions or advice. He *may* have been wrong. Everyone knows that some diviners are better than others. Maybe you will think it well to consult two or more of them – provided, of course, that you can raise the necessary fees. But the reason for continued misfortune may also be that you have yourself continued to offend, failed to make adequate amends to indignant ancestors, or broken some other rule that you had overlooked or set aside as unimportant. The system, in short, is a total one. It protects itself against predictive failure.

These attitudes towards misfortune vary from people to people. In some cases they seem to be more consistently developed than in others. Generally, however, Fortes's dictum about the Tallensi holds good for all in varying degree. In African traditional thought 'everything that happens has material causes and conditions, but [these] are effective only by grace of the mystical agencies which are the ultimate arbiters of nature and society': the

Figurine in soapstone, about 18 cms high, from Mende country in Sierra Leone. Nowadays often placed on a little clay platform at the foot of an oil palm, and used in rice fertility rites, these 'nomoli' sculptures are of uncertain origin but were possibly produced by the Sherbro in the sixteenth century

agencies, that is, which are thought of as having given birth to society and shaped its manner of survival. Whatever interrupts this ideal pattern of life is thus to be referred to some breakdown in conduct which has human and therefore controllable explanations. If the controls fail to work, this is not because the diagnosis is worthless or the methods of treatment ineffectual, but because they are inadequate or fallibly applied.

This consistent referring of the apparently accidental to the 'inner workings of life', to interaction of the principles of order and disorder, offers another large facet of what I have called a 'science of social control'. It illustrates what Horton has in mind when he writes that 'the goals of explanation and prediction are as powerfully present in traditional African cultures as they are in cultures where science has become institutionalized', and why he is justified in arguing that these traditional systems may be regarded as 'theoretical models akin to those of the sciences'. But it also shows again where the true difference lies between this 'pre-scientific science' and modern science. The second is open-ended, inherently subject to doubt, experiment or further development. The first, on the other hand, is closed and complete within itself, theoretically always capable of explaining phenomena within its own terms. Its bets are always hedged, its predictions always subject to revised explanation according to the same rules.

However obstructively conservative, it could offer great services, especially in the field of social therapy. Many anthropologists have dwelt on this. The Nyoro of western Uganda are among those peoples who have suffered much from malaria, yaws, leprosy and dysentery, all of which have been endemic, as well as from venereal diseases said to have been introduced in the nineteenth century.

Miscarriage is common, and as in pre-twentieth-century Europe, there are few families which have not lost one or more children. Often only one child, sometimes none, reaches adulthood. So Nyoro are a good deal concerned with human mortality, for illness and death are a constant background to everyday life.

Now this state of affairs

would be hardly tolerable if there were no means of either comprehending it or coping with it, and such a means is provided by a complex system of magical and quasi-magical practices and beliefs ... Whatever the misfortune which strikes or threatens, be it illness, impotence or childlessness, poverty, loss of stock or harvest, or the hatred of spouse or neighbour, Nyoro culture provides an institutionalized response ... The victim is provided not only with an explanation but with a prescription for action.

Death, the supreme interrupter, makes perhaps the clearest case. Most Africans have disbelieved in the *normal* possibility of 'natural death', which, on their view of things, is practically a contradiction in terms. This is not because they have seldom or never been able to know the scientific aetiology of their diseases. It is because their diagnosis goes beyond the immediate causes of death, and asks what the ultimate causes may have been. A hunter killed by a lion clearly dies for an obvious and common-sense reason. But they do not ask, as we should, 'What mistake or rashness did this hunter commit, what bad luck did he have?' Pressing for the 'first cause' which must explain, for them, this disturbance of the ideal equilibrium, they ask: 'What wrong has he committed; with whom has he quarrelled; who was jealous of him; in short, who has killed him?'

Those particular questions were recorded in Malawi of the Chewa. Others ask the same. The Lele of the Congo (Zaïre Republic) admit that natural death is possible.

When a man has reached the end of his allotted span he will inevitably die. But only rarely does it happen that a very old person's death is attributed to the advanced senility which strikes the outside observer as the most likely cause ... [and] in practice all deaths and most illnesses are attributed to sorcery.

They agree with the Kaguru of central Tanzania that 'most illness, death, miscarriage, sterility, difficult childbirths, poor crops, sickly livestock and poultry, loss of articles, bad luck in hunting and sometimes even lack of rain, are caused by witchcraft': are caused, in other words, by the evil ways of men. Putting it another way again, witchcraft belief is 'equivalent to ideas which have been formulated in other societies such as Fate or the Will of God'.

All this needs keeping in perspective. Actual homicide within most societies was judged by the courts as a serious crime, and punished as such, while the killing of strangers could likewise bring stiff penalties. Over and beyond the Will of God, there was also the will of legality. Yet it was the Will of God that has counted most. However virtuous and devout a Tallensi may have been, 'his death is invariably interpreted as the consequence of a failure in his or her predecessors' piety towards the ancestors'. This unleashing of retributive Fate 'may be due to some long-forgotten sin, his own or his father's ... [or] it may be an apparently commonplace ritual debt' which has not been paid.

Either way it is the result of faults which have roused the ire of ancestors always jealous for their ideal way of life.

When death strikes, then, the important thing is to explain it. All cultures have recognized this: only with explanation can death be absorbed into one's system of thought and rendered acceptable. But where the aetiology of death is little known, other forms of explanation must be found. African explanations may sound strange. Yet they have been logical, and, being logical, not terrifying. They have been concerned, moreover, with a concept of death which has generally supposed rebirth into this world – into this specific community: with an idea of death, that is, much less drastic or final than ours. The Chewa man who neglected his wife died because he had offended the social norm, and the wife was not condemned for 'killing' him: later on, the gods being willing, he would return to the community of the living in another but not lesser guise. Others in her shoes might be thought to have gone too far, and still have remained within the bounds of the 'right and natural'. In another Chewa case, interpreted by Marwick as 'impudence punished by death', a herdboy died after striking his mother's sister's husband – in Chewa terms, his family father – who had reproved him for allowing cattle to stray. The father was strongly suspected of having 'killed' the boy, but no action followed against him.

Such reasoning might appear to induce a situation of daily stress and fear. In fact, few accounts of traditional society paint any such picture. For although it is true of many societies that their world, as Beattie says of Bunyoro, is or was 'peopled by actual or potential murderers' – in the sense that someone or other is going to be thought responsible for almost every death that happens – 'it does not follow that neighbours are always apprehensive and suspicious of one another, though they sometimes are. For sorcery is situational; it only becomes relevant when things go wrong.'

Evans-Pritchard has made the same point about the Zande. He found that 'the [individual] Zande expects to come across witchcraft at any time of day or night'. So that 'when misfortunes occur he does not become awestruck at the play of supernatural forces. He is not terrified at the presence of an occult enemy. He is, on the other hand, extremely annoyed … It is the aggressiveness and not the eeriness of these [witchcraft] actions which Zande emphasize when speaking of them, and it is anger and not awe which we observe in their response to them.' For they are concerned, in their view, not with uncontrollable or inexplicable phenomena but with breakdowns of the moral order. These breakdowns are deplorable. But they can often be remedied, and always explained.

# 14 The Danger Within

Fear of divine punishment and love of Good for its own sake may be powerful conductors of behaviour. But fallible mankind has never found them enough. Africans, like others, have required less mystical deterrents to sin. Public opinion has been one of these, youthful training another.

In Chewaland, for example, notions of ideal character and behaviour have supposed that 'the good man is the meek one who pleases all, gives offence to none, and is wise, generous and sociable'. This is what public opinion has required of Chewa who want to enjoy a pleasant reputation. And although it is obvious that public opinion will often have failed to induce wisdom, generosity or sociability, its force was considerable in these small-scale societies where it was always difficult for a transgressor to 'move away to where the neighbours do not know'.

There was also training by initiation schooling and other *rites de passage* designed to instil the ideal by 'setting up values and behaviour patterns both for emulation and detestation'. Cautionary tales and fables did the same. They consistently opposed the companionable human order of the village to the outcast wilderness of the bush, equating the one with hope and the other with despair, and employing a rich symbolism to drive home the contrast.

Yet Chewa have found public opinion and youthful schooling, even when backed by mystical sanctions, nothing like enough to keep them on the path of righteousness. Individuals have continued to invite the attentions of the Devil by coveting their neighbour's wife or husband, pushing their own careers, fornicating with forbidden relatives, breaking out in acts of violence, and generally doing what they know they should not do. As well as a moral order, they have required a legal one; and there is plenty to suggest that they have been deterred from transgression as much by their jural institutions as by anything else. Yet it is precisely here, in considering the limits of jural sanction, that one finds another clue to the place of witchcraft belief, and to its often concealed connections with the social order.

It happens that the Chewa social order is matrilineal. They trace descent, and therefore succession to property and office, through mother's brothers and not through natural fathers. So litigation among the Chewa 'is generally between one person supported by his [mother's kin] and another supported by his'. But in these family matters the jural system breaks down. Criminal and civil law fall away, as with many African peoples, before conflicts within a given family grouping; and 'you have to go home and settle your quarrel there'.

This limit on jural effectiveness has distant origins in the settlement of intrafamily disputes. Very possibly, it stands for an expression of the supreme value of the moral order as epitomized in kinship relations: only ancestral sanctions, not legal and therefore profane ones, should regulate the affairs of close kin. However that may be, Chewa have accepted it. In what way, then, can family disputes be settled? Chewa find the answer in their witchcraft beliefs.

Marwick's informants 'contended that matrilineal relatives "practise sorcery against one another" because, belonging to a close-knit group, they are unable to settle their disputes by the judicial procedures available to unrelated persons who quarrel'. Being outside the jurisdiction of the courts, disputes between close kin, and the tensions which arise from such disputes, are relieved 'not by catharsis and adjustment, but by suppression; and informants believe that the smouldering hatred resulting from suppression flares up in due course in the form of sorcery'. Wronged by your mother's brother, or by your mother's sister's son, you cannot take him to the courts. So you bottle up your resentment and eventually you hate him. Hating him, you open the gates to the entry of Evil. You have recourse, or are believed to have recourse, to the machinations of sorcery.

Family resentment having this effect, Chewa deplore it. To nurse this kind of 'smouldering hatred', or, as they say, 'to keep words in the chest', is regarded 'with an almost neo-Freudian disapproval'. The fact remains that words often are kept in the chest; and the belief that they result in sorcery is seen by Chewa as a great source of trouble. One of Marwick's informants said about quarrels over succession to public office that

... Headmanship kills many people in this country of ours because, if you have succeeded in it, it isn't everybody that rejoices with you ... Sometimes the people of a family (*banja*, which in this context means matrilineage) choose a junior child to be headman of it, if they see that his character is better than that of the senior 'brother'. Thus, when the junior brother succeeds to the headmanship, the senior one seeks 'medicines' that he may kill him and seize the headmanship.

Perhaps one should add that the 'killing' would be by ensorcelment and not by act of violence.

Here again one sees how the notion of Evil has been linked, within the archetypal family unit, to god-given or ancestral rules which are not adjustable by any secular rules that men may invent. This intimate linkage has emerged from many studies. 'It is in the idiom of witchcraft,' Evans-Pritchard explains, 'that Azande express moral rules which mostly lie outside criminal and civil law.' The Lugbara offer a wide expression of the same approach.

It might be expected that Lugbara villagers would locate the cause of their troubles among all those 'sorcerers and magicians', or other upside-down folk, who live in other villages. But not at all: malevolent magic, according to Lugbara ideas, comes only from *within* one's own village or related group of villages. Witches attack 'their own' people. At first sight this may seem perfectly illogical, since a Lugbara village system, created according to a divinely given order of social relations, should logically be free of the workings of Evil. But Lugbara have their own logic about this. Their witchcraft beliefs are revealed on analysis to 'express certain tensions and stresses which are conceived ... as due to attempts to alter the divinely created pattern of authority and orderly relations between kin and neighbours'; between those very persons, in short, whose relations are governed by what is 'right and natural' and can thus be disturbed only by what is 'wrong and natural'.

Seen in this way, witchcraft beliefs become clearly functional: 'part of the complex system by which human beings are enabled to live together in an orderly arrangement of social relations'. But a merely functional explanation is not enough. For if function were all that was involved, why should Africans not have freed themselves from witchcraft fears, which nobody enjoys, simply by extending their jural institutions into the field of intrafamily dispute? Why not just stop believing in witches?

The curious case of the Amba helps to answer these questions. Like Lugbara, Amba think of witches as being upside-down people who are thoroughly inverted to every kind of right behaviour, and who do a lot of harm. Amba repeatedly told Winter 'how wonderful it would be to live in a society without witchcraft', and complained that British colonial officials who constantly talked about helping them had proved quite unable to deal with the scourge they hated most. Yet the fact is that so long as Amba ideology holds firm, witches must remain. For it is in terms of witchcraft that the Amba explain all their most intimate troubles. 'People do not fear the witches of other villages; they fear the witches of their own village.' Though balefully destructive, the danger is rootedly within.

And it is rootedly within because, so long as the Amba moral order retains authority, it cannot be anywhere else. Threats or hostile actions from outside your own moral system – with the Amba, the village lineage – can be dealt with by warfare or other commonsense means. But within your own system you are faced with the subtle and subversive battle of Evil against Good, poised in dialectical balance at the very springs of community life.

Forming its own moral universe, each Amba system has necessarily incorporated its own negation. Its right has supplied its wrong; its gods have invoked its devils. So that no matter what their social functions may be, witchcraft beliefs have also to be seen as terms in moral philosophy, and, as such, integral to the ideologies of traditional thought.

# 15 Useful Magic

These ideologies may reasonably be called optimistic, for generally they taught the supremacy of man in controlling or influencing his own present and future. Far from imposing a grim subjection to the 'blind forces' of nature, they held to a shrewd realism. *Onipa ne asem*, say the Akan: it is mankind that matters – meaning, in this context, that any man can always be responsible for himself.

Within the God-given community of the dead, the living and the yet unborn, it is the living who face the actual problems of life, and who therefore have priority. On their side the ancestors have promised that the living can solve these problems if they obey the rules. By the same token, however, the ancestors must also obey the rules. From this standpoint, the spirits become the servants of living men.

Proper manipulation of the spirits has consequently been a chief preoccupation of these societies. It has occurred in two chief dimensions of therapy. The first may be called the social dimension, while the second is that of the intimately personal. A few more examples of the first may be useful before going on to the second.

Popular wisdom has had a lot to say on the subject of manipulation or control. Thus the Kalabari of the Niger delta undoubtedly respect their ancestral spirits, but only so long as these behave according to the rules. They say, for instance, *Tomi oru beremere*, It is people who make the *oru* (the carved shrine object which a given spirit will inhabit while speaking to men); and *Tomi, ani oru ma*, People, they are the *oru*; or, along the same line of thought, *Agu nsi owi baku kwma, en duko i'o pre ba*, If a spirit becomes too violent [in its demands], they will tell him the wood he is carved from. In other words, the spirits cannot be expected to do what they are told; but they can be and are expected to behave according to reliable prediction. Otherwise they will only make themselves ridiculous.

We have looked at several cases of social therapy at the community level. Anthropologists have come across many others. The Mbugwe are a small farming people of northern Tanzania among whom there is a great deal of 'sorcery between chiefs'. General calamities, damage to entire neighbourhoods rather than to individuals, have usually been attributed by Mbugwe to the workings of chiefly witchcraft. This is how Mbugwe have explained their troubles of an epidemic or group character. 'At the same time,' Gray suggests, 'these beliefs reinforced the existing political structure by creating tensions and attitudes of hostility between chiefdoms, and by stimulating loyalties within the chiefdoms and thus increasing the solidarity of the group.' He goes on to argue that 'the complex of beliefs also functioned more overtly in that the chiefs undoubtedly attempted to manipulate them for the deliberate purpose of increasing their own political power and also the size and strength of their chiefdoms.' As elsewhere, cunning forethought could find religion very handy now and then.

The same approach was evidently helpful, perhaps crucially so, in aiding and smoothing the segmentation of communities, the splitting away and migration of junior groups from senior groups. Whenever a group of kin decided to move away from the parent group that had given them birth, they were faced with the hard fact of breaking with their lineal ancestors. This meant breaking with their moral order. So they had somehow to accomplish a move which struck against their established beliefs about themselves and their identity. They had to remould these beliefs, and become 'another people'.

What seems often to have happened is that the break was explained and dramatized in terms of witchcraft, while rebirth was consummated by appropriate anti-witchcraft action. 'Accusations of witchcraft' and the counter to them would act, in Mitchell's words, 'as a catalyst in the process of segmentation'. The term 'witchcraft' can of course be misleading: what we are talking about here is not some frantic dancing round a witches' cauldron, but an institutionalized relief of group tension and a calculated rearrangement of socio-moral norms. Lineage leader B, desiring to move away with his followers, would accuse lineage leader A of witchcraft, and anti-witchcraft action would then sanction a break between the two lineages, thus giving the new unit, as well as the old one, the comfort and reassurance of having adjusted their lives to the needs of the 'right and natural'.

This symbolic drama of lineage separation took many forms. In the seventeenth century the Italian missionary Cavazzi, writing of the kingdom of Kongo, deplored the fact that the founding hero of Kongo history was celebrated for having murdered his aunt. He found, moreover, that each successive king, upon taking the throne, was obliged to commit a similar act. In truth, the ceremony may now be seen as symbolism showing that the king had buried his personal loyalty to his own lineage, and was now, unlike ordinary men, enthroned as the guardian of all the lineages of his people. Whether or not one calls this 'witchcraft' is merely a matter of convenience. In contexts such as this, one could also call it constitutional law.

Therapy at the individual level was similarly diverse. The Kaguru are among those who have believed that no one should seek unusual wealth or power, and that anyone who did so might well have helped himself by witchcraft. 'Affluent men are often considered witches ... A prosperous man may be both dangerous to others and in danger to himself on account of witchcraft', because, intentionally or not, he has disturbed the ideal balance. Such beliefs not only tended to resolve tensions, but also to safeguard social norms and comfort the unfortunate. As Gluckman found, a Bemba who comes across three wild bees' nests in the bush is by no means necessarily to be envied.

Marital conflicts have drawn the same treatment. Kaguru often accuse their wives of witchcraft. Beidelman argues that this is because they 'feel great insecurity towards their wives, [since they] see them as independent or even as secretly hostile to them. Children belong to one's wife's clan, and a man believes that his wife teaches her children to favour her brothers rather than her husband. Women want many children and if they have few or none, they become very dissatisfied and may accuse their husbands of impotence or sterility.'

Quarrels in a polygamous household are another common field for witchcraft accusations. Huntingford found that the Nandi of Kenya have made use of witchcraft belief in cases of debt, as when a husband failed to pay instalments of bride-wealth, or the guardian of a minor refused to hand over cattle in his keeping. Resort to a recognized witch, or a threat to do so, was apparently an accepted means of securing one's rights. Where the law could not do the job for you, you could turn to the spirits. Some Lugbara, according to Middleton, even like to have a bit of a reputation for witchcraft; they find it gives them a certain if somewhat risky rise in the social register.

Social therapies of this kind were institutional, and their degree of success will obviously have varied. By and large, however, the evidence suggests that these structures of belief, and the manipulations they allowed, were persistently adequate to the material possibilities of much of traditional Africa until the nineteenth century. Could they otherwise, indeed, have achieved such authority or survived so long?

Yet it is the personal application of these beliefs that shows them at their most effective. At this point we enter a new and little known field of research, that of medical sociology. But already it is one that seems likely to prove richly fertile.

A young husband finds himself impotent not long after marriage. Applying to a traditional doctor, he is informed that his sister is a witch who has removed his testicles. Unless these are returned to him, his impotence will continue. The sister is accordingly summoned before the doctor. She readily confesses her guilt and informs those at the hearing that she has hidden her brother's testicles in an ant hill. When asked whether the ants will not have eaten the testicles, she replies that she hid them in an empty cigarette tin. With this information the doctor and his followers move to the ant hill in question, and begin to dig. They turn up an empty cigarette tin. This tin is presented to the patient by the doctor, and the patient gratefully accepts with it the return of his missing testicles. Within a year, his wife is delivered of a son.

Most psychiatric workers in Africa seem now agreed that suggestive therapy in cases of this kind, practised by traditional doctors deeply familiar with their milieu, has often obtained good results. The following exchange took place during a radio interview with Dr T. Adeoye Lambo, M.D., M.R.C.P., D.P.M., a Nigerian psychiatrist much respected for his clinical work, who afterwards became Vice-Chancellor of Ibadan University:

Is it possible to say how effective these witch-doctors, these traditional healers, are in treatment?

LAMBO: Let me be perfectly honest with you. Their treatment procedures and their entire management are, I think, vastly superior to what we are doing at the present moment in Nigeria.

To what *you* are doing?

LAMBO: To what *I* am doing: and probably to what some of my colleagues are doing.

Let us get down to figures, Dr Lambo: what is their success rate in your estimation?

LAMBO: About three years ago we made an evaluation, a programme of their work, and compared this with our own, and we discovered that actually they were scoring almost sixty-per-cent success in their treatment of neurosis. And we were scoring forty per cent — in fact, less than forty per cent.

This is not to argue that traditional methods of psychotherapy have been sufficient. Though useful in the treatment of anxiety neuroses they were and are not, according to another specialist opinion, of any help to psychotics or to people suffering from severe traumatic reactions. Within these limits, however, few modern specialists would now question the right of these methods to be regarded with respect.

It seems, indeed, that Africans long anticipated Freud and what has flowed from Freud. Their methods have been akin to modern methods: 'the order of criteria employed [by witchdoctors] to distinguish particular kinds of mental and emotional disturbance', according to Leighton and Hughes, 'are very similar to the criteria employed in psychiatry. People are said to have this or that illness according to symptoms, degree of impairment, the causes that can be discerned, and response to treatment.' Writing of Yoruba doctors, they add that 'many kinds of psychoneurotic symptoms, certain manifestations of reactive depression and a good many types of personality disorder are perceived by [these healers]'. Inaugurating the first Pan-African Psychiatric Conference in 1964, Sir Aubrey Lewis gave full recognition to the 'thesis that the psychotherapy inherent in these methods has a profound appeal and a probable validity which the sophisticated psychiatrist cannot afford to ignore, and which he will not wish to deride'.

'If it were not for the traditional healers,' a long-experienced European psychiatrist in charge of a central African mental hospital said to me one day while we were discussing these matters, 'we should be flooded out here with anxiety-neurosis cases.' And he proceeded to describe two such cases which his hospital had treated, but which, in his view, traditional healers could also have treated by their own methods and often did treat. One was of a wife who resented her husband's marrying again. She had become so neurotic as to be completely speechless, and had taken to firing huts. Her repressive mechanism had long since prevented her from reasoning about her condition. 'So we applied abreaction in the form of the so-called "truth drugs", and then it all came out.' She could release her hatred in words, and, in so doing, move towards relief.

The second case was of a type sometimes called in evidence, by Europeans in Africa, to show that Africans cannot face the modern world. This was of a man living in the capital city who came into hospital with neurotic afflictions, including spasmodic drunkenness that he was ashamed of but could not control. He was finally brought to see that his condition was a product of guilt disturbance. He had a wife in the country for whom he was failing to provide as he should.

The truth about this man, in short, was not that he could not 'face the modern world', but that he could not live at peace with it while continuing to meet the counter-claims of the 'old world'. The modern world insisted that he come to the city by himself and earn cash: the old world insisted that he support his wife in the country. In this case, as it happened, the man was earning enough to support her. In most 'settler colonies', by contrast, workers in the cities were regularly paid a single man's wage as a matter of policy, so as to keep African families out of the towns. The resultant strains are obvious. It was in helping to relieve strains of this kind that traditional doctors played an ever more important part in everyday African life during the colonial period.

Even so, how did their methods 'work'? Why, in the case of the missing testicles, did the doctor settle on the patient's sister as the source of trouble? The likely answer is that he did so because he was well informed about local gossip as well as about local beliefs and customs. Personalities apart, one could expect that this occurred in a matrilineal society where the sister's brother's son, if and when he was born, would inherit wealth or position within the family. The sister will have had her own reasons for wishing her brother to be childless, and the brother will have been aware of this to the point of depressive anxiety.

But why would the doctor accuse the sister of *witchcraft*? Clearly, because impotence is an interference in the 'right and natural' ordering of life. Its 'cause' would therefore lie in the workings of Evil: with this case, in the deliberate manipulation of Evil. Then from where would the doctor draw his power to induce belief that the missing testicles, however invisible, were 'really' in the empty cigarette tin? Here one enters the complex unities of traditional thought. For the doctor, though trained in his work, and even highly trained for several years, was less a secular than a religious figure: less a doctor in the modern sense than a priest whose authority was drawn from an explanatory-mandatory charter of belief. The doctor had authority because he had access to the explanations that lie beyond commonsense, the explanations by which Africans have looked for the roots of causality.

The training of doctors was a serious affair. In the past this craft seems often to have been divided into two chief sections, respectively practising in herbal cures and in divination or other forms of religious treatment. Today there is a good deal of blurring of the lines of division, at least in the towns where mere superstition, the broken husk of any religious system, tends to flourish amid the survival of cultures now much adulterated or undermined by contact with the modern world. That is partly why recent manifestations of the healing craft can sometimes look absurd. Raymond Prince reports a Nigerian doctor's sign which read: We Cure Mad Fellows in Twenty-One Days, and another which proclaimed, We Specialise in Everything.

Traditionally, specialists in anti-witchcraft followed the craft from father to son through several or even many generations, handing down their techniques and forms of training, their quintessential experience and habitual shrines where application could be made to the spirits. Half a century ago it was observed by Rattray, who lived among the Asante of Ghana, that training for priesthood – for doctorship – was an arduous business of three years during which the trainee must observe full continence and other testing prohibitions.

This training had much to do with the observance of ritual. And obviously so. For it was through appropriate ritual, and its associated techniques of self-entrancement and divination – of 'speaking for the spirits' – that the authority of ancestral charters was expressed. The effective force of these charters may be regarded almost indifferently as religious, magical, medical, political, social or cultural: it was, in truth, all six at once. And ritual, whether in the Gennepian sense of *rites de passage* from one stage or state of being to another, or in some other sense, was its necessary mode of execution or administration. Ritual, in other words, was purposive. 'Rituals of all kinds,' as Gluckman has said, 'were associated with efforts to ensure success and avoid disaster.'

Seen historically, these systems and their rituals of catharsis may wear an ambivalent face. They were a means of reconciling conflict within a given 'natural order': to the extent that they were successful, however, and the evidence suggests that they were highly successful, they were also a means of preventing systematic change in that order. At the same time they possessed a remarkable absorptive capacity, even when faced with sharp breakdowns or disasters. Confronted by social change, they could allow for it. They could adjust to new techniques and new phenomena.

This ambivalent force of divinely sanctioned ritual needs to be understood as one of the chief dynamics of the past. How one judges its effective value, and so its relative pressures for conservation or change, will depend on time and place and standpoint. Perhaps one may draw a parallel, distant but not essentially inexact, with modern views about trade unions. Are they forms of socially sanctioned ritual which stand for means of reconciling conflicts within capitalist society, so enabling capitalist society to continue to work and hold together? Or are they means of sharpening the employer–employee conflict to the point where resolution can demand a change of structure? Both views may be 'true': which of them you take is likely to depend on where you stand within the system.

The point in this connection is that the doctor could not be just anyone. Charlatans apart, he had to be a man duly invested with appropriate authority. To be accepted as a practitioner, he required the evidence of training just as much as a modern doctor needs a string of medical initials after his name. Then his authority could be very great. For 'ritual mobilizes incontrovertible authority behind the granting of office and status, and thus guarantees its legitimacy and imposes accountability for its proper exercise'. Told by his doctor that the missing testicles were in the empty tin, the patient had the best of reasons for believing it. Besides, what he was really getting back were not his physical organs, manifestly still in place, but the immanent force which gave them their power and would, in his now instructed view of the matter, restore his potency. Having removed the 'true' cause of his trouble, he was cured.

Yet why, after all, should the sister have confessed? Possibly her relations with her brother had long been strained, and she felt in some way guilty for this. But even if she had really wished to keep her brother childless, had she really put that cigarette tin in the ant heap – or was it perhaps the doctor with a curative conjuring trick? This last question is immaterial. The interest lies in the confession. For it leads on to the indubitable fact that many witches, as examples quoted in an earlier chapter have shown, have always been ready to confess their misdeeds, even without the pressure of threats of ordeal or reprisal.

Margaret Field, a pioneer in this area of research, has compared Ga wizardry with European experience. In sixteenth-century Europe, as the records repeatedly show, 'it became the custom, when cows aborted, swine took fever, crops failed, floods rose and people perished, to look around for a witch. It has been a matter of modern bewilderment that the guilt was almost always laid at the door of some lonely, poor and wretched old woman, hitherto submerged in humdrum insignificance. The explanation suggested by the witchcraft of West Africa is that the old woman had voluntarily asserted and insisted upon her guilt.

'This is further supported by facts which confront us in the mental hospitals of Britain today. There is no more familiar figure in the admission wards than the agitated depressive, weighed down with extravagant and unshakeable self-reproach.' And Field goes on to offer cases which are exactly parallel with those of the Ga women who confessed to killing scores of children or committing other crimes. That, for example, of a

Mrs B., a widow of fifty-five, [who] was admitted in an agitated depression. She was retarded, speaking slowly in a whisper. She covered her face, wrung her hands and moaned. The content of her speech was exclusively self-abasing. 'I have brought destruction ... I'm ashamed ... I did it without thinking ... No one else has been so wicked as I have ... Why should all these people have to suffer for me? ... All the floods and all the war: it must be me to blame.'

Very reasonably when seen against the African evidence, Field concludes that 'we have in our midst today in Britain people who proclaim ... that they are the very stuff of witchcraft'. So with more knowledge it may be that the study of African beliefs can help to elucidate not only the wizardry of a past Europe and America, but also more recent manifestations of depressive guilt; and even, perhaps, the social causality of mental maladies peculiarly modern, such as the neurosis of urban alienation with its sequels in violent anger or pain.

In the case of the missing testicles the available evidence is not enough to show whether the sister was suffering from depressive guilt. But large numbers of similar cases, reported today in contexts which suggest that they reflect the situations of the past, undoubtedly reveal symptoms of neurotic depression. It was because of this that Margaret Field became convinced while working as an ethnographer in pre-war Ghana that a key to the understanding of witchcraft lay in clinical psychiatry. Years later she returned to post-war Ghana, armed with a medical training and some experience in psychiatry, and set about investigating the work of shrine doctors. She found several thousand of these in practice. Most of the cases treated by them were concerned with symptoms of more or less intense anxiety.

These shrines were usually open two or three days a week for *abisa*. This is the preliminary consultation at which applicants make known their requests and speak of their troubles, and when the priest-doctor listens and decides whether or not to accept the case. If he or she decides favourably, the patient is given another appointment. At this second session the doctor becomes entranced or 'possessed by the spirit' which has chosen to inhabit the shrine in question. Having obtained the spirit's advice, the doctor then prescribes. 'A popular hard-working shrine', Field says of the Akan areas of Ghana in the middle 1950s, 'may deal with upwards of a hundred commonplace cases in a day.'

The sociological interest of Field's material lies chiefly in its remarkable demonstration of the links between social transition and neurotic maladjustment, a point to which I shall return later. 'Of all the supplicants who bring their troubles to shrines' – and Field examined 2,537 cases – 'the most frequent is the frustrated, unhappy, despairing man whose complaint is "I am not prospering".' Many such cases were the fruit precisely of new social problems, such as the chronic indebtedness and insecurity of lorry-drivers, or the failure of children to pass examinations at school. But there was a whole class of complaints whose nature seems to reflect the situations and practices of the past. Indirectly, they offer another facet of historical reality in a region where old accounts are notably defective or confused.

Among such cases are fears of sexual impotence, or the anxieties of those who actually suffer from it. With such examples one may reasonably take Field's material and 'read it back' into times before the great upheavals of the last hundred years. They suggest how closely the psychology of neurotic depression and its treatment must have followed in the path of traditional morality and its prohibitions or imperatives, and how patently the analysis of such disturbance confirms the structural picture of the Evil and the Good that ruled men's lives.

Considering impotency cases, Field notes half a dozen where 'the patient had two wives, the "old" and a new young one, and was impotent only with the new' – because he feared that the other, 'out of either jealousy or just resentment of neglect or ill-treatment, would make bad magic against him'. Another impotent 'had on his conscience a first wife who had died in the distress and want occasioned by his neglect, and he feared her ghost'. A third admitted intercourse with a married woman whose justly resentful husband he believed to have consulted a maleficent doctor. One became impotent after dreaming of intercourse with 'a certain woman', but gave no further details of an experience which, presumably, embarrassed him for reasons of social guilt or shame. 'In several instances the patient had a wife who had become reluctant, from which the patient inferred that her affections were elsewhere, and that the rival was making bad medicine' to stop him sleeping with his wife.

Three impotency cases were of a somewhat different kind, and help to throw light on the nature of causative belief in the past. Like the man with the missing testicles, these were patients who looked for a more obscure 'first cause'. They were men who had caught venereal infection from prostitutes. They understood the immediate cause of their disease, but remained convinced 'that without witchcraft or bad magic they would not have succumbed'; and they held accordingly that hospital treatment would be 'futile till the ultimate malevolent power' had been broken – the power which had caused them to choose prostitutes who were diseased. Here one sees why it is that many patients admitted nowadays to general hospitals still make certain, if they can, of continued treatment by traditional doctors. Modern doctors may be fully recognized as having an otherwise unknown wisdom in the cure of disease. But in traditional eyes they cannot deal with ultimate causes. Only traditional doctors can do this, because only they can reach the spirits who control these matters, the spirits through whom people conceptualize the nature of their civilization and the stuff of their experience.

If a much-narrowed idea of religion makes it hard for us to grasp these attitudes, the difficulty is compounded by our similarly narrowed notion of social responsibility. A great deal of African treatment rests upon the practice of group therapy – but of one that is not, as with us, an artificial or 'organized' affair. The group therapy of Africa has been only a specialized aspect of a total situation. This has been the situation in which the thoughts, beliefs and actions of the individual are embedded deeply in the fact and knowledge of community. The suffering might be solitary, but the treatment was social even when it was also highly personal. And this could be so not only because of the small scale of these societies, but above all because of their capacity to externalize, publicly accept, and treat anxiety by open rituals carrying a sufficient power of therapeutic relief. Society, in Fortes's words, took over the burden of adjustment which, with us, falls entirely on the individual.

African society could take over this burden, resolving individual tensions with personal advice or group tensions 'in a wave of enthusiasm and solidarity', because it rested upon an imperative morality. In our western world, as we live it today, any such basis for curative 'enthusiasm and solidarity' has long begun to crumble. Increasingly, whether we like it or not, we are left with the solitary on the couch – or, of course, to the shooting in the streets. Loss or gain? The nature of African civilization has no answer. Complete within itself, it looked no further. Progressive in its resolution of human tensions, it remained constrictive by the very totality of its terms. Within those terms there was nothing that it could not explain, no behaviour that it could not provide for. Only the irruption of the modern world, raggedly, unmindfully, has availed to break the mould of this most comprehensive work of social architecture.

# 17 Art for Life's Sake

A constant trouble for the familiar 'outside' view of Africa has lain in its insistent defining of *dissected* beliefs and activities. This view has tended to take the cultures of the past painstakingly to pieces, and then examine each part in isolation from the whole. It has thought of religious belief in its own terms, as being somehow extraneous to real life, and has consequently mistaken the place and meaning of religion in traditional society. It has studied witchcraft in detachment from the total structure, and all too often seen nothing but mumbo jumbo. It has looked at African masks in museums, and found them primitive or absurd. In the same way it has constructed theories about the arts, seeing them in isolation and asking, What did they *do*? What were they *for*?

A familiar answer has been that the arts of Africa were meant to make things happen. You drew an antelope on a wall of rock so that your arrow should afterwards find one. You performed a ceremony in order to make rain fall. The arts were a branch of magic as though these antique Africans, to quote Mary Douglas, were so many 'populations of Ali Babas and Aladdins, uttering their magic words and rubbing their magic lamps' in happy confidence, but against all the odds of actual experience, that the heavens would open and cornucopias of wealth pour down. Alternately, these arts were orgiastic, even in the solemn sense of worshipping the gods: they were meant to placate, flatter or otherwise imitate the supernatural powers. Or they were there to express 'primeval' terror, joy and other wild emotions evoked by the 'unknown'.

All these kinds of definition are more or less worthless, either because they are flatly wrong or because the arts die and lose their meaning when dissected from the context and embrace of life.

We shall get at an understanding of the arts of Africa only by an arduous effort at grasping the totality of this civilization. The effort is difficult because our cultures of urban industrialism have moved us far away. Rarely now can we experience 'cultural manifestations' which still reflect, even if distantly and partially, the rounded attitudes and approaches of a different age.

In rural Sicily not long ago I happened to be present at an annual festival to confirm the peace and welfare of the place which I was in, and called the Festival of Sant' Antonio. Fair booths and coloured lights lined the village street. Crowds of country folk were there to enjoy it. Towards ten in the evening a blast of trumpets announced the Madonna and Child, who forthwith appeared from a starlit tunnel enthroned on a gawdy dray and beclustered with electric lamps. A relaxed and yet respectful crowd stood and watched beside the church, hoisting children on their shoulders, shoving for a better view, pressing back against tables where the temporarily moneyed were eating their suppers in the velvet night and sinking their wine. Somewhere nearby a barker was shouting for a dozen large dolls splendidly dressed and hatted: *Cen-to lire la bam-bola! Guardate che ha sulla testa! Hun-dred lire the doll! Just look at the hats they've got!* To the background of his cries the Madonna and Child were lifted from their dray on poles carried by strong men, and literally danced up the steps of a glowing and expectant church. *Cen-to lire la bam-bola!* yelled the barker, and the dancing Madonna nodded her consent. Heaven and Earth were joined in happy unison.

Now was there anyone in that crowd who believed that this ceremony actually made, ensured, guaranteed the peace and welfare of the coming season? Perhaps one or two. But it will probably be right to think that most of these sceptical and toil-toughened peasants and their wives saw the matter differently: as nothing very mystical, far less magical, but rather as a customary and comfortable affirmation of the ways things 'ought to be', as a token that good tradition was going on, as an agreeably intimate if indirect statement about themselves and their identity. It was not the moment to ask them what they thought. I think if

I had done so they would have merely said, 'Well, but this is what we always do at the Festival of Sant' Antonio.' The self-evident within a culture calls for no elucidation by its members.

Far away in Dinkaland they have other festivals. They perform ceremonies concerned with rain. These they hold in the droughts of spring that are always followed, or as near as makes no difference, by rains which gradually fill up their rivers and soak their land. Having lived here for many centuries the Dinka are perfectly aware of when the rains begin. If the object of their rain festivals was to make rain happen, their natural country scepticism would surely long ago have dissuaded them from bothering with efforts to cause what was going to happen anyway. Why, then, do they hold these ceremonies?

They themselves would probably reply to a chance enquiry, like the Sicilians, 'But this is what we always do.' Lienhardt has probed further. He explains that these festivals are not to be understood as 'rain-making' rites. They are ceremonies aimed at restating the customary and comforting assurances of Dinka tradition. In them, human action moves symbolically 'with the rhythm of the natural world around them, recreating that rhythm in moral terms and not merely attempting to coerce it into conformity with human desires'. All this dancing and music-making are expressions of what is felt, thought and believed about life as Dinka know it. They are manifestations of the 'right and natural'.

A group of anthropologists were present when some !Kung Bushmen – the exclamation-mark is there for a click on the letter 'k' – were performing a 'rain ceremony'. No sooner had they finished than 'a small cloud appeared on the horizon, grew and darkened. Then rain fell. But the anthropologists who asked if the Bushmen reckoned the rite had produced the rain, were laughed out of court.' What the Bushmen were doing, apart from enjoying themselves, was not to 'magic rain out of the sky', but to dramatize their dependence on rain, their recognition of rain as an aspect of the natural order like themselves, their restatement of the primordial morality which had brought rain and Bushmen into the world together, and linked them in the nature of things.

Then there is the part of misunderstanding which comes from sheer lack of intelligent participation. Lienhardt comments,

Most anthropologists have had the experience of being laughed at for their own credulity, in taking too literally some story told by the people they have studied. It is as though, having heard it said in England that there was a man in the moon, a foreigner was to proceed to talk to the English as though they believed that.

Or as though a 'tribal African', having seen the gory agonies displayed in Crucifixion figures, were to enquire of Europeans why they nailed people on crosses.

African art, no doubt, was religious in the sense of being the expression of ideologies conceived in an age of faith. There were rain ceremonies which really were concerned with a shortage of rain: with finding out, that is, why the Principle of Evil was at work in preventing rain, or why the Principle of Good was not at work in sending it. Masks were carved for specific ritual purposes. A great deal of dancing was primarily not for fun. Skilled metalsmiths uttered prayers while pouring metal. In a deep sense the arts of non-literate Africa composed its holy books and testaments. They were the corporeal rendering of otherwise inexpressible unities between the known and the unknown. They were shared links with ancestors and gods who had shaped the world and laid down rules for its progression. If we call them 'religious arts', however, we risk falling into our own dissecting attitudes to reality.

They were art for life's sake, but also for pleasure's sake. They were subject to critical taste. Carvers were famous because they were excellent. Dancers were celebrated not bcause they knew the steps – practically everyone knew the steps – but because they danced them supremely well. Drummers were admired for the rhythms they could hear and play, rhythms so complex that an unskilled listener like myself cannot even recognize them. The great schools of sculpture were of artists who, generation by generation, embellished the affairs of everyday life. There was an exacting scale of achievement; and the criteria were aesthetic.

This variety of relevance could impel the emphasis of meaning in one direction or another, or in several at the same time. Consider the dancing of the Kalabari of the Niger delta. This people of the Niger creeks and seaways have excelled in masquerades. Each of their communities has a man's society called *Ekine* or *Sekiapu*, 'the dancing people', and each of these societies puts on, or used to put on, a cycle of from thirty to fifty plays.

At first glance these Kalabari plays may certainly appear religious. Kalabari have told Europeans that *Ekine* is 'one of the highest things'. Before staging their plays, dancers 'go down in canoes to a spot far out in the creeks known as the "Beach of the Water Spirits"' who are thought to inhabit the seaways. 'Here they call in the spirits', with suitable invocations and libations, 'telling them that their plays are about to begin and that they should come to attend them. The spirits are believed to return to the town with their invokers. This done, the *Ekine* members offer a dog to their patron goddess, with a prayer for the success of her plays.'

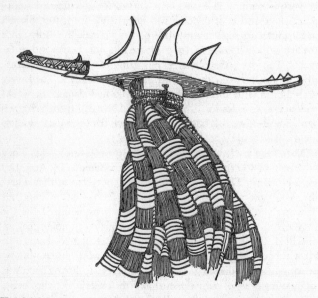

Kalabari water-spirit mask in the form of a crocodile, about 80 cms long. These maskers customarily wear a long cotton robe

But a closer look suggests another interpretation, neither religious nor moral. The invocations, in fact, are not so much concerned with a request for social benefits as with artistic success for the players.

They ask that the masker should be given nimble legs and light arms; that nothing should press heavily upon him; that his ears should be wide and clear to hear the drum; that it should seem as if he and the drummer had planned every step of the performance between them; that the drum should 'enter the dancer's legs'; that the spirit of the masquerade should possess him.

The spirits invoked are a minor lot of rather turbulent characters not generally believed to be powerful or even well-intentioned: a sort of magical coterie of dubious Bohemians normally best ignored or left alone, somewhat as though care were being taken to leave the 'serious spirits' quite outside these often uproarious occasions.

Besides this, the material of the plays recognizably reflects life as it is and not as it ought to be, and the masquerades take no particular stand on moral issues.

Perhaps the commonest theme is that of the ferocious male warrior, laying about him with matchet or spear, his violence set off by the plump, comely, slow-moving figure of his wife ... Then there is the dignified, opulent 'house head' portrayed by masquerades like *Gbassa* and *Alagba*. Or the massive, stolid character portrayed by the maskers of *Otobo* – a water spirit who is thought of as part man, part hippopotamus ... By way of contrast, there is the cunning, amoral hypocrite portrayed by *Tkaki* ... Or the sexy-good-for-nothing aristocrat *Iqbo*, of whom they sing: 'His father sent him to market to buy yams; but instead he bought a woman's vagina ...' Or again there is the native doctor *Ngbula*, grunting around with grim concentration in search of bad medicines and evil spirits: suspicious like all of his profession that people are talking ill of him, and breaking off from time to time to make ferocious charges at his supposed detractors.

All this shows that these masquerades are robustly recreational, whatever else they may also be. Horton argues that they are a case of religion serving art, rather than the reverse. He suggests that the idea behind the 'calling of the water spirits' is to help spectators to suspend disbelief about the material of the plays, and, no less, to depersonalize little-disguised dancers whom everyone knows in everyday life. Unless this can be done, as every modern parent understands who has ever seen his neighbours or children in theatricals, the dramatic effect is bound to fail. For if it is only old so-and-so making an ass of himself, there is no play; there is only embarrassment.

Apart from this, aesthetic standards are rigorous. Long training and careful organization are obligatory.

Almost as soon as they can walk male children are encouraged to imitate the masquerade performances of their elders, and their fathers or other male relatives often help them. At the age of fifteen or so, the boys pay a small sum to join *Kali Siri* – a junior replica of the *Ekine* society which operates in intervals between masquerade cycles proper.

Emphasis on artistic skill comes out again in criteria for entry to the various grades and offices of a Kalabari dancing society. These criteria 'do not involve the considerations of wealth, pedigree, and political influence which govern advancement in Kalabari society at large', but are concerned with artistic skills. Kalabari nicely make the point when they say that 'in *Ekine*, everyone is equal to everyone else. Whatever people say on the path outside, it is not our business who owns whom, or whose father is greater than whose. We are here for laughing, drinking, and for the play.'

Other elements again suggest a social content. Good playing is a useful path to local status. It is also a means of reinforcing the lineage loyalties crucial in Kalabari society. The plays, it appears, are a way of working out personal competition within the lineage system, while Kalabari 'often answer vague questions about *Ekine* by saying "It is our old-time government"'. To the extent that performance of a specific masquerade is 'an act of reverence for a dead man on the part of his descendants, it is also an assertion by them of the collective status which they derive from him'. As such, it is apt to include a great deal of spending and giving of a kind that lauds status.

So it is that the mind behind the mask was a variable and many-sided one, neither 'primeval' nor ideologically simple. It possessed and expressed a complex reality. It imagined and created in the wake of a long evolution. It spoke and worked for clear purposes. Ignoring all this, many museums still label their African collections with the word 'primitive'. But the truth is that the pre-eminent arts of Africa – dancing, drumming, carving, and the rest – had ceased to be 'simple', let alone 'primitive', in form and content or in meaning and performance at least by the time of the European Middle Ages, and probably long before. Those who deny this, or do not know it, have possibly talked more nonsense than anyone else on any African subject.

Worringer, the German aesthetician whose views are often endorsed by Sir Herbert Read, has described Primitive Man as 'a creature who confronts the outer world as helplessly and incoherently as a dumbfounded animal', and [explains that] 'artistic creation means for primitive man the avoidance of life and its arbitrariness'.

Tell that to the Kalabari dancers!

Zither, about 75 cms long, from the Kweri of Tanzania

# 18 The Dynamics of Reality

If his arts suggest that 'primitive man' was neither 'helpless' nor 'incoherent', let alone 'dumbfounded', the same view emerges from his ontology and metaphysics. A new understanding of African concepts of Being, of the immanent systematization of the cosmos according to African ideas, looks back to the year 1946. Then it was that the Dogon elders of Ogol took an important decision about a visiting Frenchman.

Imagine the reversed situation of, say, the canons of Coventry Cathedral. They would surely have behaved no differently. Faced with an exotic but agreeable visitor who was pleasantly and yet persistently eager to understand the workings of the Divine dispensation, they too would in the end have wearied of uninformed questions and simple answers. Busy though they were, they would have recognized that there are moments when theology must be explained. They would have called in the dean, even possibly the bishop.

For think what kind of stuff this distant traveller might otherwise go away and tell his own world. 'The English pay little or no heed to religion; they have splendid churches, but seldom worship in them. They claim to have some notion of a High God, but you soon find out that this God is thought of as a man, a fact which no doubt says something about their intense individualism and aversion from community control. They will not, however, admit this. Although Coventry cathedral is decorated with the painting of an enormous male figure, the priests claim that this is really the picture of a god, a suprasensible being in some way an embodiment of ancestral wisdom. They deny that this is an image to be worshipped, although it is perfectly obvious that people do in fact kneel before this image and pray to it.

'With the same inconsequence they claim they have only one

god. Yet it is just as clear that they have not one but three who are important, as well as many lesser gods. These last they call saints, perhaps because people here seldom like calling a thing by its real name. They are similarly reticent on the subject of one of their most solemn rites. This consists in eating the body and blood of their god. At the same time they are obviously sensitive to the old African belief that Europeans are, or at least were, habitual cannibals. The priests insist that this rite is, *and always was*, merely symbolic, and that what they eat is only bread and wine. I observed the rite myself, and at least on this occasion I am sure they were telling the truth.

'Of course I may be accused of idealizing a people whose reputation has been one for rapacity and violence. The fact remains that the English, no matter how their everyday behaviour may have seemed to deny it, do indeed have a religion with a place for love and non-violence, and even for modesty and respect of truth. Besides this, they have an ontology and metaphysic concerning the origins of the world. Unfortunately, we still have a long way to go in understanding them . . .'

A case for a little authoritative guidance? In 1946 the elders of Ogol decided that Marcel Griaule, whom they respected as a serious seeker after truth, should be given this kind of help. He had been asking them questions for years, and for years they had given him the simple answers, *la parole de face*. But now 'the elders of the lineages . . . met together and decided that the more esoteric aspects of their religion should be fully revealed'. For this purpose they chose a venerable colleague called Ogotêmmeli. And Ogotêmmeli devoted three and thirty days to the task.

What emerged for Griaule was an account of cosmogony according to the Dogon who live in the great bend of the river Niger south of Timbuktu. Others have since extended it.

Religious gestures . . . show themselves under analysis to be of extreme subtlety in their implications. The smallest everyday object may reveal in its form or decoration a conscious reflection of a complex cosmogony . . . The Africans with whom we have worked in the region of the upper Niger have systems of astronomy and calendrical measurements, methods of calculation and extensive anatomical and physiological knowledge, as well as a systematic pharmacopoeia.

Ogotêmmeli was able to build for Griaule a cosmic picture complete within its own terms. He showed how the concept of Being is expressed in the idea of Amma, the High God; how Being is related to Embodiment by way of its emanation, Nummo; and how Nummo, the life force conceived as Water but also as the Word, lies at the origin of all things, persons and other beings, including the first ancestors of men and women. Later on, writing in 1954, Griaule could describe this Dogon conceptual structure as revealing 'an internal coherence, a secret wisdom, and an apprehension of ultimate realities equal to that which we Europeans conceive ourselves to have attained'. If matters had been the other way round, the canons of Coventry might well have been pleased. A real attempt had been made to understand the meaning behind the symbols.

Dogon cosmological ideas are found to have entered their life at every crucial point. As Lienhardt says about the Shilluk on the other side of Africa, these ideas are 'embedded in belief and action'. They have governed the layout of villages, the practice of crafts, the ordering of everyday affairs. Dogon granaries, handsome boxlike structures roofed to a peak, have for example more than an obvious function. In Dogon ideology they portray 'a picture of the world-system ... and the way this system worked'. A granary's chief structural elements were explained to Griaule as standing for the eight principal organs of Nummo the life force, comparable to the organs of man with the addition of the gizzard, since Nummo has the speed of a bird. These organs are held in place by the granary's construction. The 'four uprights ending in the corners of the square roof were the arms and legs ... The granary was like a woman, lying on her back (representing the sun) with her arms and legs raised and supporting the roof (representing the sky).'

The dynamics of Dogon cosmogony proved to be neither simple nor linear. At every critical point, we are told, there had to be allowance for an interpenetration of the material and immaterial, of form and content, of the immediate and the enduring: an interpenetration that operated dialectically in a contrasting of pairs, a controlled tension of opposites, a continual fusing and reaction of conservation and change. Such was man

the female soul was located in the prepuce; in the woman the male soul was located in the clitoris. But the foreknowledge of Nummo no doubt revealed to him the disadvantages of this makeshift. Man's life was not capable of supporting both beings: each person would have to merge himself in the sex for which he appeared to be best fitted.

'The Nummo accordingly circumcised the man, thus removing from him all the femininity of his prepuce', while the masculinity of the woman was 'excised by an invisible hand' during intercourse with the defeminized man. Interaction brought change. Change induced its own reorganization of phenomena, and thus a new stability. The symbolism may be regarded either as an access to reality or the everyday garb of hidden meanings. Its actual appearance would in any case be merely diagrammatic. The point was nicely made by Ogotêmmeli when expatiating on the structure of the world system. The ordered cosmos, he said, could be seen in the shape of an upended basket with a square base, each 'side' having ten steps from base to top. On these steps all creatures had to find standing room.

Griaule objected: 'Only some of the animals and vegetables were on the building. Where were the rest?'

'Each of those mentioned,' replied Ogotêmmeli, 'was as it were a file-leader. All the others of his kind were behind him ...'

'How could all those beasts find room on a step one cubit deep and one cubit high?'

'All this has to be said in words, but everything on the steps is a symbol, symbolic antelopes, symbolic vultures, symbolic hyenas ... Any number of symbols could find room on a one-cubit step.'

The symbolism of a 'concert of opposites' at the root of life and growth is clearly of great antiquity in tropical Africa. The Bambara of the middle Niger, for example, say they derive their ontological conceptions from the Keita lineage which appears in history at the end of the first millennium A.D. This Bambara system explains creation as arising from the Void, *fu*, by the action of *gla*, the creating but uncreated 'principle of fundamental movement of the cosmos and all that therein is': a principle, that is, of continuous creation. 'Full of its emptiness, and its emptiness full of itself', *gla* began the work by uttering 'a voice from the Void', the Divine Word which created its double, *dya*, thus endowing Life with dialectical force. Out of *gla : dya* there came *zo*, the symbol of human consciousness, and *yo*, the symbol of purposive thought. From these the universe was ordered and took shape.

Whatever the precise symbolism, it is the interacting duality that is always fundamental. Bambara sages, for example, project this duality into their conceptual universe as Heaven and Earth represented by two great spirits, Pemba and Faro, whose inter-action spells conservation and change. Pemba is the force or being of things, but Faro, master alike of Water and the Word – as with Nummo of the Dogon – is the shaper and reorganizer of the world. Pemba–Faro are thus the dialectical pair who sym-bolize, as we might say, both Being and Becoming, things as they are and things as they will be. Bambara welfare demands respect for each: for the 'given order' guarded by the ancestors, but also for the power of change, dynamic impulse of Pemba–Faro, which makes the world go round, drives the stars upon their courses, and advances the affairs of men.

The forms vary, not the content. Thomas has described the cosmogony of the Diola of southern Senegal as resting upon three primary concepts. First is that of *participation*, supposing a totality where 'everything belongs' and has its place, ordered and classified: the principle of Being. The second he calls *le couple dichotomie-complémentarité* in which may be recognized the principle of interaction: the principle of Becoming. Thirdly there is a principle of *solide optimisme*, a 'philosophical opti-mism' deriving from the life-force which, product of Being and Becoming, projects the Past into the Future and assures both identity to the person and continuity to the group.

How far do these or similar ideas spread across Africa? No detailed answer is yet to hand. But the general answer is that they are in some degree universal to the continent. They are aspects, in Lienhardt's words, of 'a kind of knowledge and theory of the nature of the universe and of man'. In the 'most usual sense' of the word philosophy according to *The Oxford Dictionary* – of a department of knowledge concerned 'with ultimate reality, or with the most general causes and principles of things' – they comprise the philosophies of Africa.

Accept their strange garb: and these systems can wear a curiously modern air. Over the past hundred years and more the old static categories of the Christian cosmogony have given way to concepts of the universe where matter takes form in motion. Yet this dynamism is what African philosophy has also supposed. However different the symbols, there may even be 'a logical resemblance between the gods of primitive peoples and the ultimate particles and other theoretical entities' of modern physics.

'Certainly the properties to which the savage mind has access are not the same as those which have commanded the attention of scientists', Lévi-Strauss has commented. 'The physical world is approached from opposite ends in the two cases: one is supremely concrete, the other supremely abstract; one proceeds from the angle of sensible qualities and the other from that of formal properties.' Independently of each other, they have 'led to two distinct though equally positive sciences: one which flowered in the neolithic period, whose theory of the sensible order provided the basis of the arts of civilization (agriculture, animal husbandry, pottery, weaving, conservation and preparation of food etc.), and which continues to provide for our basic needs by these means; and the other which places itself from the start at the level of intelligibility, and of which contemporary science is the fruit. We have had to wait until the middle of this century for the crossing of [these] long separated paths.'

It is in considering this 'meeting of the roads' that one may begin to see, for example, how the treatment of mental sickness, notably depressive neurosis, could travel to the same curative terminals from starting points as different as those of traditional thought and modern science. If psychoanalysis supposes that consciousness operates at different levels, and according to different and even opposed motivations, traditional thought in Africa has likewise assumed, in its 'concrete' conceptual terminology, that a man has several souls with different purposes and possibilities

Fortes has described how the Tallensi think of these matters. An individual embodies several categories of spiritual agency.

First comes the *segr*, which presides over the individual as a bio-logical entity – over his sickness and health, his life and death. Then comes the *nuor yin*, a personification of the wishes expressed by the individual before his arrival on earth. The *nuor yin* appears specific-ally concerned with whether or not an individual has the personality traits necessary if he is to become an adequate member of Tale society.

An evil *nuor yin* 'serves to identify the fact of irremediable fail-ure in the development of the individual to full social capacity'. A good *nuor yin* 'identifies the fact of successful individual development along the road to full incorporation in society'. Thirdly, with *segr* and *nuor yin*, a successful individual – what we should call an integrated personality – incorporates the agency of two or three benevolent ancestors who guard his for-tunes.

Here, argues Horton, 'we have a theoretical scheme which, in order to produce a deeper understanding of the varying fortunes of individuals in their society, breaks them down into three aspects by a simple but typical operation of abstraction and analysis'. Such processes may reveal 'striking resemblances be-tween psychoanalytic ideas about the individual mind as a con-geries of warring entities, and West African ideas about the body as a meeting place of multiple souls'.

Though couched in mythopoeic terms these approaches to reality, these 'theories of the actual', were linked to practical use. They bore on the craft of community relations as hoe culture bore on the growing of food, or weaving on the production of clothes. They were ideological supports for socio-moral charters of a specific form and content, conceptual offspring of a particu-lar time and place. Anything but arbitrary, they were 'the reli-gious extrapolations of the experiences generated in the relationships between parents and children in societies with a social organization based on kinship and descent', and, one may add, of an economic organization embedded in subsistence and mutual aid. Within the kinship continuum, they offered 'a finished whole which embraces all activity, whether social, tech-nical, or economic'.

Strong for conservation, they were saved by their inbuilt dynamism. The individual was integrated with his community; but he was also systematically opposed to it in the pattern of a 'concert of opposites' whose interaction made the stuff of daily life. Man was the product of the system, but he was also its dominant force. 'They consider man, *muntu*, as the central living force,' Tempels has said in a well-known passage about the thought of Congolese peoples, 'the being who has life at its best and most elevated. Man is the supreme force ... dominating animals, plants, and minerals. These lower beings exist by divine decision only to be of help to man, their superior.'

Hence what Thomas, writing of the Diola of Senegal, has called a 'curious compromise' – present perhaps in all peasant societies – between the ethics of community solidarity and the striving egotism of the individual. Man is the subject of spiritual agencies which control him. But he may also, by appropriate action, control them in turn. In this flexibility of thought one may see the basic reason why African peoples, time and again, could so well adjust themselves to outside influences, Muslim, Christian and the rest, and absorb these into their own world structure.

But there was, as we have seen, a strict limit to this flexibility. It could exist only within the boundaries of the given system. However much this thought might allow for the dialectical workings of the life-force in its power to build and shift the lives of men, it left no place for structural speculation. It had, to repeat Horton, 'no developed awareness of alternatives to the established body of theoretical tenets'. All their beliefs, says Evans-Pritchard of the Zande,

hang together ... [in a] web of belief [where] every strand depends upon every other strand; and a Zande cannot get out of its meshes because it is the only world he knows. The web is not an external structure in which he is enclosed. It is the texture of his thought and he cannot think that his thought is wrong ... Or, to put it another way, they reason excellently in the idiom of their beliefs; but they cannot reason outside, or against, their beliefs because they have no other idiom in which to express their thoughts.

This completeness is persistently revealed. There can be no place for 'accident', in our sense, because any admission of the accidental would undermine the all-embracing nature of the explanation, and so question its mandatory power to shape behaviour in every circumstance. There can be no place, equally, for predictive failure. All these cultures accordingly possessed a range of valid excuses for such failure: that the conditions of oracular consultation had not been properly fulfilled, that countermagic was at work, that the case in question was only part of a larger case still to be examined. Alternatively, new and inexplicable phenomena could be allowed for by assuming a temporary breakdown in the 'right and natural', and taboo mechanisms were available for this. Horton has a good example. He recalls a Kalabari story about the coming of the Europeans who, for reasons not only of their pigmentation, were undoubtedly a strange intrusion in the Kalabari natural order. 'The first white man, it is said, was seen by a fisherman who had gone down to the mouth of the estuary in his canoe. Panic-stricken, he raced home and told his people what he had seen: whereupon he and the rest of the town set out to purify themselves – that is, to rid themselves of the influence of the strange and monstrous thing that intruded into their world.'

It was not denied that unpredictable chaos could and did exist outside the ordered classifications of the 'right and natural'. On the contrary, it was generally accepted that chaos would advance and overwhelm a given community if it should persistently depart from the saving order of its own world view. Many myths of origin explain the great difficulty encountered by the fathers of creation in bringing this order out of primeval confusion. Annie Lebeuf has told how the Fali of Kamerun dramatize this in their legend of the Tortoise and the Toad, who twice failed in their attempt to launch the world – that is, the Fali world – upon an ordered course. Only then did God step in and classify all things and beings according to their place; and then at last the society of Man could grow and evolve.

Ogotêmmeli made the same point to Griaule when talking about speech. 'Its function was organization, and therefore it was good; nevertheless from the start it let loose disorder.' The problem was to master this disorder. It was mastered for the Dogon by the concepts of their cosmogony: by the ideological projection of an order in which alone the Dogon could survive and prosper, and from which any great departure must return them to chaos, and so to disaster.

Hence the rejection of alternatives was compulsive. Alternatives were denied because they had to be. To question established tenets could not be the act of a reasonable man. Horton has another illustration. An Ijo man was asked by a Christian missionary to abandon his old gods. He replied. 'Does your God really want us to climb to the top of a tall palm tree and then take off our hands and let ourselves fall?' Wherever established tenets have an absolute and exclusive validity, Horton comments, 'any challenge to them is a threat of chaos, of the cosmic abyss, and therefore evokes intense anxiety'.

Many writers have drawn attention to this necessary demand for a mutual compatibility between all aspects of understanding, all interpretations of experience. It was this demand, Adesanya writes of Yoruba metaphysics, that was

the main weapon of Yoruba thinking. God might be banished from Greek thought without any harm being done to the logical architecture of it, but this cannot be done in the case of the Yoruba ... [Or] in modern times, God even has no place in scientific thinking. This was impossible to the Yoruba ... Philosophy, theology, politics, social theory, land law, medicine, psychology, birth and burial, all find themselves as logically concatenated in a system so tight that to subtract one item from the whole is to paralyse the structure of the whole.

Colonial intrusion swept aside taboos. The Kalabari might 'purify themselves' of the first European they saw; afterwards they had to make do as best they could. There are many dramatic examples of what happened when 'outside chaos' really got into its stride, and before Africans had time to adjust to its consequences by developing new defensive mechanisms, by accepting Christianity, or by otherwise 'moving into the modern world'.

In 1895 there were disturbances in the Brass area of the Niger delta. They arose because European traders under official British protection were beginning to monopolize trade at the expense of African traders. 'The rules in force' under the influence of the Royal Niger Company, concluded Consul-General Sir John Kirk, 'are practically prohibitive to native trade, and the Brass men are right in saying that this is so.' But being right did not help them. Finding this, those Brass chiefs who had come under Christian influence or had accepted Christianity began to turn back to their traditional beliefs. A slightly earlier consular report explained why.

'Some years ago the Christian party was much stronger and more powerful than its opponents, [but] many chiefs who were brought up as Christians have now gone back to fetishism, [and] the reason for this [is] that they had lost faith in the white man's God, who has allowed them to be oppressed, and their trade, their only means of livelihood, to be taken from them without just cause or reason.' Faced thus with a situation in which the white man's God appeared a fraud, the Brass chiefs went back to the reassurances of a system of belief and action which could, at least for them, explain everything. They had lost their trade because they had departed from the ways of their ancestors; and now their ancestors had decided to punish them, and must be suitably appeased. Theirs was to be a characteristic reaction against colonial conquest and upheaval. Meeting the onslaught of cultures within which 'a developed awareness of alternatives' had become a mainspring of action, these closed societies had either to retreat within their own ramparts, shutting their eyes to the new and strange, or else give way and perish.

Today we live in a time when many such societies have perished, and others must go the same way. Even with good evidence to hand, it is hard to imagine their old puissance and validity. Too much has happened, too much has changed. Those who would praise them may say with the Swahili poet of old Pate, recalling the vanished splendour of his city and the men who lived there:

> All the world paid them homage
>> And their world was straight ahead of them
>> they walked with heads held disdainfully
>> and eyes closed in scorn.
> Swinging their arms and arching their necks
>> while behind them and in front crowds accompanied them
>> everywhere they lived there were seats of honour
>> and troops of soldiers to attend them.

> Their lighted houses were aglow
>   with lamps of crystal and brass
>   the nights were as the day
>   beauty and honour surrounded them . . .

But those who would understand them have to hold in mind the evolving interplay of clans and peoples across these limitless lands, the onward drive of thought through twenty centuries. The growth of this civilization was an odyssey in space and time, but it was also an odyssey of the mind, a far-steering journey beyond the hills of the familiar and past the forests of the known. None of its limitations can lessen this truth.

Down those long rivers of experience the canoes of kinship-and-descent held firm in all the falls of doubt and floods of tropical profusion. These people voyaged long, wearing out their craft as they went, displacing them with models of the same type and yet enlarging these, modifying them, demanding new qualities. They achieved good destinations. They passed wide reaches of calm water where life became immemorially quiet and clear, so that later on, faintly remembering, men sighed for a 'golden age' that nothing could regain. At other times they suffered shipwreck, partial or complete, and paid for it in harsh disaster. Yet they swam ashore and built again until at last, emerging from the immense and ancient mileage of the past, there opened to them the oceans of another world; and here their craft foundered and sank in furious storms, leaving them to drown or go aboard vessels of an entirely different shape and build. Then it was that the skills they had learned and the resilience they had kept were tested in the hurricanes of the twentieth century.

The stuff of cultural history in this continent rests in those ancestral vessels of kinship-and-descent. But it rests as well in all the shifts and alterations, failures and successes, that were made or met with on the way. The dynamic of this civilization lies not only in its formative elements, social or ideological, but also in its mechanisms of change.

# Part Four: Mechanisms of Change

People cannot persist in a state of anarchy, and need a person to restrain them. He is their ruler. Royal authority is an institution that is natural to mankind.

IBN KHALDUN (1332–1406), *Muqaddimah*, i, 381–80 (trans. F. Rosenthal)

Then Turi set out with the men of Vuga, a very great army, young men and elders, with two war horns and his flute, and his signal horn . . .

*Habari za Wakilindi* (trans. R. Allen)

# 19  From Elders to Kings

Many peoples by the fourteenth century had developed forms of rule that were personalized in the leaders of dominant descent-lines: these ritual and political leaders had titles, such as *mansa*, *mai*, *oba* or *ntemi* which meant much the same as Europeans of the same period understood by emperor or *kaiser*, king or *könig*, *roi* or *re*. Some of them had few subjects and small power, being little more than 'chairmen' of councils composed of descent-line spokesmen in a cluster of villages. Others stood at the head of large systems, even of vast systems: although not autocrats, these great kings were rulers of wide prestige, and some of them acquired an intercontinental fame.

Living at the court of the emperor of Mali in 1352, the Moroccan scholar Ibn Battuta found *Mansa* Suleyman 'a miserly king, not a man from whom one might hope for a rich present'. In his memoirs of a few years later he recalled having expected the *mansa*'s hospitality gift to be 'robes of honour and money'; but when it was brought to the house where he was staying with the chief judge of Mali, 'Lo! it was three cakes of bread, and a piece of beef fried in native oil, and a calabash of sour curds.'

His disappointment will have been all the sharper because the kings of the western Sudan were renowned for their generosity in gifts. Only a little earlier another Mali *mansa*, while travelling through Cairo on pilgrimage to Mecca, had undermined the price of the Egyptian dinar by the quantity of gold that he and his following had thrown upon the market. It was Mali gold that fuelled the trade of half the civilized world, and was now providing the metal for Europe's first gold currencies since Roman times. Enthroned beneath a wide umbrella topped with the golden figure of a bird, the emperor was said to rule over a kingdom 'four months' travel in length and as much again in breadth'. A king like that, one might reasonably think, could do better than cakes of bread and a calabash of curds.

Ibn Battuta was better pleased with the pomp and brilliance of the *mansa*'s court and ceremonial. He describes how on days of audience the king 'comes out of a door in the corner of the palace, preceded by musicians with gold-and-silver-chased guitars and attended by three hundred slaves'; how 'he walks in a leisurely fashion'; how 'he halts and looks round the assembly, then mounts his throne in the sedate manner of a preacher ascending a mosque pulpit', but to the sounding of drums, trumpets and bugles.

Here at these big assemblies one could catch sight of the kingdom's men of power and office ranged on either side of the silk-emblazoned throne, sombre in their stance and dignity: strong lineage chiefs, governors of provinces, commanders of cavalry, judges and men of God, tellers of oracles and other folk of high appointment; as well as drummers and dancers furiously performing or waiting to begin, Turkish pages bought in Cairo, tall guards and strutting grooms, fine hunting dogs on leash and riding horses housed in splendid harness; and all these, jealous of their pride of place, amid a host of hangers-on and hopeful applicants compressed in throngs and arguments about the royal scene.

We are clearly far from the direct simplicities of village rule. That kind of governance might still continue in the countryside, true to the ways of the past and loyal to ancestral shrines, self-perpetuating in its economy of 'subsistence' and touched by long-range trade or other waves of outside influence only in a minor way. Elsewhere the processes of centralizing change had manifestly travelled far. Strong rulers had taken power, courts had gathered, bureaucracies were in formation. Even a brief stay in towns which had now become capitals or wealthy trading centres was enough to show the visitor of those days that old equalities had given way to new servitudes. Communities, or at any rate urban communities, had fractured into hard divisions of power, influence, and privilege. Individual freedom of action in such polities had become in all respects relative, even rare.

In trying to explain how the early village governments of Africa grew into kingdoms, and how these kingdoms multiplied or spread, the historians of Africa are in much the same unhappy position as those of Europe. More can be said about the early Anglo-Saxon and Frankish kings and kingdoms than about their African counterparts of the same period or somewhat later. But not a great deal more: if the royal names are in the European genealogies, some are obviously the work of pious or political imagination, while others are mere labels for monarchs and reigns whose lives and doings remain otherwise in darkness.

The situation in Africa is worse for this early period because the documents are fewer, while tropical archaeology, mainly because there was seldom any building in stone or brick, holds small hope of adding much detail to the little that we have already. In some cases there are long genealogies available, but these require a sceptical eye. Generally, the evidence points to a few broad conclusions. Institutions of personalized government, of recognizable kingship in one form or another, seem to have begun to emerge in tropical Africa around the middle of the first millennium A.D. Certain kingships undoubtedly existed by the eighth and ninth centuries, and what we know of them suggests that they were not of recent formation. It is probably fair to say that the history of kingship in the tropical regions, as distinct from the Nile valley, Ethiopia and the Maghrib, begins little or no later than that of Anglo-Saxon and Frankish Europe.

Once launched, these institutions showed a remarkable continuity. There are some famous dynastic examples. In Kanem-Bornu – the Chad region with north-eastern Nigeria – the Saifuwa lineage is said to have provided rulers without interruption for a thousand years until the middle of the nineteenth century; and the evidence, here, is fairly good. Much the same is true of the rulers of the central kingdom of the Mossi in modern Upper Volta. The great Keita lineage provided Mali with its founding rulers and has remained of eminent influence ever since. In central Africa the lineage of the rulers known as Mwanamutapa enjoyed a not much less remarkable longevity.

These kingships were thus the product of a long and unbroken line of growth. Potential within earlier types of Iron Age society, were never radically changed until very late in time. Their institutions repeatedly *modified* the kinship-authority patterns of their peoples, and the social charters which were at once the foundation and emanation of these patterns; but they did not go beyond them. Even when kings began to appoint office-holders by merit or achievement rather than by birth, the older links and pressures remained pre-eminently strong. Only in the nineteenth century did the 'kinship continuum' begin seriously to break down in face of socio-economic change and its consequences for royal accumulation of power.

But how were royal institutions launched in the first place? Even with our lack of detailed information it is possible, hypothetically, to see the answer in a series of stages. First there is the transition to settlement, thanks to farming and ferrous technology. Settlement brings larger units of self-rule as people grow in numbers. It also brings a productive surplus which allows for a greater division of labour, and craftsmen who add to the variety of everyday life. There comes a need for stronger government 'at the centre', even if the centre be no more than a council of descent-line elders. One or other descent-line takes the lead, ritually and then politically. Embryonic kingships are born.

To these pressures others are added as populations continue to grow and spread: a need for better defence against intruding neighbours, a call for more efficient leadership in wars of conquest or migration, a constant demand for ritual adjustment between migrants and those already in possession. Forms of centralized authority continue to crystallize. These processes are well established by A.D. 1000, at least in certain areas.

After A.D. 1000 the needs of group leadership, whether for ritual, political or military purposes, are expanded by fresh opportunities of trade, especially long-distance trade, among peoples favourably placed for this. A host of variable factors add their thrust. Small kingdoms grow into large ones. New rivalries develop. Islam brings a strongly shaping influence; later on, so do the Europeans. By A.D. 1600 the early processes have moved into a great diversity of local elaboration.

Viewed in more detail, however, the history of these institutions reveals no such simple line of growth. The formative conditions varied enormously in their relative influence and timing. Here we are up against the sheer size of the continent and its ecological diversity. High annual rainfall, good soil or pasture, natural wealth whether vegetable or mineral: these were crucial ecological factors in the growth of population, whether by local expansion or incoming migration, and so in the development of institutions. Where these factors were present, as in the southern uplands of Uganda, or the hills of the western Rift, or certain regions of forest or savanna, the early systems flowered and greatly changed. Elsewhere, amid scorching semi-desert or barely penetrable forest, in regions of great natural difficulty where men could socially survive only within strictly limited patterns of group behaviour, the early systems changed more slowly or much less. Sometimes, as with the Bushmen and the Pygmies, they barely changed at all.

This variability of impact applied to other factors in the development of institutions. The ancient kingship of Ghana emerged in the far savannas of the western Sudan in large response, so far as one can see, to new trading opportunities after the Arab conquest of north Africa in the seventh and eighth centuries, while its origins may have lain in older response to the trans-Saharan trade of Carthaginian and Roman times. By contrast the political structures of the central African Shona appeared, at least as a strong confederacy under central leadership, only in the fifteenth century; though once again, so far as one can tell, partly in response to new trading opportunities which then came inland from the East Coast. Along the Indian Ocean seaboard the city-states of the Swahili had evolved after the ninth century as links in the trade of the Eastern world; just so, after the sixteenth, did the city-states of the Niger delta take shape as links in the trade of the Western world. The cultural history of Africa is therefore one of greatly unequal development among peoples who, for definable reasons such as these, entered recognizably similar stages of institutional change at different times.

The history of the Nilotes, pastoral peoples who speak the languages of the eastern Sudan, illustrates this very well. They appear to have crystallized as a distinctive grouping in their remote plains (of modern Equatoria and Bahr-al-Ghazal) at least by the middle of the first millennium A.D., and to have reached by about 1000 – but the date can be no more than an educated guess – a point of growth where they were too many for the land they held. Obscure migrations followed. Out of these came the ancestors of the Nilotic peoples of today. Some of them, including the Nuer and the Dinka, settled along the upper Nile and its tributaries. Here they reached a balance with nature which called for no far reaching developments of institutions. They remained content with what anthropologists have called 'minimal government'. But others moved on towards the south.

These Luo-speaking folk moved south in nomad bands of warriors, women and children, driving their cattle on unknown trails, fighting opposition whenever they must, or absorbing strangers into their ranks whenever they could. In course of time they came into what is now northern Uganda, country not much different from their former homeland, and gave rise to populations who are the Acholi, Lango, Alur and others of today. Some of these evolved small kingships, probably as a means of ruling non-Luo peoples already in the land.

But other Luo groups continued again towards the south and came into country where larger kingships had already taken shape. These Luo turned their backs on 'minimal government'. They were not content with small kingships, but helped to form powerful dynasties. Still other groups of Luo went farther on their way. Those who went farthest were the ancestors of the Luo of Kenya. These moved into high rainfall areas between the eastern shores of Lake Nyanza and the Kenya highlands. Here they 'gradually evolved an economy which differed little from the hoe agriculture of their Bantu neighbours'. So the history of Luo settlement in these areas 'is largely the story of how the immigrants changed the general landscape; and, on the other hand, how the environment modified their mode of life'.

Another Luo branch, clans known collectively as the Padhola, remained in the forests and uplands of south-eastern Uganda. These again show how local factors could prove decisive in shaping the patterns of everyday life. Wherever they found empty or little inhabited country suitable for raising cattle, they reverted to the immemorial Nilotic pattern of their pastoral ancestors:

they continued, in other words, to apply the social charter of their forebears. But where the Padhola had to fight for land, the charters of the past proved inadequate. They evolved, and continued to evolve, new patterns.

'We see a few colonists arriving in search of new homes', Ogot writes of them:

We see them moving about for five generations before deciding on a permanent locality. We next see them subduing the forest and defending their settlements against wild animals and external foes. When conditions become intolerable, the settlers, at least for a while, live banded together in villages surrounded by trenches for protection. They practise subsistence farming, discover new crops such as sweet potatoes, while at the same time they continue to look after their flocks.

For a long while these people have had little or no consciousness of forming a distinctive entity. But gradually they acquire a group loyalty. This is then fortified by a new ancestral cult appropriate to a changing way of life, the cult of *Bura*. And when later, in the nineteenth century, new invaders arrive in the shape of the Ganda from the west and the British from the east, 'we see the Padhola resisting their intrusion under the leadership of Majanga, the chief priest of *Bura*', not yet a king but clearly the embryo of one.

In what follows I have taken a few outstanding patterns of institutional development, among those best studied during the past twenty years, with the aim of illuminating this diversity of change and its underlying unity of response. No 'full catalogue' is possible at this relatively early stage of historical research, nor could it perhaps be meaningful within the limits of a single volume. What can be done is to suggest the decisive lines of growth: to relate these not only to each other but also, in some degree, to the development of centralized structures elsewhere; and to provide the basis for an understanding of the major institutional crisis of the nineteenth and twentieth centuries, discussed in my concluding chapters.

# 20 The Nature of Kingship

If little can be said in detail about the emergence of kings and kingships, much can be inferred about the nature of these persons and institutions. One conclusion is that like circumstances in different places repeatedly produced like results. Diffusion of ideas from the Nile valley or north Africa may have played some distant part in shaping tropical developments. But diffusion of ideas, even where it really happened, was always less important than processes internal to a given region.

Some of these can be defined. Ogot and others argue that kingships evolved most regularly wherever an incoming minority, marching for new land, had to extend their rule over settled peoples who lived within different lineage frameworks. So the dynasties which appeared in the wake of Luo intrusion into Uganda 'evolved as a result of a small, well-organized group successfully imposing its rule over a disorganized majority'. In these circumstances, 'any political set-up based upon kinship ties cannot work. The minority group, in order to maintain its rule over what is usually a hostile majority, must present a united front.' Their means of doing this is kingship. Thus at one end of the spectrum the Nuer, remaining a unitary society composed only of Nuer, evolved no centralizing institutions because they needed none; while at the other end, in the 'conquest kingdoms', there emerged a plural society consisting of dominant Hima and subject Iru, of dominant Tutsi and subject Hutu, and of other but comparable pluralities, all with kingships.

A second conclusion is that the trend towards centralization of power – away from segmentary government in favour of kingship or its equivalent – seems always to have taken the same broad line of advance. All these historical monarchies, whether great or small, very old or quite new, belong to the same basic type. This type used to be called 'divine'; more knowledge has suggested that 'ritual' would be a better adjective. They were first and foremost repositories of ritual power. Their authority rested mainly and consistently upon its place in a given people's beliefs about themselves and the world. Kings were ritual specialists who had accumulated power in societies which had passed beyond the early subsistence level and had developed, whether in isolation or by the stimulus of migrant-resident accommodation, the need as well as the possibility of centralizing institutions.

Thus the original nature of kings is to be sought in ritual specialism associated with the guardianship of ancestral charters. In a whole great range of centralizing systems which emerged about a thousand years ago, and whose customs are fairly well known for the last two or three centuries, the rulers were supposed never to appear in public in any way that could present them as ordinary men. They must eat privately, unseen except by privileged servants; and they must live privately. The greater among them were furnished with palaces of stone or clay. Each had his sacred symbols of office: spears of copper, ornaments of gold, other ritual paraphernalia. In many cases they presided over sacral fires from which it was supposed that all other fires symbolically derived. When they grew senile or otherwise unfit to rule they were killed – or at least it was said in the rules that they ought to be killed – or quietly deposed so as to preserve the ritual virtues of their office. The examples are many, and some of them are very old.

These kings, then, were not 'divine' in the sense of being regarded as gods. They were political and therefore earthly persons as well as ritual and therefore spiritual ones. The two sorts of quality hung inherently together. These qualities could be separated whenever a failing in the first appeared to threaten the second, and they often were; but their spiritual quality remained always paramount. For what they did was to subsume in their persons the many ancestral powers formerly invested in a more or less large number of lineage leaders, and so enable a people's unity to survive. They were, in other words, the guardians of a social charter which contained a network of otherwise separate charters. Willingly accepted only when legitimate, they could not become so except when recognized as standing at the ritual apex of their people's socio-moral order.

Hence the accent on 'divinity'. For the king's existence as a political person or military leader was a secondary thing: over and beyond these secular functions, he had 'to maintain harmony between society and its natural environment by means of ritual action' of a regular kind which he alone could take. 'His duties in this sphere were threefold: to perform the daily rites for which he was uniquely qualified by office; to provide for and direct

Imaginative reconstruction of an ancient burial chamber, at Igbo-Ukwu in eastern Nigeria, excavated in 1960 by Thurstan Shaw. Composed by the excavator and artist working together, the reconstruction is based on detailed finds combined with ethnographic data which may be relevant. It shows the corpse of a sacral ruler, such as one of the Eze Nri of Iboland, seated in a wooden-lined tomb on a wooden stool studded with copper. His bronze and copper regalia and the other objects were found in positions which suggest the manner shown. Caroline Sassoon depicts it at the moment when the wooden roof was being closed with boards

the activities of other cults; and to sustain and control his own spiritual potency.' These words about the kingship of the Nigerian Jukun have a wide application, and not only to Africa. 'In fact,' writes Bloch of medieval western Europe, 'the king ... (had) three fundamental duties and scarcely any other: to ensure the spiritual welfare of his people by acts of piety and the protection given by the true faith; to defend his people against outside enemies ...; and at home, to safeguard justice and peace.' The forms of kingship might be different: the content in Africa and Europe was essentially the same.

Hence, too, a correlation between the king's character and the people's good. Ideally, the king should be strong and comely, generous of mind, bold in warfare, cunning in council and devout in everyday life. He should epitomize a people at one with its moral order, at peace with itself, at every point in harmony with the ancestors 'who brought us into our land and gave us life'. From this it followed that he should never go on reigning when his powers had failed, or when, as al-Mas'udi said of an East African monarchy a thousand years ago, he 'became tyrannical and departed from the rules of justice', and thereby ceased to conduct himself as 'the son of the Master'. Then he had to go, no matter how prestigious he might be.

Reality was obviously not ideal. The king might indeed embody the will of God: the means by which he got his throne or kept it were likely to be anything but God-given. Great dynasties might persevere for centuries, with one king following another at the holy shrines, encompassed by respectful servitors and counsellors, hedged around by walls and galleries of pious solitude, sighted with religious awe by multitudes of ordinary people and saluted in the dust by any who approached his presence. But he might still have to fight for his throne in a most immoral way. He might have to intrigue against rivals, wade to power through bloodstained battles, rule with force or deviousness. The legend of 'perfect kingship' in traditional Africa has no more substance than the old English notion that Anglo-Saxon kings had ruled a golden age, and that royal beastliness came in only with the Norman conquest.

Yet ritual sanctity could excuse all this, whether in Africa or

Europe. What counted was the 'true succession'. Having seized the Anglo-Saxon throne, William the Bastard had to be careful to show himself the legitimate successor of Edward the Confessor: as latest in the 'true line' of God-protected ancestors and accepted as such by the Archbishop of Canterbury, head of the English priesthood. William had to prove that he stood in harmony with the 'right and natural', since no peaceful government could have otherwise seemed possible. If Anglo-Saxon England accepted conquest by four thousand Norman knights, it was less for their military strength than for their careful accommodation with the Anglo-Saxon socio-moral order. African conquerors behaved no differently in the kingdoms they took or founded.

Only from this standpoint can one hope to understand how small groups of migrant warriors were able to impose their rule upon much larger numbers of residents. For what they actually imposed was not *their* rule, but a rule modified by accommodation with the customs of the peoples among whom they settled. We have seen this in the case of the Kongo; the parallels are legion. During the sixteenth and seventeenth centuries new kingdoms were formed in the Congo Basin. Relating these events, the traditions say that junior chiefs split away from their Luba homeland and marched with their followers to found new states. Yet in every case the traditions tell a story that is parallel with that of the Norman conquest of England or the Kongo conquest of the lands to the south of the great river. Superior military power at a crucial point had always to be reinforced by ritual acts of compromise which secured, for the newcomers, the legitimation of an existing order. Out of these accommodations came systems differing from the Luba kingdom as much as Plantagenet England differed from France of the House of Valois; but the differences, in Africa as in Europe, remained of form and not of content.

Methods of confirming the legitimacy of these new systems push the parallels still further. Among these methods was the stubborn or ingenious ensuring of the unity of lineage tradition. Just as the kings of England saw to it that their bards should link them with Adam and hence with God, so too did the kings of Africa rearrange the facts to suit their needs. That is why royal genealogies tend to become unreliable once they reach back beyond a few generations. It is also why, whenever a sudden break occurred in the traditional structure, with one system of authority being displaced by a manifestly different one, means had to be found of providing divine authority for the change. A celebrated example is the means of legitimation that was found for the Asante kingship shortly before 1700.

The Asante kingship took authority over a number of related Akan groups hitherto without organic unity among themselves. These groups had increasing reason, after about 1650, to unify themselves so as to throw off their tribute subjection to more powerful neighbours, and the better to exploit their opportunities for long-distance trade. But their separate group loyalties, each linked to a different ancestral system and its living representatives, stood in the way. Their traditions tell how two outstanding leaders, Osei Tutu and *Okomfo* Anokye, the one a military and the other a priestly leader, were able to bring these systems together under a new kingship.

Choosing a moment when Akan groups were under strong pressure from their overlord of neighbouring Denkyira, Osei Tutu and *Okomfo* Anokye called an assembly of chiefs and other leading men. Anokye told them that God wished them to be united in loyalty to a single line of power: in Akan symbolism, to a single ancestral stool or ruler's seat. As evidence of God's will, he caused a Golden Stool to 'descend from Heaven' and gently alight on Osei Tutu's lap. This Golden Stool, Anokye explained, was the symbol of their welfare as a single people. It embodied all their hopes of health and strength, survival and prosperity. No ruler was ever to take his place upon the Golden Stool, but its guardianship would be a necessary condition of kingship.

The spiritual attributes of the Golden Stool were thus accepted as subsuming those of the separate rulers' stools of each constituent group. By this religious fiction the Asante Union could be launched upon its way. But having launched it, Osei Tutu and Anokye at once took legal steps to strengthen the union. It was forbidden to remember the separate group genealogies or at any rate to recite them in public. This 'law of common citizenship', as an Akan historian has called it, became a potent element in building one of the most powerful states of African history. 'Ritual' and 'politics', here as elsewhere, marched hand in hand. Whether as the Golden Stool, the sacred spears of Central African kings, or the crown and sceptre of the monarchs of Europe, possession of the royal regalia provided the ultimate justification for political action. They were seen as the decisive instruments for transforming powers gained by superior force, intrigue, or good fortune into moral rights peculiar to the king.

Succession customs offer another set of clues to the nature of kings and kingships. Even where succession was the outcome of warlike rivalry and the slaying of rivals, much care was taken to prevent any formal or admitted break in the line of transmitted power. 'The king is dead, long live the king!' was the ruling sentiment here as well: again not primarily to avoid 'disturbances', but to insist on the continuity of ancestral descent. If the king's person embodied the spiritual and therefore material welfare of his people, the king must never die. But since it was obvious that the king would indeed die, and that some time, even if brief, must elapse before a successor could be installed, suitable fictions had to be employed during this interregnum to preserve unbroken the moral order of which the king was the manifest apex and prime representative.

The customs of the Mossi of the Western Sudan display all this with a dramatic vigour the more impressive for the Mossi kingdom's being so venerable in years. By the sixteenth century their system had become 'a constellation of minor kings revolving in the orbit of a supreme ruler. The latter's enthronement, his daily life and his death, were all occasions for elaborate ceremony reflecting the Mossi ideology of kingship.' His functions were eternal; it was inconceivable to a Mossi that a king – or rather a king's 'soul' or spiritual essence – should decay or die. 'Such an occurrence would presage the end of the kingdom, the end of the world.'

In positing an immortal 'king's soul' as the essence of kingship and the necessary condition of Mossi welfare, Mossi ideology remained true to a total system of explanation. It equated the Mossi kingdom with the world, and the royal palace with the centre of the world. Here the king lived within a tight network of mandatory custom, and could never leave it during his physical life. His days were ordered by detailed ritual attended by ranked courtiers and ministers according to their duties and their needs. 'A remarkable feature of the system', Zahan explains, 'was the precise positioning of the dwellings of important courtiers around the palace; another was the strict protocol which allocated to each minister and dignitary his exact position in the outer court when they assembled to pay their respects each morning.'

Even so, the king did die. How then avoid disaster during an interregnum? Ritual solutions were provided. The king's physical demise was announced when he was clearly near the point of death. His eldest daughter was at once installed with her father's regalia and even wearing her father's robes. She presided over the burial rites and 'ruled' for a year. At the end of the year she was dethroned in favour of another intermediary. This was a man who had long lived in the palace and was invested with the authority of 'carrying the king's soul'. Then the next king was elected from among the royal candidates – an election settled by political and other down-to-earth considerations – and the 'carrier of the king's soul' at once departed. He could never see the king again, and was usually charged with governing a distant village.

Other customs and arrangements buttressed the king's indispensability. The Mossi were 'past masters in the art of incorporating diverse groupings into their politico-religious system', and 'experts on drawing together all the invisible threads of the economy to the centre of their kingdom – the king'. They took care, for example, to demonstrate that the welfare of the economy was inseparable from the king's welfare. 'The market was not simply a place for the exchange of goods; it was an area of security and order, the equivalent of the world', at whose centre the king reigned by ancestral sanction. 'This explains why at the death of the king the peace of the market was violently disturbed by armed retainers from the palace. The market was transferred elsewhere and did not resume until a new king had been installed.'

Customs of organized disorder, rubbing home the dangers of kinglessness, are reported from other peoples. Among the Gonja of northern Ghana Goody has observed that 'at the death of a divisional chief, the market of Salaga [a trading centre of much importance in West African history] became a bedlam. Young men rushed in, overturned the traders' stands and stole their wares. For three days misrule continued, providing a dramatic demonstration of the supposed consequences to the society and its complex network of trade if it were to be permanently without kings and kingship': as well as making, Goody adds, 'public expression of the inevitable resentment to which authority gives rise among those excluded from office'. A warning: but also a useful safety-valve.

In Dahomey, another West African kingdom, the royal heir was installed as quickly as possible, but

the interregnum was always marked by several days of wild anarchy: royal wives killed each other so that they might accompany their husband to the grave; ordinary subjects were at liberty to indulge in all kinds of delict – theft and major crimes – without the slightest intervention of the law. Only the accession of the new king put an end to this disorder – adequate proof of the state's need for a head.

Kings such as these, even when they reigned at the summit of strongly centralized systems, could not do as they wished. Power might accumulate within their hands, but it remained within the ancestral framework. Usurpers might seize thrones: to stay on them they had to obey the rules. And the rules – the constitutional rules – were repeatedly developed in the direction of 'checks and balances' to control the growth of centralizing power. There is perhaps no more fascinating subject in the history of African institutions.

'No one who has studied or worked in any political system', Gluckman affirms, 'can fail to be impressed by the Barotse's penetrating insight into relations of power.' He describes a Central African system in which every position was balanced hard-headedly by another: the king against his council, ranked members of the council against each other or against their deputies, and all enclosed within an explicit duality which 'must have arrived at its complete elaboration over a long period of time, with more and more accretions of officers and institutions'. Thus the leading executive official, the state *ngambela*, also had his own *ngambela*: this deputy or 'second' was 'a councillor holding a permanent title who is specially charged, beyond other councillors, with restraining the state *ngambela* whose interests he primarily represents'. Thus *ngambela*ship was a generic concept denoting an assistant or deputy but also a protector against superior authority. And this concept and practice of *ngambela*ship was applied, by a system of interlocking restraints, to 'all situations in Barotse life which involve the delegating of power'.

For 'the Barotse are apparently terrified of giving away power' and

always think of the dual pressures of the ambivalence of power on an individual. If royalty be seated among commoners to protect the people, its bearer may become puffed with power and abuse it. He cannot be checked by another prince, since princes are in theory rivals for power; therefore when he has a deputy who restrains him and who acts in his absence ... this deputy is drawn from the ranks of those who interlink commoners and royalty. And both of these title holders must be in judgement soft and gentle, withal firm in supporting the law, even beyond what is demanded of other judges.

Hence, again, a clear theoretical separation between king and kingship. Both might be identical so long as the king obeyed the rules. Once he departed from them, however, the king endangered the kingship – ideologically, the state – by transgressing the boundaries of the 'right and natural', and thereby allowing the intrusion of Evil. This is the sense of al-Mas'udi's tenth-century description of the kingship of 'the Zanj'. It was no different with the Barotse. Their founding traditions are perfectly clear on this. They 'emphasize that the king was bound by the law, and that if a king ruled cruelly his council and people were entitled to rebel against him and to try to dispose of him'.

In all this the parallels between Africa and Europe are so close that they help to explain each other. Thus the Norman kings of England acceded with oaths which bound them to a solemn covenant with the people, or at any rate with those who had power among the people. Its essence lay in 'the maxim that the power of a king who acts as a tyrant is illegitimate', a maxim that was applied right down the scale of political power. This meant that an aggrieved party, whenever denied redress, was 'entirely within his rights in declaring his obligation of vassalage at an end, making war upon his lord, and coercing him by every means in his power to do him right'. Legitimate power lay in the office sanctioned by ancestral norms, not in the person; and the person lost his right to exact obedience once he abused that office.

Magna Carta in feudal England made resoundingly the same point that al-Mas'udi had defined for the 'kingdom of the Zanj' two centuries earlier. It was no new principle that King John was forced to admit on the field of Runnymede: in England, it went far back beyond the covenant of Henry I that was 'thrust beneath his nose' on the eve of that memorable gathering. It drew its strength from the immemorial 'obligations of princes' in Anglo-Saxon times.

The crucial chapter in Magna Carta was number sixty-one. Later on, when the power of princes became threatened by new and most unprincely voices, this chapter was conveniently forgotten: in Gluckman's words, it was afterwards 'omitted from reissues owing to its largely revolutionary character'. But it stated the Zanj principle of kingship round and clear. By it, John agreed that any future failure of his to redress grievances at law should justify the barons 'with the community of the whole land, [to] distress and harass us [the king] by all the ways in which they are able; that is to say, by the taking of our castles, lands and possessions, and by any other means in their power ... And whoever of our land pleaseth may swear that he will obey the command of the aforesaid twenty-five barons in accomplishing all the things aforesaid, and that with them he will harass us to the utmost of his power; and we publicly and freely give leave to everyone to swear who is willing to swear; and we will never forbid anyone to swear.' Legitimate civil war, as in Africa, could not be treason.

In England, of course, it became treason as soon as the barons had to face the other way – in Gluckman's reading of the evidence, with Edward III's Statute of Labourers of 1352. This statute 'for the first time made it treason to levy war against the king', being linked to yeoman demands for higher wages, and to similar demands by the journeymen of English towns whose agitations shook 'the harmony of the medieval City Guilds' by causing 'social and economic cleavage between master and man'. After the big peasants' revolt of 1381, another enactment also made it treason 'not only to compass the king's death, but also his deposition', and held that 'anyone who procured or counselled the repeal of the statutes passed in that Parliament should be guilty of treason'. With this defence of class stratification the English kingship was headed for autocracy, and so for the rebellion of 1642 and all that followed.

In Africa, by contrast, the 'checks and balances' generally held firm until the nineteenth century, chiefly no doubt because class stratification was far less advanced than in Europe. This is true even of those kingships, such as that of the Jukun of Nigeria, which earlier writers thought were autocratic. Better analysis now shows that the Jukun king's constitutional position 'reveals that although his office was pivotal it was not autocratic. His constituted authority could only manifest itself through the hierarchy of officials, and his own attempts to enhance his power were balanced by the attempts of others to do the same.' There remained a constitutional right to overthrow Jukun kings whose conduct threatened the structure.

How often they really were overthrown remains unknown. What is interesting, in any case, are the reasons by which Jukun tradition justified deposition. Kings were supposed to be killed if they broke any of the royal taboos on personal behaviour, fell seriously ill, or ruled in time of famine or severe drought: whenever, that is, they could no longer be regarded as fit guardians of the 'right and natural' according to Jukun belief. For the Jukun king's mere executive function, one may repeat, was not enough to ensure his people's welfare: first and foremost, 'he had to maintain harmony between society and its natural environment by means of ritual office'. He might rule well: it was none the less accepted, if evil came, that he had not ruled well enough. With this we are back to the essential distinction between kingship and king: to the concept that the office was always far more than the man, and that the man, if necessary, must be sacrificed to the office.

These unities of thought can be traced at many points. English medieval lawyers were at pains to distinguish the king's 'body natural' from his 'body politic', the one being mortal but the other 'the corporation sole of the perpetual dynasty' and consequently immortal. Mossi jurists, as we have seen, would have had no trouble in accepting exactly this: their own ideas were no different. They buried the king's 'body natural', but they saw to it that the king's 'body politic' was always manifestly there.

Such parallels go closer still. The Mossi preserved a dead king's 'body politic', his *dignitas* in English terms, in the form of his eldest daughter posing in the royal robes. With the death of Edward II in 1327 the English adopted the custom of placing a royal effigy on top of the coffin: made of plaster and padded leather, and dressed in the coronation garments, this effigy represented the royal *dignitas* which never died, but was ritually transferred to his successor. The *dignitas* of bishops and other persons of sacral authority was represented by their tombs in much the same way. Thus the immortal part of sacral office was transferred, as Kantorowicz says, 'from one incarnation to another'.

Jukun express the same idea with *juwe*, by which they understand 'the indefinable spiritual potency which is the quintessence of kingship ... immortal and indivisible, manifesting itself in the bodies of kings and in their very commands' – just so long, that is, as the king was seen to be a fit vessel for this spiritual force.

Dominant concepts of law belong to the same underlying unities. In African law, it would seem, the fundamental principle has lain in a contractual liability to conserve what I have called the 'ideal equilibrium'. This equilibrium being expressed in every aspect of the social fabric, any action tending to harm others becomes a threat to the whole society, and must be purged by appropriate counteraction. Right behaviour is accordingly seen in terms of debt: of a negative liability on the individual not to do what is wrong, but also a positive liability to do what is right.

Within a given balance of power and status, purging and punishment are consequently a matter of compensation. It would even be possible, Gluckman comments, 'to write about Barotse law largely in terms of debt, whether one were dealing with transactions, obligations of status, injuries, or offences', and he feels this to be true of the general structure of all African law. Putting it another way, 'legal issues and moral issues are constantly confounded ... and a man's rights to his legal dues may depend on his fulfilling his moral obligations sensibly and uprightly' – fulfilment of these obligations being seen 'in the constant discharge of obligation, the rendering of service and of material help'.

But much of European law was no different. The contract of vassalage was essentially a matter of obligations, and it was not sufficient for right behaviour to abstain from doing wrong: it was just as necessary to do right. Ideally, at least, the contract was expressed in a duality of debt. Africa might be far away; it was evidently not so far as we have often thought.

Unity and continuity within a diversity of forms were insistently present. Change brought kings on the scene and elevated them to high authority; yet the kings were strong only in the measure that they conserved, or could be thought to conserve, the ideal harmonies of old tradition. Law became elaborate and the charters were greatly altered; yet the governing ideas behind them stayed at the heart of the matter. Even the exceptions or the apparent exceptions, at any rate until the nineteenth century, can now be seen to prove this rule.

# 21 Conquest and Clientage

It may be some while yet before we have a universal history nourished by all the new knowledge of the last fifty years, so that the particular structures and institutions of Africa or Europe, or any other major region, may be considered systematically as variations upon common themes. At least we are approaching this kind of world synthesis. Time has worked inversely on the essential differences and distances between 'them' and 'us': the more the facts pile up, the smaller in their essence do these differences and distances appear.

They did not always appear great. During their early years of discovery along the African seaboard, the Portuguese thought they had come upon kingdoms very like their own. Were they, after all, so much mistaken? The king of Portugal was astray in thinking that his royal friend and brother of Kongo stood at the apex of an aristocratic hierarchy like his own. All those prestigious titles recommended in the *regimento* sent from Lisbon to the *Mani*-Kongo in 1512, with its princes and dukes and counts and marquises, derived from a social stratification of a depth and nature not present in Africa. Yet it can now be seen that the chief stratification of feudalism – the distinction between lord and vassal, or patron and client – had its clear development in Africa as well as Europe. If the forms of these relationships were extremely different, being shaped by sharply divergent systems of power, their content – what Bloch has called 'the ties of dependence' – were sometimes remarkably alike. The concept of kingship shows this. So does the relationship of patron and client.

It shows this, moreover, in cases where no external influences came in to move the wheels of change. Further on I am going to look at the consequences of external influence: of the trans-Saharan trade and Islam, of the Atlantic trade and Christianity, as well as of the influence of interregional borrowing and reaction. Here I want to consider briefly a series of kingdoms which emerged in the hill country of east-central Africa, and did so in apparently complete isolation from factors external to the region.

Without being feudal in the European sense of the word, these kingdoms displayed several aspects of feudalism. Subjection of a peasantry; land grants (in Africa, usufruct grants) in place of wage rewards; the supremacy of a class of specialists in warfare; ties of mutual dependence between lord and vassal; a dispersal of political power and hence a continual danger of disorder. These elements of medieval society were all present in the kingdoms of the Rift valley hills, as the work of Maquet, Kagame, Oberg and others has now amply explained.

The impetus of their development, like that of western Europe, seems to have lain in conquest by small intrusive groups over settled majorities. In what is now southern Uganda, the Hima warrior lords of old Bunyoro, and the somewhat later Hima-Luo lords of Kitara imposed their sovereignty upon a much bigger population of Iru farmers. Like the Tutsi kingdoms in the hills towards Lake Kivu, southward down the western spine of the Rift, they evolved complex patterns of dependence. Their ideology of lordship and clientage was distinguished by its ceremonial dignity, its sacred rites, its intricate ordering of everyday relationships, its cattle symbolism, and its epic though unwritten literature.

Little but legend is known of their origins, though conquest seems to have stood at their root. Traditions generally agree with archaeology that the first Hima kingship in southern Uganda had emerged by about A.D. 1350, while the Tutsi kingdoms further south probably took shape at about the same time, or perhaps a little earlier. Lord and client stratification deepened with the passage of time. By the 1920s the ruling caste of Tutsi royals and warriors in Ruanda composed about ten per cent of the population, Hutu peasants about eighty-five per cent, and Twa Pygmies, occupying a position so low in the scale of social value as to be considered more or less completely 'irresponsible', though not by themselves – about five per cent.

At the summit stood a ritual kingship. Its powers were ideologically absolute since the *mwami* or living king was the spiritual personification of society: he *was* Ruanda in the sense that he derived from Kazimuntu, the common ancestor of all mankind. Created by God – by *Imana*, the Creator 'conceived as an intelligence, a will, an emotivity' – Kazimuntu had begotten many children. Among these were Gatutsi, Gahutu and Gatwa who, as their names indicate, were the ancestors of Ruanda's three ethnic groups. These groups' subsequent inequality is explained in Tutsi belief by the statement that Kazimuntu chose Gatutsi to rule the land and beget its line of kings. Thus sanctioned, the living *mwami* was hedged about with ritual rules and prohibitions. His regalia was indispensable to his kingship. No man could become *mwami* without having possession of Kalinga, a ritual drum that was never beaten (just as the Asante Golden Stool was never sat upon), but was honoured in a variety of ways appropriate to success in battle, such as its decoration with the genitals of enemies slain in war.

One of seven surviving figures of long-horned cows in wrought iron, this one about 20 cms long, from regalia of the kingdom of Karagwe in north-western Tanzania. Recorded by Speke and Stanley in 1861 and 1876, they belonged to a large apparatus of ceremonial metal work, including spears and stave-holders for hibiscus flowers, now preserved by the Tanzanian government

In practice, the king was not an autocrat and could not be one, although changes in the nineteenth century tended to enlarge his executive powers. He had to act within a fairly rigid social structure, pay attention to the guardians of royal tradition, and solicit the views of leading Tutsi nobles. He could choose his successor among his sons, but the choice might be contested after his death; civil wars of succession were evidently frequent, and they certainly were among their neighbours to the north. But this avoidance of any automatic succession by a chosen heir helped in fact to conserve the system. Though at some cost in bloodshed among rival royals, it meant that the whole structure of dependence was regularly renewed and given fresh life. There was none of that seeping away of power which afflicted the kings of Europe when automatic succession at the top, by primogeniture, began to spread down the pyramid of fiefs and powers, and barons could found dynasties of their own. 'Grants of tenure' were revocable with each new *mwami*; and every Tutsi 'baron', to keep his 'fief', had to renew and prove his allegiance.

The system had a number of subtleties concerned with the use or abuse of power. Each new king was given one of four royal names which were always, it is said, chosen in the same order of succession. Of these four, the three who were named Cyilima, Yuhi and Mutara were called 'peaceful kings'. 'They were forbidden to cross the Nyabarongo, a river which runs through the middle of the country ... So they were unable to give personal leadership to military expeditions. Wisely, this rule gave the country a breathing space after a warlike reign, and an opportunity to assimilate newly conquered territory.'

An official scapegoat allowed for royal blunders and brutalities. Being a sacral person, the king was above criticism. Essentially good in nature, as befitted his divine ancestry, he could not be said to be a bad king. In this the Ruanda were at one with English constitutional law in holding, with Blackstone, that the king 'is not only incapable of doing wrong, but even of thinking wrong: he can never do an improper thing: in him is no folly or weakness'. But the king of Ruanda could, of course, receive bad advice. His failings were accordingly referred to the evil ways of his 'favoured counsellor', an official of the great council who was always named as such.

These arrangements will have comforted the Tutsi. The Hutu and the Twa no doubt saw things differently. Their lives were less agreeable. Having no political rights, they looked to their Tutsi overlords for aid and protection, and chose or changed these lords for perfectly hard-headed reasons. But while the Tutsi ruling caste did 'no manual work and [had] leisure to cultivate eloquence, poetry, refined manners, and the subtle art of being witty when talking and drinking mead with friends', the Hutu had to labour for these elegant rulers as well as for themselves, and they did not find it easy. 'On a very poor soil, with technologically primitive implements, it [was] necessary to work hard to secure the surplus production required by the Tutsi.'

The main link in this structure was *ubu-hake*, an institution variously translated as 'paying court to a superior'; 'stock-rent'; 'recommendation' in the feudal European sense; or 'contract of pastoral serfdom'. It seems to have possessed elements of all four of these, and was concluded between a superior, *shebuja*, and an inferior, *umugaragu*: between a patron and a client. This tie of dependence existed between Tutsi and Hutu, as well as within the Tutsi caste, and was expressed in terms of cattle. A client undertook to graze his patron's cattle and otherwise to work for him in exchange for certain benefits. These benefits included political protection as well as usufruct of the cattle in question: milk, male calves, meat and the hide of dead cows. A client could also use *ubu-hake* cattle in order to become the patron of someone else: he could, as it were, sublet them on his own account. In return, he had to pay homage to his patron, serve him in military and other duties, carry messages, provide occasional gifts of beer and other products, and repair a patron's house or fencing.

Similar ties existed to the north, and notably in the Hima kingdom of Ankole in southern Uganda. Like the Tutsi, the Hima were a cattle-raising warrior folk who had imposed their rule on a more numerous peasantry, the Iru. The two groups have long become physically difficult to tell apart, and speak the same language; but the caste system remained intact until very recent times. Being only about one-tenth of the population, the Hima found it paid them well. 'Although the agricultural technique of the Iru did not produce a great surplus, it could produce under pressure enough beer and millet to make domination profitable.' So the Hima lived with their cattle, 'and forced their serfs to give them as much beer, millet, and labour as possible without destroying their source of supply'.

These structures were indigenous. There is no reason to suppose diffusion from far away. Intrusive groups could either dominate or extirpate, and it was clearly preferable to do the first. Out of this came their need to weld extended-family units into a political organization capable of exercising domination. 'At bottom,' comments Oberg of Ankole, 'this new relationship was based on Bahimaship – upon race and cattle-ownership. But this special bond had to be created, had to be consciously entered into. It involved leadership, cooperation, submission to authority. It gave rise to kingship and the dynastic principle, the organization of military forces and chieftainship. In short, it welded the Hima into a state.'

In Ankole the organizing principle was parallel to the Tutsi contract of *ubu-hake*. It was called *okutoizha*, which Oberg translates as 'clientship'. A Hima cattle-owner 'would go before the *mugabe*, or king, and swear to follow him in war and would undertake to give the *mugabe* a number of cattle periodically to keep this relationship alive'. It could be broken at will by refusing homage, although a client's elbow-room for manoeuvre would depend, in practice, on a number of surrounding factors which included the relative strength of his lineage.

Clientship imposed various duties, chiefly war service. 'Every Hima, even if he were not a member of a military band, had to go to war when called upon. Any cattle which a Hima acquired through a private raid were claimed by the *mugabe*, and a part of them had to be handed over to him.' Clients had to visit the king's residence with homage payments from time to time; and 'whenever a Hima died, his heir had to report to the *mugabe* and renew the bond of clientship by giving a "cow of burial"'. Here, too, the system allowed no seeping away of power through automatic succession.

'In return for military service and the payment of homage, the client received protection. First, the *mugabe* undertook to shield the cattle of his client from cattle-raiders and to retaliate when his client suffered from raids. If a client had lost all of his cattle through raids or disease, the *mugabe* was obliged to help the man start a new herd. Secondly, the *mugabe* maintained peace between his clients.'

The Iru, like the Hutu, had no such freeman's rights. Their toiling for their lords opened no road to the sweets of office. They were barred from military service – and thus from its gains – and their social inferiority was fixed by law. If an Iru was killed by a Hima, his family could not exercise the right of blood revenge. They could go before the *mugabe* or some other great lord, and complain of the crime; but they could not do anything about it themselves. Yet the family of a Hima killed by an Iru could legally kill another Iru without further ado. As in other caste societies, the upper crust might take concubines from the lower, but not dignify them by marriage. 'Iru concubines were especially common among Hima chiefs and gave rise to a class of half-castes known as *Abambari*' who were usually considered as Iru. One thinks of the offspring of black concubines taken by whites in South Africa. They, too, as 'Coloureds', have been subject to a similar caste demotion, and are treated today as Africans.

But these Ugandan rigidities, in contrast to those of modern South Africa, were softened with time; and the evidence suggests that the castes had become greatly blurred at the edges by at least the middle of the nineteenth century. Even before that, the ecology of Ankole had helped to give the system a different emphasis from that of more purely pastoral Ruanda. The chief reason for this lay in the spread of the East African banana, *musa paradisiaca*. An Iru peasant who took over cattle from his Hima patron acquired a valuable source of manure which helped to expand the supply of food. Not being slaves, the Iru were able to push for readjustments in their favour as their economic position strengthened.

There were obvious limits to adjustment. Social change was possible, and apparently took place in favour of the crop producers. But the whole ideology of statehood rested upon a sanctified kingship whose integrity and authority were conceived as vital to the social weal. In upholding these the traditions run unbroken from the fourteenth century, and probably much earlier. Moreover, up to the crisis of the late nineteenth century, the use of power was always balanced by built-in checks and counterpoises, while the crop producers lived within a society where distant power could seldom reach them, and where near power could be moderated by practical arguments of personal acquaintance and common interest.

Wars were many, but on a scale so small as to be hard to imagine as wars today. What fighting really meant in these kingdoms is displayed in their heroic poetry with its flourishing of spears and praise-names:

I Who Am Clear Headed faced the spears together with the Ceaseless Fighter;

I Who Am Agile came up alongside them and with me was Katwaza,

I Who Am Eager for Battle made a vow on an ant hill with the The Tamer of Recruits;

I Who Am Not Disobeyed broke my bow in my impatience ...

I Who Am Not Put To Flight passed on to the battle at Rufunza and so did Katemba;

I Who Do Not Tremble set to work with my spear ...

I Who Do Not Ask For Help stood fast in the narrow way ...

Bold names, great deeds: they were the essential stuff of conversation in these pastoral kingdoms whose ancient framework, composed behind horizons far outside the reach of the European world, seems so closely to reflect the tone and temper of the Middle Ages.

## 22 Trade and Islam

Wherever external factors moved the machinery of change, they began with long-distance trade: with the brave small ships of Indian Ocean sailors, defying the seas of the Zanj, or camel caravans that set their courage against the wastes of the Sahara: with these and their commercial influence, and afterwards their Muslim impact in every field of life.

The trade was old, far older than Islam. By 500 B.C., and perhaps long before, Berber enterprise had taken horse-and-chariot trails to the tropical lands beyond. Merchants from Carthage had trafficked down the far west coast. Timgad and Volubilis had been Roman forerunners of Sijilmasa and the great Arabo-Berber entrepôts of later times. It was the sea captains of Ptolemaic Egypt who first opened up the east African seaboard.

But the great period of the long-distance trade began with the maturity of Islam after A.D. 900. Then indeed it spanned the world from Cadiz to Cathay, drawing all Europe within its range and driving far into inland Africa.

Egypt was the pivot of this worldwide system. Thousands of business documents have survived to tell the tale. Fortunately preserved in Cairo for almost a millennium, though only lately available to scholarship, they open the view upon a system of safe and regular travel, long-term credit and long-range dealing, whose size and scope were not again to be achieved for many centuries. Their details are very convincing.

A travel-wearied merchant of Alexandria relaxes in his bath one Friday afternoon towards the year 1100, and then, before sitting down to dinner, scribbles a note to a partner in Cairo.

I have just arrived from Almeria in Spain. Your business friend in Moroccan Fez sent me there a bar of gold – certainly from the Sudan – so as to buy Spanish silk for you. I thought this not a good idea, however, and am sending you the gold instead. At the same time a friend of your business friend delivered me a certain quantity of ambergris which I also forward herewith. He wants you to send back five flasks of musk of the same value. Please sell the ambergris when you get this letter and buy the musk, because I have to send it off at once.

Ambergris from tropical African waters, gold from the western Sudan, silk from Spain, musk from Asia: and all the subject of a small transaction done incidentally for friendship's sake.

Those were the years when the Fatimid rulers of Egypt found a place of influence and even of prestige for a new merchant class. Taking their rise in the cities of the Middle East, they it

East African trading vessel of a design common to the Lamu archipelago and the Bajun Islands. Of great antiquity, this *mtepe* type of coastal vessel was used for many centuries. Held together not by nails or other metal clinches but by palm-fibre lashings, these ships could be as large as 70 tons. The one shown here is from a model in the Fort Jesus Museum at Mombasa

was who increasingly shaped the policies of the Muslim states, developed commercial law and custom, and gave the civilization of Islam its strong emphasis on the bourgeois virtues of saving and sobriety, avoidance of waste or ostentation, and respect for scholarship, welding this wide world into a unity of culture where men, or at any rate some men, could enjoy an unexampled freedom of travel.

As in medieval Europe, Jewish trading communities played an often key role. Integrated within Arab or Arabo-Berber society without losing their cultural identity, they embraced these new opportunities and many served in high positions. Ali Killis became the first vizier of the Fatamid empire. Abu Zikri Kohen from Sijilmasa in Morocco was a leading representative of Cairo trade, who made prolonged journeys to India while retaining contact with his homeland. Halfon ben Nethanel Dimyati had extensive business in Egypt, Yemen, India, Morocco and Spain. When Ibn Battuta went on his famous travels to east Africa, India, China and the western Sudan two centuries later, he was following well-beaten trails.

Africa had begun to be affected by the long-distance trade of Muslim times soon after Islam's early conquests. The first Muslim trading settlements on the East Coast date from about A.D. 800. But their full development came only two or three centuries later, when they became the scene of a specifically African variant of Muslim culture, the civilization of the Swahili. In west Africa, or rather in the western Sudan, steady if as yet infrequent caravans were linking both sides of the Sahara at least from the foundation of the Maghribin trading states of Tahert and Sijilmasa in the eighth century; and the consequences and development of such contacts were to be enormous. It is not too much to say that here in the western Sudan the long-distance trade, and all that it meant in terms of commercial, political and religious change, presided over the birth and life of dynasties and empires.

Gold was the core of the trade. Other exports played their part, notably ivory, as well as the domestic slaves that figure in every account of medieval trade. But as along the East Coast – where ivory was possibly more important than gold – the slaving component was comparatively small. Though contrary to a familiar opinion, this view of the slave trade is heavily supported by the Egyptian documents. The Cairo papers from the tenth to the latter part of the thirteenth century often refer to the buying and selling of slaves for use as servants or as business agents, but never, it appears, to a slave trade of any importance. Even more convincingly, perhaps, the *Minhadj* of al-Makhzumi, a detailed account of Egyptian commerce and port customs dating to the late twelfth century, has no single word about the slave trade. This can be explained for the trade in east European slaves by the fact of widespread Christianization of the Slav peoples during that period. But this is an explanation that will not hold for Africa. Contemporary records for Moslem Spain, moreover, strongly suggest that the import of black slaves was only for the domestic purposes of the wealthy, and so was on a minor scale. That slaves in those times were in fact always a prized and expensive luxury is clear from the Geniza documents, while al-Bakri, writing in 1067, notes that a black cook in Awdagost, south of the Sahara, cost a hundred pieces of gold or more, a small fortune for that period.

In all these contexts the very word 'slave' can be grossly misleading. Usually it has been translated, but without further explanation, from Arabic texts using the word *'abd*. But *'abd* was understood to convey a status very different from the trans-Atlantic slavery of later years. This was a status, as Goitein says, that could convey 'great economic advantages as well as social prestige', for 'a slave fulfilled tasks similar to those of a son'. Aspects of it might be cruel and terribly degrading, as with the making of eunuchs, but it was seldom the chattel slavery of the Americas.

Even when one takes into account the growth of 'slave-militias' – but never, except in ninth century Iraq, of large-scale slave plantations – it remains obvious that trans-Saharan slaving was on a scale too small to give the trade its impetus and influence. And this, with some partial exceptions, stayed true of later times. The idea that the overland slave trade was on anything like the same scale as the Atlantic slave trade is an historical myth.

It was the gold trade that really mattered. Three factors, in this connection, help to explain why the trading towns of the western Sudan, the western Sahara, and the Maghrib now acquired their great chance of growing into wealthy cities. One is that traditional supplies of gold, worked since Roman times and before, were running short in Europe and the Middle East. West Africa could offer a major new source. A second factor was the virtual closing, for climatic and other reasons, of the old trans-Saharan route which had long linked Egypt with the western Sudan by way of the oasis of Kufra to the region of Lake Chad and beyond. At least from the time of Ahmad ibn Tulun, governor of Egypt in A.D. 868–84, this southern route gave way increasingly to the easier route through north Africa and the western Sahara. A third factor, during Fatimid and Ayyubid times (969–1250), lay in Egypt's increasing need of gold for the payment of Eastern imports.

By the tenth century, accordingly, the north-western entrepôts were acquiring an importance still larger than before, and one that was further enhanced by the growth of Muslim civilization in southern and central Spain. Among these Maghribin entrepôts Sijilmasa in southern Morocco retained a key position, being 'at the entry of the desert'; and once again the Cairo documents illustrate the point. They show that sea transport was highly developed between Egypt and the western Mediterranean, while 'in winter, when the sea was closed, up to three caravans passed from Sijilmasa ... through Kairouan, Tripoli and Barqua to Egypt'. Along with these there were commercial postal services, including a privately-managed courier link which operated throughout north Africa and western Asia. For several centuries it was to be the gain or loss of control over these trading cities, especially Sijilmasa and afterwards Tlemcen, Fez and Marrakesh, that would go far to decide the rise or fall of states and dynasties in the Maghrib.

The same effects were repeated further south. Valuable trading towns sprang to life. They became the pivotal centres of large political systems, so that the history of Ghana, and afterwards of Kanem-Bornu, Mali, Songhay, and many lesser states, was inseparable from the opportunities and needs of the long-distance trade. They fed the trade with the north, and were repeatedly influenced by its consequences.

As early as A.D. 951 the traveller Ibn Hawkal heard in Sijilmasa reports of Ghana that led him to describe its king as the wealthiest of all the kings on the face of the earth, and as one whose forebears had reigned there since 'ancient times'. The same man claimed to have crossed the western Sahara to the city that was then the greatest of the southern entrepôts, Awdagost – a long vanished town whose foundations lie beneath the Mauretanian settlement of Tegdaust, which has narrowly survived – and to have seen a merchant's receipt on account of trans-Saharan trade for the sum of 42,000 gold dinars, a very large sum for credit transactions in those times or even today.

The rulers of Ghana enclosed this city of Awdagost in about 990 within their own system of trade and tribute, following what appears to have been a consistent policy of monopolizing the long-distance export–import trade. Not for nothing was their title *Kaya-Maghan*, Lord of the Gold; writing on good information in 1067, al-Bakri has shown how insistently these rulers milked the trade by their customs duties. Minted in the Maghrib, their gold had become by the eleventh century the most valued currency in the whole great system of trade centred on Cairo.

The actual process of centralization is far less clear than the means and the motives. What seems to have happened is that a leading Soninke lineage acquired power in the western grasslands over other lineages and vassal peoples. This may have occurred at any time after about A.D. 500, and possibly before. Rejecting Islam after its first missionaries – merchants in all probability – had appeared in the eighth or ninth centuries, these Soninke rulers held firm to their own ancestral charters. They welcomed Muslim merchants to the towns they commanded, and allowed these useful visitors to settle in urban quarters of their own, where they built stone houses after the Maghrib fashion. Thus the kings of Ghana can be seen as ritual leaders who gradually extended their power into the secular arena of conquest and the gathering of tribute from envassalled neighbours. But to internal factors making for centralization of power – including, one may think, a desire to monopolize the relatively short-distance movement of salt, always an important African commodity – the trade in gold and north African imports added others of compelling attraction.

Other empires followed Ghana in the western Sudan. In all of them the long-distance trading factor remained of supreme formative importance. But the nature of the kingships changed. Partly they changed because of their own internal dynamics: as in other regions, kings and princes acquired not only the possibility of more power and 'divinity', but also the taste and ambition for it. This growth of centralization, buttressed later by the rise of 'king's men' in appointive bureaucracies, was a primarily indigenous process. Yet it was dramatically aided, shaped and sharpened by the intrusion of Islam.

Muslims must probably have sojourned in the towns of the Sudan during the late seventh century, coming from Egypt by the long east–west route through Kufra. But they were few and of little or no influence upon royal courts or markets. The first real impact came by Berber transmission from the central and western routes across the Sahara. At this time, the traditions say, Islam was accepted by several kings whose commercial positions were important at the southern end of the trails, notably the kings of the middle Niger city of Gao, later to be the centre of the Songhay empire, and those of Kanem-Bornu. Westward, the kings of Ghana resisted conversion; and with good reason. For if they too had excellent relations with the Berber traders of the north, they faced invasion by other Berbers who were also Muslims. These were the Almoravids of western Mauretania who challenged the Ghana empire around the middle of the eleventh century, seized Awdagost in 1054, invaded the Soninke homeland in the 1070s and eventually sacked the capital itself. But the Almoravid intrusions were short, even if they were painful, and there is little evidence to suggest that they opened the road to Islam among the non-Berber peoples, except in Senegal. The larger Berber impact was made peacefully, and by the vehicle of trade.

It is easy to see why. Those very techniques of credit, literacy and commercial practice which had given merchants their influ-

ential place in the Muslim polities of the north were useful here
as well. Across the years they drew the cities and their courts and
commerce into the world of Muslim culture. They gave a metropolitan relish, a flavour of distant trails and legendary capitals,
to the quiet provincial life of the western Sudan. It became a
custom yielding much prestige for rich men and rulers to go
upon the pilgrimage to Mecca and see the magnificence of Cairo.
These pilgrims returned with more than prestige. They brought
new ideas and fashions from the East. Schools of learning were
established. Scholars travelled back and forth. Royal courts acquired clerks and literate chanceries. The fame of Sudanese kings
spread out across the Muslim lands.

Yet for a long time this influence was peripheral to everyday
life. The roots of Muslim faith and scholarship flowered slowly,
and only in the towns; not until the eighteenth century would
Islam make much impact on the countryside. By far the greater
number of the peoples enclosed within the great imperial systems of Mali, Songhay and Bornu remained true to their own
faiths, and continued to live by the laws and customs these had
formed. Their rulers continued to draw the weight of their
authority from the leadership of great lineages, and to rest their
claims on popular loyalty in the sanctioned charters of tradition.
For most of their subjects these rulers remained *primus inter
pares* among a host of lesser lineage heads, and, as such, the
fount at which the wisdom of the great ancestral spirits could be
sought.

The kings had therefore to ensure their traditional legitimation, and to carry out their traditional duties. Even the inno-
vating emperor Musa (reg. 1307–37), a most powerful monarch
who thought it worthwhile taking forty large loads of gold on his
celebrated pilgrimage and is said to have meditated ending his
days in Mecca, applied Muslim policies and customs with a
tentative hand; performed the rites and ceremonies of Mandinka
religion; and, though making many conquests, embarked on no
wars of religion. And the almost contemporary Cairo writer
al-Omari, who used information from Egyptians who had lived
in Mali, tells us that the emperor was regularly required to
preside over traditional courts and settle witchcraft cases.

But Islam now exercised a deepening influence in the towns, and from this there developed the great equivocation which was so often to decide the fortunes of these Sudanese systems. Islam and traditional religion came increasingly in conflict. With all his caution and care for compromise the same emperor Musa much extended the application of Islamic law, placed a *qadi* at the side of every provincial governor, and adopted Egyptian-style protocol and rules of precedence. The central machinery of the state became ever more emphatically Muslim. The emperor's officers, soldiers and bodyguards were given land and other gifts in the manner of the *iqta* which 'enjoins a king to distribute lands to his courtiers, sometimes together with the whole product of regional taxation'. The way was clear for new social divisions.

Changing economic pressures lay at the base of this. These flourishing towns no longer lived within anything resembling the traditional 'subsistence economy' of the countryside. Accumulation had begun to be possible in new ways, breaking down the old unities of 'tribal life'. This is the point at which deepening stratification begins to give rise to labour exploitation, in some ways comparable to slavery, as a means of production for a privileged few. To these privileged few the regulating hand of Muslim law and custom could help to buttress their positions; and it was used with an increasing awareness of its value.

From about 1450, accordingly, the central problem of imperial policy lay in the need to balance the interests of the cities, with their merchants and officials and their growing interest in accumulation, against the contrary interests of a largely egalitarian countryside. More and more, the power of the rulers rested in their command of the cities: more and more, as kings were able to increase their demands for services or labour, there opened a cleft between the city and the village. The problem of bridging it was variously tackled in each of these great systems. But it was never resolved.

This shift towards 'non-traditional' types of kingship can be seen decisively in the efforts that were made to systematize new legal codes.

What was at least the forerunner of regular enslavement for productive purposes now appeared. In 1450 we have the Hausa king of Kano, Abdullahi Burja, sending out military expeditions for the capture of countryfolk whom he obliged to work for him. Following the practice of his liege of Bornu, Burja is said to have settled these in special villages where they produced for his needs. In the end, according to tradition, he had as many as twenty-one such settlements of a kind which had certainly not existed in earlier times.

His successor Muhammad Rumfa (reg. 1465–99) went further. Rumfa's ambitions reached to the building of a luxurious palace and the establishment of a semi-professional army, or at least a large troop of long-service soldiers, who, being mainly of captive origin, stood outside the lineage framework and were answerable to the king's person. These were innovations needing considerable legal adjustment, and Islam clearly held the answer. Muhammad Rumfa accordingly asked the advice of a north African scholar, al-Maghili, then teaching in Kano. Al-Maghili wrote for him the *Risalat al Muluk, The Obligations of Princes,* to explain how an up-to-date Muslim ruler should organize his affairs. It marked the beginning of a systematic Islamization of Hausa government.

Other rulers followed suit. A little later al-Maghili performed the same service for the much stronger ruler of the Songhay empire, Muhammad Turay (reg. 1493–1528) in a series of 'Answers to Questions' which became famous in the western Sudan and are used in its Quranic schools to this day. These 'Answers' tell much about the central problem of balance between Muslim town and traditional countryside. They consider the question, a crucial one in those days, of a people who have nominally accepted Islam but remain loyal to the old faiths: attack and enslave these pagans, says al-Maghili; and the advice to embark on religious war is followed for the first time on any scale. They rehearse the Muslim rules for property inheritance, another issue of great potential conflict among populations accustomed to settling inheritance in quite different ways. They deal with the standardization of weights and measures, betraying once again the change in economic life that is now gaining strength. And what to do, in view of Muslim customs, with the abomination of unmarried women walking nude in the market-place and other ticklish social matters? 'So give us legal ruling about these people and their ilk,' the emperor had demanded, 'and may God Most High reward you!'

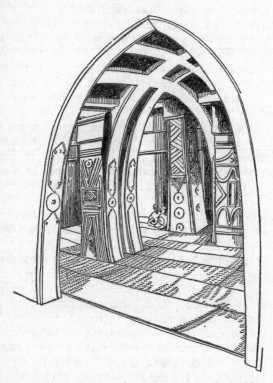

Mosque of Zaria, northern Nigeria, built by the master-builder Babban Gwani in 1860

But it was one thing to have the ruling and another to enforce it. Compromise persisted. As long as three centuries later, in 1804, we find the Fulani leader Uthman dan Fodio still citing al-Maghili's 'Answers' in order to support the legality of holy war against Hausa rulers who were also, as they claimed, Muslim rulers.

Stratification steadily deepened. Tribute-payers were thrust down into a position little different from serfdom. Technically 'free peoples' found themselves placed under heavier restraints. Raiding for slaves increased; and all this, perhaps together with a growing demand for domestic slave labour in the Ottoman empire (which had enclosed Egypt and north Africa early in the sixteenth century), helped to enlarge the small but steady overland slave trade.

Court expenses rose. Royal dwellings became more splendid. Long-service soldiers equipped with imported guns and with costly horses dressed in quilt and mail became a major tax upon the state. 'The cost of royal government was always increasing as royalty became more royal ... New and larger palaces were built, navies and munitions became more expensive, lay bureaucrats replaced their clerical predecessors who had been paid in benefices, all prices rose.' *Mutatis mutandis*, this description of late Tudor government applies just as well to Queen Elizabeth's contemporary in Bornu, King Idris Alooma, or to the rulers of the Songhay empire. All these monarchs might well have echoed James I's complaint to his council in 1607, that 'the only disease and consumption which I can ever apprehend likeliest to endanger me is this canker of want, which, being removed, I could think myself as happy in all other respects as any other king or monarch that ever was.'

Majesty became ever more expensive in these kingdoms. Going out to meet ambassadors from the Ottoman sultan towards 1600, the emperor of Bornu took with him a flashing troop of soldiers 'all mounted after arraying themselves and their horses in armour, cuirasses, shields and their best apparel', a scene which inspired its memorialist, the courtier Ahmad ibn Fartua, to apostrophize his readers with the words: 'O my wise friends and companions! Have you ever seen a king equal to our Sultan or like him at this time when the Lord of Stambul, the Sultan of Turkey, sent messengers from his country with favourable proposals.' No doubt: but it did not come cheap, and the many who had to pay – and to pay in ways that were new and painful –

will have taken a different view of all this wealth-consuming splendour.

Sharpening stratification took a characteristic administrative form in the shift from appointment to office by right of birth to appointment by service, merit, or achievement. Kings increasingly relied on officials drawn from the ranks of enslaved men who had no effective lineage loyalty which could lessen their obedience. There came the regular appointment of eunuchs to high office, men whose mutilation had deprived them of any personal interest in the conservation of lineage. So it occurred that Europeans, arriving later on, could find 'slaves' in positions of great responsibility as ambassadors, generals, or chief ministers. This in turn produced fresh problems, and led to new constellations of power.

For these 'slaves' could be ambitious. In the Bambara states of the middle Niger, during the eighteenth century, 'slave' generals seized the throne repeatedly. But constitutional ways of absorbing such problems were gradually developed. They took shape in the rearrangement of older checks and balances.

In the Hausa state of Zaria, for example, there developed a constitutional system which regularly counterpoised those who were appointed by right of birth to those who were appointed by merit. The army was commanded by a traditional chief, but its supplies and administration were in the hands of a eunuch minister who was the king's appointee. Even the capital city was divided between these two great men, the *madawaki* and the *galadima*, each of whom ruled half of it as a fief held of the king. Being a eunuch, and thus with no separate lineage interests, the *galadima* could be relied upon to side with the king against a rebellious *madawaki*, while the *madawaki* could similarly be relied upon to ensure that the *galadima*'s powers remained within bounds.

When a king of Zaria died, an electors' council picked a successor; but in this too the checks and balances were carefully at work. The majority of men on the electors' council consisted of *mallams*, men of learning, who were debarred from political office, including the kingship. They could accordingly be expected to choose a king who would rule with a minimum of strife, from which they normally had nothing to gain. Once elected, the king had considerable powers, but could act in controversial matters only by playing off one set of officials against another.

On any major issues, the king was by custom obliged first to consult his senior household officials, and next, the *rukuni* or senior order of the public officials, that is, the *madawaki* and the three eunuch *rukuni*, *galadima*, *wombai* and *dallabu*. If all these agreed on the course to be pursued, the king could not resist their advice and in fact the power of the state would be against him if he did.

In these and other ways the influence of traditional structures slowed and modified the concentration of power. However persistently kings might enlarge their sovereignty – and this they did in many of the forest states outside Moslem influence, as well as in the Sudan or among the Moslem city-states of the Indian Ocean seaboard – the ancestral frameworks fought a long rearguard action: not until the nineteenth century were they seriously undermined. The 'king's men' might gain steadily in influence and authority. But the lineage chiefs who drew their own from immemorial shrines could not easily be set aside.

Local or short-distance trade, spurring the diversification of goods produced by specialists, helped to give society its early division of labour. Long-distance trade deepened this effect. Both increased the power of chiefs and the authority of kings. This can be shown for every major region, though by no means for every people.

Central Africa experienced the same general sequence as the Western Sudan. Down the long East Coast the Swahili city-states, by the thirteenth century strongly Muslim in their tone and accent, could handle gold and ivory from the inland peoples, and send back to them Indian cottons and other useful manufactures. Responding, the inland peoples expanded their own production, hunting the elephant far and wide, opening thousands of gold-bearing deposits. By 1450 the greater part of the central plateau – an area about the size of western Europe – was enclosed within a series of producer-states whose interests were marginally but perhaps crucially influenced by the long-distance trade.

Any such trade required a certain degree of central direction. It also called for defence of caravan trails. Ritual leaders went into trade, but they also went into warfare; and kings emerged. The process had its own momentum. If a chief could expect a tusk of every elephant killed in his people's territory as part of his 'emoluments' – the example is from Malawi – then he had an interest both in extending his trade and enlarging his kingdom. Many saw the point and pressed it home.

The forms varied far more than the content, at least outside the Muslim sphere. No matter how energetically they drove the trade of their kingdoms, the kings were not capitalists. They might accumulate, but were invariably expected to disgorge their wealth in regular gifts to deserving persons: that is, to kinship-segments over whom they ruled. Good kings did this wisely or sufficiently well; bad kings paid for their greed by hostile plots and deposition. Even in a kingdom as centrally organized as eighteenth-century Dahomey, where the king controlled a state economic sector of considerable importance as well as monopolizing all trade with Europeans on the coast, it remained mandatory on the monarch to share out his proceeds at 'annual customs', where generous handouts could maintain the general balance of the state.

Within these limits the forms varied with local opportunities and personal ambitions. Individual rulers or sets of rulers introduced new methods of rule, expanded their power at the cost of their peers, drew within their orbit of authority a widening range of everyday affairs, and made claims on sovereignty that were sometimes in strong opposition to the custom of earlier times. The institution of kingship thus acquired its own dynamism. Initially a leader among other leaders of descent-lines, the king was elevated by the sheer pressure of group interests who would look to him for favours, depend on him for advancement, until he became much more than *primus inter pares*. But once supreme he was able to buttress and confirm his supremacy by fresh acts of prestige, wars for tribute, the engrossing of wider areas of trade and revenue. I am not saying that this line of growth in royal power was always a conscious one. But it was surely far more deliberate than historians have generally allowed. The great 'ritual kingships' of sixteenth-century Africa and later, reinforcing their secular authority by an overwhelming spiritual prestige, will have owed as much of their 'divinity' to calculated planning by interested parties as to all or any of the postulates of religion.

There is the striking case of Buganda. Its kings had emerged as elected leaders of councils of chiefs who were each other's peers. Not until the fifteenth king, according to Ganda traditions, was royal authority able to stand outside of and above the lineage network. But then, by a continued taking of new powers, these kings became strong enough to make and change law and custom which, at least in theory, the ancestors had laid down as immutable. By the nineteenth century the Ganda kings could even be despotic.

The ancient kingdom of Benin in southern Nigeria makes another example. At some time around 1400 the Bini royals broke away from the elective succession they had taken over from their neighbours in Yorubaland, and declared for primogeniture. Though checks and balances continued to operate in matters both of policy and administration, the nobles lost their power of deposition. Other changes followed. By 1600 the king was a figure of towering prestige, and his palace a maze of courts and chambers inflated by an atmosphere of majesty through which other men approached him in ceremonial self-abasement. Little by little, and to a point that was exceptional among African peoples, the 'royal party' and its priesthood had advanced their theocratic case. And when in 1897 the British at last invaded this kingdom, they were met by the staunch resistance of men at arms, but also by priestly confusion and frenzied human sacrifice: very much, indeed, as in that earlier theocracy of Mexico where God and his representatives had taken all the power, and left the gates but poorly guarded to the Spanish.

At the same time one needs to see these systems within a total situation. Powerful kingships were not mere impositions: they reflected an evolving socio-economic reality. When early Yoruba society took shape in western Nigeria a thousand years ago, people settled in farming communities in the forest. As Yoruba towns grew larger and more prosperous in this fertile land, each of them developed parallel and similar institutions under their local lineage leaders. These institutions were organized on the concept of *Ebi*: they projected the state as the replica of a family. Yoruba ideology supposed a family of spiritual beings, gods and lesser gods and ancestors, under the supreme and immemorial aegis of Olodumare, and saw this as being repeated on Earth in the 'founding model' at Ife, and then in every other Yoruba town.

From this model flowed all legitimate authority. At the head of these communities stood the Oni of Ife, with the obas of all the other towns ranked in order of seniority below him, according to the supposed foundation dates of their communities. Thus the Oni of Ife held the apex of politico-religious authority in that he derived from the founding-hero, Oduduwa, who was, in turn, the instrument of God. While the many Yoruba communities lived more or less independent lives, they continued to pay homage to the Oni's spiritual primacy. So their political unity – in so far as any existed before the Oyo empire of about 1700, and on this opinions differ – was the unity of a vastly extended 'family' under chiefs whose duties were also social, religious, or economic, and who reproduced within each town a similar structure of authority. Within this hierarchy all Yoruba could find a place; and it is obvious from the great longevity of these systems that the place was generally acceptable.

Into this simplified picture one must read the richness of Yoruba cultural life. Each town had its royal palace and dominant shrines, its town-quarters reflecting lineage unities, its manifold officials whose appointment depended on their positions in the lineage structure; and all this was enshrined in beliefs of luxuriant versatility and all-embracing relevance. The fact of aristocracy – and the Yoruba systems can reasonably be called aristocratic – was constantly modified by the politico-religious framework.

These systems were admirably organized for local production and short-distance trade. Excellent forest farmers, the Yoruba had other ingenious skills. They were notably advanced in the techniques of cotton dyeing: only when Europeans had learned the dyeing art from India could they produce anything to rival these glowing robes of Yorubaland. They were shrewd workers in iron and brass: for tools but also for objects of ritual and decorative art. Each town had its guilds of craftsmen, often with specialized reputations. Markets organized at four- or eight-day intervals were a central part of their life, and many of these markets became famous for a long way round. Even today a visitor to Ibadan's textile market, opened at fourteen-day intervals, will find an impressive range of quality and variety from craftsmen near and far.

After 1650 the long-distance trade proved once again a powerful factor in political change and the greater concentration of royal authority. The nobles of one of the youngest of the Yoruba states, Oyo in the grassland country towards the river Niger where it flows from the north-west, embarked on the building of an empire. Capitalizing on their favourable position between the

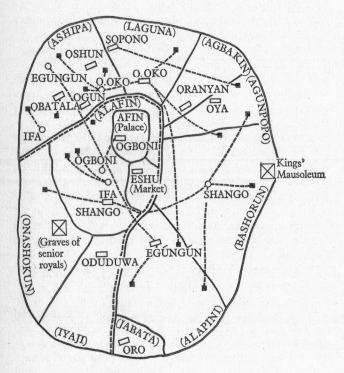

Key:

| | |
|---|---|
| ▭ | Central temple |
| ○ | Secondary temple |
| ◼ | Domestic shrines |
| ----- | Links in hierarchy of cult organization |
| ——— | Ward boundaries |
| ===== | Boundary of royal section of Oyo |
| | Ward heads (royals or Oyo Misi) in brackets |

Pattern of distribution of temples and domestic shrines in Oyo forest country and the north, these Oyo Yoruba were able to insert themselves most advantageously into the trading system of the Sudan. Their own outstanding capacity for artisan production, especially in textiles, had pointed the way. They had long sold their cottons to the north. Now they transformed themselves into the leading middlemen for exchange of northern and southern goods on a wider scale, dealing in the produce of the forest country and the manufactures or metals of the Sudan and north Africa.

The Oyo Yoruba had other advantages. While tsetse fly prevented them from breeding horses for cavalry warfare on the Sudanese pattern, they became wealthy enough to purchase regular supplies of cavalry mounts from the north. These they used to gain equality with their strong northern neighbours of Borgu and Jukun, then to impose their hegemony on other states near the forest fringe, eastward into Nupe and westward into Dahomey. With this, the northern Yoruba communities who spoke the Oyo dialect became closely unified under the king of Oyo city. There emerged another large system of trade and tribute, but with interesting features of its own.

The *Ebi* or family concept of structure was retained, although this clashed increasingly as the empire grew in size and outlying provinces were placed under king-appointed governors, with the contrary principle of centralizing imperial power. The whole structure had characteristic intricacies. Persistently hierarchical in its basic framework, Oyo government evolved 'on a system of checks and balances centring around four powerful figures': the Alafin or king, the Bashorun, the Oluwo, and the Kakanfo. In theory all powers issued from the Alafin as the spiritual embodiment of ancestral force and legitimation; but in practice there was clear division of powers between the 'executive', composed of the Alafin and his appointed lieutenants, and the 'legislature' of leading descent-line heads who were necessarily chosen by birth.

As time went by, more power accrued to 'king's men' who were often drawn from the ranks of those who had lost their civic rights for one reason or another, and had become bondsmen or 'slaves'. The king's three main lieutenants were 'the Ona Efa, the chief judge in dispensing imperial justice, the Otun Efa, the administrative head of Shango, a cult which worshipped the Alafin's deified ancestors, and the Osi Efa, the controller of palace finances who set and received the tributes and tolls of the empire as well as heading its intelligence service'. Conquered or subjected states were not made into integral parts of the Oyo system. They were left under their defeated or vassal kings or nobles who were watched and controlled, in turn, by two special appointees of the Alafin, the one for civil administration and the other for propagation of the Shango cult. Sometimes these two responsibilities were combined in one man.

But the *Ebi* concept imposed a firm limit on imperial authority. In practice the Alafin could govern only with the good will of his leading nobles, the Oyo Mesi or 'Council of Notables' of whom the Bashorun was chancellor or chairman. He might try to split their unity of attitude, but he could not pack their ranks by royal appointment; and they had influence at several crucial points. They could overturn the king's decisions, and even at need depose him. For they held, in the person of the Bashorun, the headship of the Shango cult and thus controlled the 'decisions' of the divine ancestors.

Here again one sees with startling clarity how fundamentally alike these cultures were, no matter what distances might separate them. Whenever influential sentiment ran strongly enough that way, a Bashorun could 'discover' that the ancestors had lost confidence in a reigning Alafin because – again to recall al-Mas'udi's words about the East African 'kingdom of the Zanj' in the tenth century – he was said by his failings 'to have ceased to be a fit representative of God'. Then the Bashorun sent the king a gift of parrot's eggs, and the king, at least in theory, at once killed himself, but was in any case deposed.

Yet the checks and balances worked both ways. Otherwise the king of Oyo might quickly have become the mere creature of his Council of Notables, the Oyo Mesi, and they could have deposed him at will. This they could not do because of the leaders of the Ogboni Society. These formed another council of notables who were elected by leading descent-lines and commanded influence throughout the Yoruba sections of the empire. Their chairman was the Oluwo, an appointee of the king; and the Oluwo was the official priest or interpreter of the great Ifa oracle. One of his attributes was to decide whether or not the divine ancestors really 'agreed' with a Bashorun's decision to send parrot's eggs and cause an abdication. The Alafin, in other words, possessed his own check on the Council of Notables through his standing with the Ogboni. Much the same deliberately ambivalent position, clearly the outcome of a long development, governed the powers of the Kakanfo or army leader. He and his seventy war chiefs, the Eso, swore allegiance to the Alafin in his own person, but care was taken in a nice symmetry to see that power over their promotion remained with the Council of Notables.

Much therefore turned on the personalities of leading men. A forceful Bashorun could dominate a vacillating king, while an ambitious king could usually find ways of making his will prevail. The history of Oyo is full of the clash of turbulent nobles, of rivalries for power and fame between leading men who sought to make the system serve their personal advantage. These troubles were long contained. But towards 1800 the inner balance began at last to break down, partly by reason of the personalities then in play, but mainly because imperial rule now conflicted critically with the *Ebi* concept of 'family structure'. Having remained a congeries of semi-autonomous states within the imperial system, the more distant peoples and then the nearer ones began to win more elbow-room by exploiting rivalries between the king and his nobles. A century and a half of more or less unified rule had brought, in other words, no concept of single nationhood. These centrifugal pressures were then sharpened by disasters in warfare with neighbours. There followed a long series of wars of succession in which one Yoruba state after another looked for combinations of its own, seeking the leadership that Oyo had lost, until the British arrived and made peace after the fashion of another empire.

With local variations, other states and imperial systems evolved under much the same pressures of change. They could be small and tightly-knit, as they often were among the republics and monarchies of the western seaboard in response to the Atlantic trade; or they could be large and loosely held together, as among the Wolof of Senegal. Taking their rise soon after A.D. 1300, the Wolof formed several states, the most important of these being the kingdom of Jolof, a western boundary-state and occasional tributary of the empire of Mali.

When you sail south 'and reach the river of Senegal', wrote Duarte Pacheco Pereira in about 1506 after several years along the coast, 'you find the first blacks, and this is the beginning of the kingdom of Jolof, which is about 375 miles long and 175 miles broad ... The king of Jolof can put about 10,000 horsemen in the field, and 100,000 foot soldiers.' Fifty years earlier the Venetian Ca' da Mosto had written of the way of government in this kingdom. It was markedly similar to that of Oyo a century later. The Burba or king of Jolof was chosen not only by birth, but 'three or four lords (of whom there are many in this country) choose a king whom they like ... and who reigns as long as he pleases them. (But) they often dethrone their kings by force, and (on their side) the kings often try to make themselves so powerful that they cannot be dethroned.'

Again like the Yoruba, the Wolof were united by cultural ties but formed no concept of single nationhood. Each Wolof kingdom, Jolof towards the inland country, with Walo, Kayor, and others along the seaboard, retained the primacy of its own interests, or rather of the interests of its nobles. As the Atlantic trade got into its stride after 1650, the imperial authority of Jolof was gradually undermined and destroyed. The coastal Wolof states, especially Kayor, took advantage of their proximity to the sea-traders; and the later history of the region is largely the record of Kayor's successful rise to power and rivalry with neighbours. Into these wars of dynastic succession the French gradually inserted the wedge of their own imperial intrusion, just as the British were to do in Yorubaland.

Constitutionally, Wolof checks and balances were evidently less evolved than among the Yoruba, but basically of the same order. In Kayor, for example, powers were effectively divided under the king between the nobles, chiefly of the seven great families who had legitimate right to present candidates for the kingship, and a number of powerful dignitaries who, as 'king's men', were sometimes of captive status and worked as governors and court officials. A skilful king could manoeuvre between nobles and officials for the enhancement of his own authority. A feckless king, on the other hand, soon came to grief.

These kingdoms were constitutional in being the product of ancestral charters projected in the local rule of law. To say that they were constitutional, however, is not to say that they were democratic. In their maturity they lost much of the democracy which continued to inspire and move the village governments of Africa – even when, as among many of the Ibo, these village governments were active in trade and production for trade. The mechanisms of centralization, whether by conquest on other pressures, might evolve imposing systems, and sometimes very large ones: they also went hand in hand with a steady loss of social equality, with a stratification which thrust large numbers of men and women into tribute-paying or work-providing bondage. It was typical of this development that the collapse of the great Songhay system, after Moroccan invasion in 1591, should have been rendered irreversible by the revolt of its own subject peoples. And when Uthman dan Fodio called for holy war upon the Hausa kings in 1804 he was able to strike a social as well as a religious note, damning the kings as profligates 'whose purpose is ... to obtain delights and acquire rank' at the cost of ordinary people.

Yet it remains true that the Fulani rule in Hausaland which followed on Uthman's *jihad* was at least no less authoritarian, and given to the 'collecting of concubines and fine clothes' or 'the devouring of the gifts of influence, booty, and bribery', than the Hausa rule which had gone before. Until the nineteenth century, however, constitutional tradition generally remained a powerful restraining influence. No doubt it is this that explains why the more successful kingships could endure for so long. No matter how royal power might accrue, there were effective brakes on its abuse.

From another angle, the strength of tradition can be seen as a kingship's weakness in a changing world. There is plenty of evidence to suggest that kings and their advisers, ever more aware of new dangers from outside, well understood the need for

tighter forms of unity than could be coaxed from the mere conflation of separate lineage loyalties. Some of them did indeed
contrive a great deal towards achieving a concept of nationhood
that could override the separatisms of tradition. Perhaps the kings
of Dahomey went further in this, but they were not alone.

As it turned out, the leap from this type of system to nation-
statehood could not be made by way of kingship in Africa, any
more than it was made by way of kingship in Europe. These
kingships may be thought to have realized their full potential
within the possibilities of traditional culture. Strong in their
ancestral framework, they presided over much that was ingenious and brilliant. They partook fully in the life and vigour
of African civilization. They helped to clothe this civilization in
luminous diversities of custom and appearance. But their evolution had its limits, and these were reached by the middle of the
late nineteenth century. Soon after, with colonial invasion, they
were finally disrupted by upheavals of a duration and magnitude
such as Africa had not known before.

# 24 The Crisis Opens

'I do not know the cause of this sudden revolution,' Prime Minister Lord Salisbury complained to a British audience in 1891, 'but there it is.' The chief commercial nations of Europe had coiled themselves into a frantic spring for colonies in Africa, and the only thing that seemed to count was who should get there first. The noble Prime Minister and other elder statesmen in Britain and continental western Europe strongly disapproved. They believed that African colonies were bound to prove an expensive nuisance. But the public, or at any rate the public that politically mattered, thought otherwise. By 1891 this public had thought otherwise for a long time, and had regularly had its way. However mysterious the reasons might appear to Salisbury and his like, the fate of Africa had taken a new turn.

Yet the crisis of modern Africa did not open with this new imperialism. If colonial invasion afterwards piled turmoil on confusion, the colonial invaders were absent from the opening scenes of the drama. Towards 1850 the ancestral charters were beginning to break down, although not everywhere or at the same speed. The fact was often blurred by their breadth of development. Within them lay long centuries of growth and the rise of many-sided cultures. Civilizations of no small technological ingenuity, of fine artistic achievement, and, perhaps above all, of genial and persistent resolving of the conflict of individual and community, had flowered in systems of proverbial wisdom and belief. Offering hope and consolation in all the great things of life and death, these could seem in their venerable power to stand outside the ravages of time.

Yet even before 1850 these systems had come severely under strain. Though the old ways could still satisfy and easily enclose those peoples who, like the Karimojong or Lugbara, still lived beyond the margins of a world in change, there were others who found themselves, like their contemporaries in western Europe, caught in a 'sudden revolution' whose causes must have seemed no less mysterious.

Much remains to be explained about this initial period of transition or adjustment to an accelerating process of change. Its root cause seems to have lain in a disturbed ecological balance. For these societies were now the victims of their own success. The evidence suggests that in certain regions, and possibly in many, the density of populations had reached or even risen beyond the optimum consistent with traditional farming. Whether from this or from soil exhaustion, which amounts to the same thing, a critically large number of peoples appear to have begun to suffer land shortage. This was, of course, a shortage within patterns of extensive agriculture. It occurred only in certain regions, and nowhere to the point at which the needs of survival imposed any radical change in systems of production. Even today, in an Africa vastly more populous, the easy availability of land remains a chronic discouragement to more intensive cultivation.

Exact data are invariably missing. We shall presumably never be able to make any exact comparison between the sizes of population in sixteenth- and nineteenth-century Africa. Yet the signs point to a rising rate of growth which cannot be fully explained by the efficacy of existing productive systems. Some new factor seems required. This was possibly the spread of American food crops after about 1600, especially maize and cassava. These relatively high-yield and disease-resistant crops were being widely harvested in tropical Africa by about 1650, and they continued to spread. They could support a somewhat denser settlement; but the consequent growth in population called in turn for more land, and did so, it appears, with a sharpening rivalry.

One large region which seems to have experienced this interplay of population growth and land shortage was south-eastern Africa, since before A.D. 1000 a homeland of the southern Bantu. These Nguni-speaking farmers and their Sotho-speaking neighbours to the westward had gradually filled up all the good farming land between the Indian Ocean and the central plains of the

Orange river. Nguni groups were settled at least by 1400 as far south as the eastern part of the present Cape Province. By 1700 they were well established along the Great Fish river, and were steadily bringing more land under stock and cultivation. But then another factor intervened. After 1750 they were unable to extend their land not only by reason of the southern ocean, but also by reason of an advancing front of Boer and British settlement moving northward from the Cape of Good Hope.

Out of this situation there arose a crisis special to the region, but which eventually influenced much of central-east Africa as well. While peoples in the far south, Xhosa, Pondo and their neighbours, stayed where they were and defended themselves, often very well, against Boer and then British encroachment, those in the north saw violent upheavals. These erupted soon after 1800 under a forceful paramount chief, Dingiswayo of the Mtetwa, in what afterwards became the Zulu empire. Dingiswayo set out upon a long campaign of unification of major tribal segments, being wont to say, according to tradition, that 'it was never the intention of Umvela, the father of the human race, that men should live at enmity with one another.'

Just how far Dingiswayo really understood the fuller challenge of his times is a matter for debate. In any case much flowed from his initiatives. And what he started in the way of unification was completed and carried further by the celebrated Shaka, who built an empire. The wars thus raised were grossly destructive. But they brought in their train other movements of unification, notably that of Sotho fragments who coalesced under the dynamic leadership of Mosheshwe into the Basuto nation. Further consequences of Nguni migration were felt as far northward as Lake Tanganyika.

These states were new, but they were still based on the old patterns, reshaped and modified. What might eventually have happened without European intrusion remains another field for speculation. Perhaps the centralizing tendencies evident in certain powerful states, such as Asante in the west and Buganda in the east, might have become generalized to the point of radical structural change, with the rise of new ruling groups and the further crystallization of classes leading to new types of economic

243

system and political organization. What did in fact happen, and repeatedly, was the effort to reorganize large regions, whether in the west or centre or south, into a further evolution of the inherited framework: by the action of powerful leaders, especially in the Sudan, or the rise of new kings or proto-kings where none had existed before.

Even with older kingdoms there was a new accent on aggressive competition. The Swazi state in south-eastern Africa, for example, was well developed by 1700. Rank was ordered primarily by birth, and power had centralized in an aristocracy whose apex was a ritual kingship. Within the Swazi structure there was peace. But it was bought at an increasing price. Warfare became 'essential to maintain the type of society that developed with the consolidation of kingship, and the main avenue whereby commoners could achieve power, wealth, and fame'. In modern terms the wars might often be no more than quick raids by small parties of warriors; all the same, they grew in frequency and size.

Another example is the Ganda kingdom in southern Uganda. 'It was in war', we are told of its later years, 'that lay the sources of their wealth such as livestock, slaves and ivory: in sum, the very things of which there was a shortage in Buganda.' More power could bring more loot, but also more revenue from trade. And when King Mawanda added eastern Kyaggwe to his dominions, and King Junju annexed Buddu, they did so partly to increase Buganda's supply of iron and ironsmiths, hitherto in short supply. Palmerston and other contemporaries would have had no difficulty in following the royal argument; in other terms, after all, it was their own. The ministers of Louis XIV might have understood it even better: gathering more power and wealth at the centre, the kings became more arbitrary and difficult to restrain.

Other pressures thrust the same way, not least a great expansion in the overseas slave trade after 1650. Since the available pool of chattel slaves was either very small, as in the Sudan, or almost non-existent, as in most of Africa south of the Sudan, this expansion meant a growing warfare in pursuit of captives who could be sold as slaves. Whatever common folk might think, the kings and their henchmen had little hesitation in meeting such demands; often they hesitated not at all. They went into eager partnership with the European slavers. Once involved, they found it hard and then impossible to extricate themselves, even when they wished to do so. For the slave trade became the only certain way in which they could acquire European goods, especially fire-arms. And fire-arms became more and more necessary to self-defence as one people after another took to using them.

Offensive wars for the taking of captives implied defensive wars against neighbours of the same mind: either way the demand for guns grew by leaps and bounds. From this interlinked buying of guns and selling of captives there flowed a destructiveness that was qualitatively new. No longer merely or mainly for the control of land, trade or tribute, warfare became an instrument of sheer survival, and was increasingly used with a bitterness that seems to have been rare in earlier times.

More than one large coastal region was deeply marked by this eruptive circuit of supply and demand. The case became clearest in eastern Africa, where a new Arab slave trade spread inland after about 1830. At the same time the Portuguese, baulked of West African slaves for Brazil by the anti-slavery patrols of the British navy, turned avidly to Mozambique for alternative sources of supply. By 1850 tens of thousands of captives were being taken out of the inland country. And as this slaving spread so also did the new trade in fire-arms.

These fire-arms were sought by the slave-trading caravaneers, by new trading states which now took shape in the inland country, and by a host of other peoples for attack or defence.

In 1847 the missionary Johann Krapf saw coastal caravans going up into Masailand that had as many as one thousand guns among the soldiers who escorted them. A few years later ... one European firm in Zanzibar was selling as many as 13,000 guns a year for use in the interior. In 1883 it was estimated that the Nyamwezi ruler of [the inland trading state of] Unyanyembe, near modern Tabora [in Tanzania], possessed as many as 20,000 guns.

Up to the 1870s they were all muzzle-loaders, frightening enough but unreliable and short of range. In European trading circles they were known as 'gas pipes', and King Shaka of the Zulu was not the only African commander who thought that spears were much to be preferred. Yet they had their effect, as may be guessed from the fact that every year during the 1880s perhaps as many as 100,000 of these guns were going inland from Zanzibar – not all, of course, to be used in military and slaving purposes, but also in shooting elephants for the ivory trade. By this time, too, imports included a few of the much improved breech-loaders which the Germans had so successfully used against the French. Altogether it has been estimated that about one million guns of various types, more than four million pounds of powder, and many millions of rounds of ammunition were imported into eastern Africa between 1885 and 1902, by which time British and German imperialists were anxiously trying to halt a trade which could only make their conquests more difficult. Much the same picture is true of western Africa.

These pressures piled their weight on the deepening crisis of structure. Just as kingships sought for a solution in greater centralization of power, so also did many of the segmentary societies – those who never previously had found a need for kings or even proto-kings – turn in the same direction. Peoples with 'minimal government' who lay in the path of trading caravans or of raiding armies saw that for them, too, new strength required new unity. Some of them in central-east Africa had already learned their lesson from the northward-thrusting Ngoni after 1835. 'Segmentaries' in southern Tanzania, for example, came together under strong kingships such as that of the Hehe. Others allocated more power to ritual leaders, and with like results. Others again, such as the Kikuyu and their neighbours in Kenya, developed embryonic forms of central control in the person of appointed war leaders, *athimaki* among the Kikuyu, prefiguration of later commanders who were to lead many thousands of Kikuyu forest fighters during the great anti-colonial rising of the 1950s. Ritual leaders among the Nandi, *orkoyiit*, were endowed with powers capable of welding segments into a common front; so were the *laibon* among the Masai, and the *ruoth* among the Kenya Luo, and notable war leaders such as Horombo and Rindi of the Chaga.

To this fragmentary sketch of social change towards new forms of organization, towards centralization of power, one could add much supporting detail. In the Sudan, historically a region of large political systems, the nineteenth century witnessed an attempt, or rather several attempts, at recovering some of the socio-political unities of the past. These were made by outstanding leaders, working mainly in the central Muslim tradition, such as the western Fulani (Tucolor) leader, al-Hajj Umar bin Said; the eastern Fulani leaders Uthman dan Fodio and his far more political son, the Amir-al-Muminin Muhammad Bello; the Mahdi of the Eastern Sudan, Muhammad Ahmad ibn Abdullah, whose conceptions went as far as unity for the whole Sudan; the Almamy Samori Turay in the region of the Niger-Senegal headwaters; and lesser figures such as Ma Ba and Mamadu Lamine.

Spanning nearly a century, the efforts of these men and their followers ranged from a re-statement of old ideas to the evolution of new structures. Elsewhere, on the side of innovation, one may add the strongly centralizing trend in Asante, with its literate chancery after 1850, its growing civil service, its widening state trading sector, and comparable developments in other states, or the growth at certain points of semi-capitalist forms of enterprise, especially in the Niger delta states, along the Leeward coast, and in Senegambia. In the light of such evidence it can well appear that much of Africa was now involved in processes of socio-economic change that were qualitatively different from any which had gone before; and that new structures and new unities stood upon the threshold of the times.

But years of experiment would clearly be required to body forth these new things. The ancestral charters still held firm, often even in the Muslim Sudan, their prestige seemingly irrefragible, their power of absorption beyond question. When the priests of the Kenya Luo affirmed that the first Europeans they saw, 'red strangers' as they called them, were the embodiment of ancestral spirits now returned to show men better ways of life, they were saying no more than that ancestral charters could once more be made to adjust and absorb.

These charters had often done this in the past: why not again?

They had carried men far within their own creativeness, and had been repeatedly adjusted to new problems. Deeply woven by an interplay of factors indigenous and foreign, old and new, the fabric of African history had revealed a wide resilience of combinations and permutations. Migration and new settlement; the articulation of power in a multitude of patterns; a corresponding evolution of structural subtleties; great influences from outside whether ideological or material; slaving and enslavement and the massive import of fire-arms, or the nagging presence of European encroachment: all these and much else lay in the record of absorption. The strong line of ancestral tradition had never yet snapped nor even, for the most part, seriously frayed.

Now it is clear, with hindsight, that no mere modification of the old solutions could any longer meet the case. The real problems after 1870 were of a kind and scale that could not be solved,

From at least the twelfth century the Swahili of the East Coast developed a distinctive Islamic architecture. This is a nineteenth-century tomb at Ununio, north of Dar-es-Salaam, with ornament incised in plaster. The domed pillars on such tombs were a fairly common feature

or even contained, within the frameworks and productive systems of the past.

New systems were needed if Africa was to sustain its growth, or even its independence, in a world of radical economic and social change. Whatever was of value in the old frameworks, their moral vigour, their humanism, their accent on man's social being, could eventually survive in new forms: the dross, the misery or the brutality of frustrated belief, the blind conservatism, would in the process fall away. But meanwhile the old systems were powerless to meet the brusque and rending challenge of industrial production.

The time required to make this hard transition of structures from one world to another was not to be available. There came instead the shattering arrival of the Europeans whose colonial impact and presence, prolonged over sixty or seventy years, made more than tinkering impossible. Africans thereafter continued to adjust and evolve, even in the cultural suffocation of the 'settler colonies'; but not until the present day, and now in situations rootedly different from any of the past, having gone through much and learned much, could they begin to approach their basic problems of systematic change.

## Part Five: The Deluge and Today

Behold, the hire of the labourers who have reaped
down your fields, which is of you kept back,
crieth: and the cries of them which have reaped
are entered into the ears of the Lord of Sabaoth.

James, v, 4

Our society, our economy, and the dominant
ambitions of our own people are all very different
now from what they were before.

J. K. NYERERE

# 25 From a Guerrilla Diary

'There is no new entity born out of colonialism,' wrote Frantz Fanon in one of his impassioned editorials of 1958 for the Algerian nationalist weekly, *El Moujahid*. A simplification, of course: like all cries of anguish. Much has come out of colonialism in Africa. But a new *entity*, a new shape to civilization? On the morrow of independence, in 1960 and after, it was possible to think so or at least to hope so. Later, with one new regime after another in more or less dire emergency, it was difficult to do either.

Yet these years since about 1870 have in any case produced a situation in which new entities can at last emerge: new frameworks and structures, that is, which are capable of matching Africa with the modern world. The Africa of today is extraordinarily different from that of a hundred years ago: even where the old things and ideas seem most alive they may often be found, on looking closer, only to be shells of their former meaning. Already these shells enclose a new reality.

The extreme situations of modern Africa may be those that show this most easily. Here, in the wars of liberation against Portuguese rule in Guinea-Bissau, Angola and Mozambique, it has been possible to see the old and the new in direct and dramatic juxtaposition.

Early in October 1967 I landed in guerrilla territory on the coast of Portugal's west African colony, where the waves of the Atlantic wash in among dense mangrove thickets.

*October 9.* Last night a long night half-mooned. We came up an arm of the creeks with a man pole-sounding on either beam and crying out depths while the ocean tide cradled us closer to the trees. I stood by the rail with him for a while. He was calling a deep and personal cantata: *Bra' giu'do, Me'o bra' giu'do ... Brass exactly, half-brass exactly*; and it couldn't, I thought, have changed in centuries. Just such a voice and just such a man, stone black as a moving statue but for points of brilliant silver when he turned up his face to the night, crying at the skipper on the poop above him, would have patiently sung in the caravels of long ago, edging their keels through rippled water the colour of dark violet, steering beneath tropical stars to a hazardous landfall.

But this landing of yesterday was like nothing in the past among these Guinea creeks and seaways; our boat was no caravel but the *Tres de Agosto*, a stout small vessel of steel with a cannon mounted on the bow ...

This contrast between the place and the occasion keeps on hitting me. Here we are living in thatched huts no different from any other huts that villagers have made for timeless years. Yet the boxes piled outside are 75 mm shell containers. Last night we ferried from the *Tres de Agosto* in dugout canoes low on the water as they always are, with the freeboard kissing the brink at every explosion of the paddle. Then we walked up from the beach to a shadowed waiting line of men who might have been just the same as the Portuguese encountered five centuries back, but were carrying modern weapons. At the same time they're men who very much belong here. Like the crew of the *Tres de Agosto* last night – or on the countless other nights they remember in this war of independence, reminiscing, gossiping, endlessly swapping their stories – they aren't returned exiles or mercenaries or members of some specialized élite: they're village Africans and the sons or grandsons of village Africans from one or other of the little towns of this colony. They're completely *of the country*: local and indigenous, unmistakably ...

Village Africans? Going by what Verhaegen has recorded about the Congo revolts of 1964, they ought to believe in supernatural protections, in spells to turn away Portuguese bombs or reduce bullets to water, in charms against the white man's wizardry. Maybe. But I can't see any sign of that. Cabral said, 'Yes, there was a lot of talk about magic in the beginning,' and smiled as though at a problem usefully solved: 'But now they've learned that it's better to take good cover and shoot back straight.' So where, in that case, are the old charters with their overhang of magical belief? I don't know. What these units have are not spirit mediums but political commissars. And what the political commissars teach and tell, so far as I can see, is hardheaded stuff about discipline, sanitation, military tactics, political strategy ...

*October 15.* We have been over near Beli where the Portuguese have one of their beleaguered garrisons. Miles of waterlogged pasture and waist-high rivers, a tiring trot. Outside Beli the nationalist units are in semi-permanent encampment for the rainy season. They are all villagers by origin, very young most of them, from the so-called 'primitive' Balante, a segmentary society without chiefs. I find it interesting, and a matter for inquiry, that the segmentaries should so often have fought colonial invasion far longer than the centralized states. The Balante were fighting the Portuguese, off and on, well into the 1920s, and they number about a third of the whole population. You'd think that dispersal of authority would mean failure to unite in resistance, but it doesn't seem to have worked that way: here or anywhere else. There's the example of the Tiv in Nigeria ...

Few of these soldiers look over twenty. Their commander is an exception, an 'old man' who may be as much as thirty-five which is a pretty advanced age in guerrilla terms, Yamte N'aga. But he too is absolutely local, indigenous, *of the country*. Yamte counts as a senior warrior in the Balante age-grade system. Has gone through the late-initiation rites appropriate to the status of village elder. Mostly, Yamte holds, 'the Balante do not think that senior men should go to war. We leave that to the young men.' His being an exception is quite a thing that's talked about.

What else do they talk about? Once again, so far as I can tell, not much fuss about charms, no great superstitions – and certainly none of those drugs reported from the Congo. Yamte talks mostly about the war. He's an old soldier who served in the Portuguese army, and he likes to make up tall stories which he tells with the gravity of age, about many aeroplanes shot down and suchlike wonders that do occasionally happen. Yesterday, coming back from Beli, we lay out across a stretch of dry rock, resting as the sun went down, and heard a lot of these stories. Everyone enjoyed it no end, even I who got them only in French from Yamte's Guiné Créole.

Over there in the camp outside Beli it was much the same. The young men showed me their large mortars and their various automatics, and posed for a group photograph, and asked me about far-off things that concern the wide world. Two of them brought out primers and exercise books, and were proud they were learning to read and write, something else the war had brought them.

They have a foot in both worlds, the world of the village, the 'primitive' Balante village, and the world of warfare for national independence, for modern education, for a new freedom. But their

# 26 The Great Transition

These scraps from a 'guerrilla diary' have a place here, perhaps, because the situations they describe make a more than usually clear illustration of certain crucial aspects of change in the 1960s. The Balante age-grade system, certainly of great antiquity, is adapted to a war of national independence. The Balante ancestral charter, undoubtedly no younger, is adjusted to beliefs and attitudes of a kind entirely new to this country.

Positive aspects of resistance, these adjustments pose interesting questions.

By what stages of thought and experience did Yamte N'aga make his journey of discovery from the ways of the past to the ways of the future? How did the crew of the *Tres de Agosto*, or those gun teams shooting up at bombers dropping napalm and high-explosive, or the youthful volunteers besieging Portuguese garrisons in the mosquito-laden forests of the south and the tawny grasslands of the north, enlarge their skylines from village boundaries to the limits of a world in radical change? By what routes did the ideas of nationalism and the command of new challenges, but also the perception of a need for new forms of unity between the individual and society, become the essence of their talk and the proof of distance travelled since the old gods failed, and the old ways went down in chaos or defeat? Generalizing within a continental context over more than a century, what can be said about this necessary but so difficult transition from ancestral charters to modern ideologies and systems of self-rule?

The following chapters attempt the outline of an answer. This cannot be anything like definitive. For that, much more will have to be understood about the actual experience of Africans during the colonial period. Little enough is known as things are now.

If social anthropologists before the 1950s prepared the ground for serious study of African society, most of them did so from a synchronic approach; and much of their work has remained of little value for comprehending historical processes of change. If historians were busy in the field, they were looking at the colonial period from a European rather than an African point of view.

Lately, however, the position has improved. With more information, the general movement of thought and action becomes less uncertain. Landmarks can be seen and followed with some assurance of not seriously losing one's way. In this respect the difficulty lies mainly in classification and selection, because these landmarks are expectably of various kinds and, if followed carelessly, can lead to confusion. This long and obscure transition has taken place, and continues to take place, at different levels of consciousness, and in different forms in different regions.

In these circumstances I have chosen to follow a line of landmarks which plot the movement, at least in a broad way, of what Africans did during the immediate pre-colonial and colonial years, and in the years that immediately followed, rather than of what was done to them. Along this route it can be seen that those who made the running acted and reacted in resistances which do indeed trace a general movement of transition in something of its true and criss-crossed complexity. It may be possible, in other words, to build a synthesis of recent African development that will be essentially accurate.

This particular approach has perhaps another advantage. A familiar view has presented colonized Africans as the more or less helpless recipients of European impact. Yet the truth of the colonial period can often be found, one now sees, only by looking at European enterprise in relation to African reaction. This interwoven truth can of course be viewed from many standpoints. What I propose here is to look at it from the standpoint of a crisis of institutions, and of African efforts to meet this crisis. This in turn implies a concentration on certain aspects of the colonial scene: on resistance rather than collaboration, although, of course, collaboration in the form of accommodation could also be at times a form of resistance. Much else will be omitted, notably the stages and contrasts of European colonial policies, themselves to some extent controlled, at least in the British and French colonies, by the nature of African responses.

Several transitional phases can be detected. They begin in the immediate pre-colonial period with changes which derived from pressures – whether of population growth or economic movement – that were largely internal to late Iron Age society. They continue, as colonial pressures rise, with a defence of the old charters, the old systems of self-rule, that was no different in its motivation from that of the past. Just as in earlier times, kings like the monarch of Asante put armies in the field to fight invaders who happened to be European, or else, again as in the past, they strove to contain the Europeans and keep the peace by diplomatic and commercial means. This has been called 'primary resistance'. There was much of it in every region of the threatened continent.

Primary resistance was a direct reaction, made face to face with the invaders. But other types of primary resistance occurred only after the invaders had begun to establish their presence and authority. These 'delayed primary resistances' tended to occur when the reality of colonial occupation had destroyed early African delusions about its beneficent nature and intention, especially in 'settler territories' such as Rhodesia. Even when still primary in their structure and ideology, many delayed resistances also revealed an ability for reorganization and re-statement within new conditions, and in the face of new challenges. They were, in short, partly transitional to new types of adjustment. Thus the Ndebele and Shona peoples who rose against white settler expropriation in 1896–7 were able to use their old beliefs and systems in types of resistance that were no longer quite the same as in the past.

But here again the picture is confused and complex. In many cases these delayed resistances of a primary type were warlike and 'straightforward' in their aims, while in other cases they were not. No few of them took the traditional form of anti-witchcraft movements. Their aim was to call in the regenerative beliefs of the past against evils of the present that were barely understood in terms of what had really happened, or not so understood at all. Often it was seen only that the force of Evil had somehow got the upper hand: that maleficent witchcraft, whose rooting out was now deplorably forbidden by white rule, was freely roaming the land and seeking whom it might devour; and that the wise and proper course must therefore be to reactivate sanctions which the force of Good had enjoined in times before the coming of the whites.

Such ideas are a *leitmotiv* throughout the colonial period: but no longer, after the 1920s, a dominant one. Increasingly, types of primary resistance give way in the 1920s (and occasionally earlier) to kinds of adjustment that are new in content as well as form, and are genuine modifications derived from contact with the outside world. These one may call 'intermediate resistances' of action and reaction. They are the subtle link between the old charters – often still persuasive in their power to sway men's sense of what is right and wrong, of what should be defended and what should be attacked – and the new charters, national and modernizing, whose outline begins to take shape in the late 1930s and 1940s.

A further phase, preliminary to political independence, is reached with the practical embodiment of these new charters of nationalist assertion in the 1950s. Intermediate forms of resistance continue to have their effect: so too, as people defend themselves as well as they can or know how, do some of the primary forms. The history of the Belgian Congo, for example, suggests that primary and intermediate forms of action and reaction continue well into the 1950s, and with profound effect on the ideas and methods of Congolese nationalism. By the late 1940s, however, these older forms of resistance are fast merging in most British and French colonies into an entirely new apparatus of self-affirmation which consists in political parties, trade unions and, eventually, concepts of nation-statehood.

None of this occurred in isolation from colonial pressure or outside example. Searching for exits from a subjection that was far more than physical or economic, Africans took the deep imprint of what Hannah Arendt has called the 'tribal nationalism' of Europe. European rule had reduced the many hundreds of pre-colonial states to some four dozen colonies. Given the colonial framework of reference – especially for élites trained in Europe or instructed in Europo-centric history – it was perhaps necessary that the independence movements should have accepted a solution which supposed the transformation of these four dozen colonies into four dozen nations. Later years would show that this inheritance, once acquired by governing élites, was going to prove a severely retarding obstacle to the kind of wide federations or confederations which could alone give Africans a strong basis for industrial growth in many fields. But the colonial powers had no interest in promoting more rational forms of interterritorial unification. The question of achieving them was never really posed, though it was sometimes thought about.

Nor was this long transition a merely serial progression from one stage to the next, with one set of ideas neatly discarded in favour of another. Emergent élites might move to new positions: village folk often refused to move with them. Besides, the colonial impact varied greatly in form and force. Constitutional change towards renewed African equality became at least thinkable in many British territories early in the colonial period; so also, if later, in some of the French territories; at no time at all, and no matter what might be the African response, in those of Portugal. And then, throughout these years, there remained the force of old beliefs, especially of those which saw European incursion as a fundamental interference with the moral order; and these beliefs repeatedly made themselves felt.

Thus new resistances in the Congo, during the 1960s at a time of merely formal independence, could think it useful and even necessary to issue and use bullet-liquefying charms and spells. These magical aids drew their force not, or not mainly, from blind superstition, but from the belief of those involved that the war they were embarked upon was essentially a war for the restoration of a 'right and natural' order, which had suffered evil interruption.

In another context the same kind of historical influence may be traced among African nationalists in Rhodesia who have named their land Zimbabwe, in honour of their ancestors, and called their new war against the whites by the same name, Chi-Murenga, as during their resistance of 1896–7. In so doing they speak to reasonable ideas about the way the world used to be, and about the way, however changed in form and content, it ought to be again. They act in the spirit of Chaminuka, the grand ancestral spirit of their distant forefathers. 'We are going to Rhodesia', ran the words of an oath taken by freedom fighters in 1965, 'We are going to Rhodesia to fight so that we take our country, the country of Chaminuka, Chaminuka our lord. We shall never betray Chaminuka and Nehanda Nyagasikan. Whatever happens to us or to anybody, no matter how the situation develops, we shall never betray Chaminuka and Nehanda Nyagasikan.' The continuity is truly impressive, for it was to Chaminuka and his sister Nehanda that the old prophets of the Shona prayed in times long before any European had voyaged south of the Equator.

This continuity of belief makes the story of transition anything but simple. From primary, delayed primary, intermediate and later phases, but with many crossings and interminglings, it is a transition that gathers force in our own day and will hold the centre of the stage for at least the remainder of the twentieth century. It is a transition, too, that continues to change in form. Late in the 1960s the ideas of political reformism, of an assumed extension of European models in African guise, were already beginning to be questioned for their failings and inherent problems.

Now it became possible, here and there, to detect the emergence of another phase. The guerrillas in the Portuguese colony of Guinea might be few and their country very small: the nature of their experience, the quality of their ideas, the lessons they followed, could be inversely large in meaning. Under fresh coercive pressures – whether from the weakness or corruptibility of new ruling strata, from the various disillusionments of the 1960s, from the steep rise in population that was fast outstripping any comparable growth of production – it now appeared that the European models on the one hand, and, on the other, the ideological romanticism of an 'African personality', of an ideal 'African community', of an African socialism' somehow freed from the problems of its realization, were alike beginning to make way for a firmer grasp of reality. The years ahead will tell us more. What, meanwhile, can be learned about this continental process from the years that are past?

# 27 The Kings Resist

Peoples in contact with Europeans during the nineteenth century were aware of their danger. If nothing else, the history of the fire-arms trade had taught it to them. 'He who makes the powder', observed a king of Dahomey, warning his commercial officers to be patient with testy European visitors, 'wins the war.' The general approach of most of these kingdoms was to show enough strength to contain European ambitions within what were regarded as reasonable or inevitable limits, and then to make treaties of trade and friendship which, it was hoped, the Europeans would keep. Useful variations on this policy were found in playing off one set of Europeans against another. The kings fought only when all else failed.

Asante policy under Osei Bonsu (reg. 1801–24) displays primary resistance in many of its facets, both backward-glancing and forward-looking. The first British governor of the Gold Coast trading castles along the Asante coastline, Sir Charles Macarthy, thought Osei Bonsu a barbarian, and had little opportunity to learn better, for he lost his head in a disastrous battle with the Asante army in 1824. In monarchial terms, as it happened, Osei Bonsu was an unusually progressive ruler. He took over an empire, somewhat larger than modern Ghana, that was already beginning to outgrow its means of exercising central authority; and he tried to solve this problem by administrative reforms. In this he followed a notable predecessor, Osei Kwadwo (reg. 1764–?77), who had reinforced the central power by appointment of 'king's men' over against office-holders promoted by right of birth.

Osei Bonsu again strengthened royal control by creating three new stools of the Ankobia Stool, or, translating, three new departments of the imperial Ministry of Home Affairs. He improved the functioning of the Gyaasewa Stool, or Ministry of

Economic Affairs, by extending its activities and introducing the use of written records by Muslim clerks imported from the north. He professionalized the diplomatic service by making it fully appointive, and 'completed the conversion of the Cabinet or Privy Council from a fixed body of hereditary members to an *ad hoc* Council to which members were invited according to the nature of the business to be transacted'.

So far as imperial government was concerned – though less for the metropolitan provinces – 'by the middle of the reign of Osei Bonsu the preponderance of the old aristocracy in political affairs was completely shattered'. One may note in passing that these reforms were all undone after the British conquest in 1900. Then, 'without its king, without central government, Ashanti reverted to its pre-Kwadwoan segmentary structure, and only with the emergence of the Republic of Ghana in 1961 were some of the fundamental lines of Ashanti development once again to be taken up, adapted to a wider mid-twentieth-century context'. The interruption of the colonial period had put things back by more than a hundred years.

In the middle of this reforming reign, in 1817, British officials were invited to Kumasi from their base at Cape Coast; and a treaty of trade and friendship was signed with them. To Osei Bonsu the British, like the Dutch, were a remote people who had settled themselves in a few coastal forts upon the southern boundary of his domains. As such, they were of marginal importance in the balance of his imperial affairs. Advantageous in that they sold fire-arms and powder and bought gold and ivory, these Europeans were potentially irritating for their troublesome tendency to make alliance with coastal vassals in subversion of Asante authority. They should be mollified and made use of on a proper basis of exchange; but they should also be contained.

The remainder of the century played out a drama motivated by these principles of policy. In 1821 the British Government took over direct responsibility and possession of the British commercial forts and stations along the coast. In 1824 their first governor embarked on hostilities with an Asante army and was sharply defeated. In 1826 another clash went the other way. In 1831 a new treaty was signed. Rather more than thirty years later the story was repeated over again, but this time with the British and their coastal allies stronger than before, while Asante government had failed to find a peaceful way of integrating its southern vassals solidly within its imperial structure.

In 1872 the government at Kumasi finally gave way to imperialist agitation at home, and sent an army southwards under Amankwa Tia with orders to bring the coastal vassals to heel. This army suffered reverses, and was smitten with smallpox and dysentery. General Tia asked for permission to break off the campaign. But the Asante king had no wish to preside over a defeat in a war that he had previously opposed. By now his own prestige was at stake. 'You wished for war,' he replied, withholding his permission, 'and you have it. You swore you would not return till you could bring me the walls of Cape Coast, and now you want me to recall you because many chiefs have fallen and you are suffering.'

Faced with this refusal, Amankwa Tia tried his own hand at negotiation. He intercepted three warlike ultimata from the British commander, Sir Garnet Wolseley, and wrote a conciliatory reply. He pointed out that there could be peace if only the British would stop supporting Asante's breakaway subjects, on this occasion the small near-coastal states of Asin, Denkyira, Akim and Wassaw. 'Those four nations belong to the King of Ashantee and they refused to serve the King, and they escaped unto you' – that is, to the military protection of the British forces centred on Cape Coast. 'But the King did not send me into Cape Coast, and when you deliver Asin, Denkyira, Akim and Wassaw unto me' – in other words, their chiefs and commanders – 'I shall bring unto the King that there is no quarrel with you: I send my love to you ...'

But Wolseley had arrived to 'take command of the situation', and proceeded on his way. Underestimating his task, he began the invasion of Asante. It proved a difficult campaign, 'the most horrible war', Wolseley afterwards affirmed from a considerable experience of foreign battlefields, 'that I ever took part in'. Eventually his troops struggled into Kumasi, which they fired, but found no king, no government, and precious little loot. Theoretically the war was won, but back in London, ruefully reciting the cost, there were official voices who once again argued for

British evacuation of the whole country. Yet if evacuation had seemed 'impossible' in face of British public opinion before the war, it appeared even more so now. Retiring from Kumasi, the British stayed in the south. The Asante rebuilt their capital and once more tried their policy of containment and resistance. They were overcome by another British invasion in 1900.

The same pattern occurred elsewhere, perhaps nowhere more clearly than in the western Sudan.

Here, after the 1840s, the scene was dominated by the efforts of al-Hajj Umar bin Said, a Tucolor of Futa Toro in northern Senegal, to build a new empire from the successor states of the vanished but still venerated imperial structure of Mali. Like the kings of Asante, Umar had no objection to European presence along a distant coastline which he could never claim to control as Asante claimed most of the Gold Coast. In 1848 he suggested to the French on the Senegal seaboard that they should give him a trading monopoly in imported fire-arms against a grant of free movement for French merchants through the interior. But the French, like the British, were no longer much interested in conciliation: they were beginning to think of conquest. They refused the offer and pressed on inland. Umar stayed with his policy of containment and resistance. As late as 1855, discounting the force of an imperialism that was now becoming popular in France, he observed that 'the whites are only traders. Let them bring merchandise in their ships, let them pay me with a good stipend (*tribut*) . . . and I will live in peace with them.'

It must have seemed a reasonable policy. It was backed, after all, by years of experience which had generally confirmed its estimate of the balance of power. Europeans had traded on the Senegal coast for centuries, and never shown any concern for conquering the interior. But Umar's policy failed to account for the 'unreason' of the new imperialism. The French kept up their pressure. Umar died in 1864 and was succeeded at the head of a grasslands empire by his son Ahmadu, king of Segu on the middle Niger. Ahmadu continued with his father's policy. He fought the French when he had to, but tried for peace. A general treaty of trade and friendship, signed in 1866, allowed commercial privileges to the French while forbidding them to build forts in Ahmadu's dominions. Ahmadu spoke for other rulers of his time when he drily remarked that the difference between the two sides was that 'we like the French but do not trust them, while they trust us but do not like us'. Seldom perhaps was the temper of this European imperialism, powered increasingly by a racialist contempt not felt by Africans for Europeans, more accurately described.

Containment proved impossible. Resistance was bitterly maintained for many years, and was finally overcome by the French in campaigns of much bloodshed, culminating in the fearful expeditions of Voulet and Chanoine in the 1890s. This deplorable pair, condemned in France but anticipating other settlers and soldiers whether French or not, 'left a trail of fire and blood behind them as they burnt villages and executed friends and foes alike'.

Later apologists for conquest might meditate a little on Voulet and Chanoine. They were exceptional in Africa for the scale of their brutality, but they were not unique. What was said about them could have been said, and sometimes was, about no few others in this business of invasion. 'Cruel, violent, undisciplined, degraded by colonial life,' wrote a French observer in 1899,

the officer in the Sudan ... suffers from promotion madness ... Men like these, left as masters of countries where distance and communications render control of them impossible ... become real monsters ... The exercise of unfettered command, the opportunity for abuses of the most appalling sort, without the least fear of punishment, make them hard on the native and impatient of their orders ... The Voulet affair is absolutely typical, in that it is the monstrous but logical culmination of such habits.

The very ferocity of some of these conquests was to have its effect on the pace and possibility of African adjustment.

What happened to Ahmadu likewise struck down another strong figure of those years, the Almany Samori Turay. He, too, fashioning a new state in the rolling country between the forest fringe and the Niger grasslands, sought to contain the French by treaties of trade and friendship, and to fight them off when they refused to be contained. But he, too, fell victim to an imperialist appetite that now demanded full possession.

Like Osei Bonsu in Ashanti half a century earlier, Samori was an innovator: 'more of an innovator than a preserver', in one recent opinion, since 'he was in the process of bringing a fundamental change both to the patterns of society as well as to political and economic organization'. In contrast with al-Hajj Umar who had stood foursquare in the old Muslim tradition, Samori was to this extent one of those late-nineteenth-century rulers who may be seen as pioneers of nation-statehood. His political system has been said to have contained 'most of the apparently essential ingredients of the modern state: a complex and detailed administration run by an appointive bureaucracy ... an efficient and loyal standing army ... and finally an unambiguous focal point for loyalty and an unmistakable single source of effective power'. This may be claiming too much for Samori and his system: it remains, however, that his state took shape on new principles of organization. Even within the language of religion, the unity of ancestors was giving way to the unity of secular control.

Among the 'small societies', the segmentaries, general reaction to European arrival was much the same as in the centralized states, but the product of a different rationale. What the segmentaries looked for, now as in the past, was to be left alone by the various powers around them. If they had to accept 'protection' they preferred a superior power who would leave them, if necessary against tribute payment, to their own devices. They were ready to buy peace, but they wanted fair value for its price. If the superior power in question was distant, or even foreign to the land, so much the better. If its agents made all sorts of grandiose promises, better still: the promises might not be worth much, at least they might be worth something. None of the eager European crooks, speculators, careerists or men of principle who travelled into Africa in search of 'treaties' ever found much difficulty in getting them from the segmentaries.

But these treaties of protection turned out to mean one thing for the 'small societies' and another for the Europeans. For the former they might suggest a possibility of gain and a reinsurance against loss; but for the Europeans they were intended, as against other Europeans, to establish 'effective presence' in preparation for territorial enclosure. As soon as this became clear, the segmentaries fought back. Having no central power which left them leaderless when overthrown, the segmentaries sometimes fought harder and longer than the centralized states: their battles of defence may have been smaller, often no more than stiff little skirmishes between a few dozen men on either side, but they were probably more numerous.

After about 1890 there emerged a general realization that the nature of European intentions was quite different from what the Europeans had said. Much oral tradition reflects this awakening to reality. Literary sources for contemporary African opinion are still rare outside the writings of those few Africans who had managed to secure a Christian and therefore literate education. They may become less rare as more is known about the Muslim literature of that period. No doubt the case of al-Hajj Umar of Kete Krachi – not to be confused with the Umar bin Said of fifty years earlier – will not prove unique. Until the scholars of Ghana University came upon his trail a few years ago, nothing was known outside his own culture about this important poet and pedagogue. Yet it seems that al-Hajj Umar of Kete Krachi, a trading town of northern Ghana, was a writer of influence and talent, and well able to stand among the notables of Sudanese learning since remote times.

He wrote a great deal. Living until 1894 in Salaga, that 'Timbuktu of the south' which had inherited much of the old intermediary trade between the central forests of west Africa and the central Sudan, he had good reason to know about the movements and pressures of the French, the British and the Germans. In one of his poems, composed in 1900–1901, he 'enumerates their mistreatments of Africans in more than two hundred places on the coasts and in the interior of West Africa', and says:

I've set out this poem in rhyme ...
For the profit of intelligent folk ...
Anyone with brains will heed it ...
A sun of disaster has arisen in the West.
Glaring down on people and populated places.
Poetically speaking, I mean the catastrophe of the Christians.
The Christian calamity has come upon us
Like a dust-cloud.

At the start of the affair, they came
Peacefully.
With soft sweet talk.
'We've come to trade,' they said,
'To reform the beliefs of the people,'
'To halt oppression here below, and theft,'
'To clean up and overthrow corruption.'
Not all of us grasped their motives,
So now we've become their inferiors.
They deluded us with little gifts
And fed us tasty foods . . .
But recently they've changed their tune . . .

Anyone who probes the story of these years, as research is now beginning to reveal it, will see the themes of containment and resistance played out repeatedly by kings and chiefs and village governments who tried in their several ways to reduce or absorb European penetration. In the end the Europeans were the masters because they always possessed superior military means and organization, though by no means always able to bring these into action. But primary resistance was widespread, stubborn, and prolonged. And when primary resistance failed, men turned to other ways of self-defence, and tried again to defy the fate which had come upon them.

A fine example from Lamu, north-eastern Kenya, of a *siwa*, or ceremonial horn that was part of regalia in the coastal states of Kenya and Tanzania. Ivory: about 2 m long

# 28 Twilight of the Old Gods

A South African lady writer living in London completed an angry novel in February 1897, and sent it to Fisher Unwin, who bravely launched her book upon an unsuspecting public. Some years earlier Olive Schreiner had made an agreeable reputation with an autobiographical novel of life on a South African farm, a simple and yet lyrical account of rustic fortitude and human error. People had spoken of a South African Brontë, and had hoped for more.

But her new book, *Trooper Peter Halket of Mashonaland*, was received with regret, even with a sense of outrage. It was unashamedly political. It bitterly deplored what Englishmen were doing in the newly discovered lands north of the Limpopo river. Many were shocked by the frontispiece, a photograph which showed white farmers in Matabeleland standing with evident satisfaction, as a good day's work well done, round a tree from whose branches three Africans were hanging by the neck.

Critics disliked this brash excursion into politics under the guise of art, while the residents of South Kensington, where it was stated in the preface that the author was living, were startled to discover a neighbour of such virulence, not to say doubtful patriotism. Miss Schreiner's new book was considered in the worst of taste and really quite hysterical, suggesting as it did that if Christ the Lord came back to earth He would actually support the Matabele and Mashona, and not the English. This was far more of a new thought then than later, and it was appreciated even less. Bold men who had gone out to civilize Africa at the risk of their lives should not, it was said, be attacked in this way, even if some of them might be wild fellows not too nice in their methods: for you cannot, after all, make an omelette without breaking eggs.

Today one can see all this rather differently.

In 1893 the Ndebele or 'Matabele' cattle-raising state in the western and west-central areas of what would become Southern Rhodesia was invaded by troops of the British South Africa Company. This armed occupation of 'Matabeleland' had been initially undertaken to establish control of a country thought to be rich in minerals, especially gold; but the nature of the occupation changed almost from the start. Soldier-settlers were determined to have land and cattle, no matter what Rhodes and his fellow-capitalists might do about mines and railways. There followed an African disaster far worse than the Ndebele leaders had imagined in their darkest moments. In the three years between 1893 and 1896, Matabeleland

witnessed a dispossession of Africans and a development of white enterprise unparalleled anywhere else in Central and East Africa ... Virtually the whole of Ndebele land and by far the greater part of Ndebele cattle passed into white hands. Here an African economic system was taken notice of; and having been noticed was expropriated.

In some ways it was even worse in the east central and eastern areas of the country, 'Mashonaland', where Shona-speaking people had lived for more than a millennium. Here there was no conquest but gradual infiltration of settlers after 1890 together with a handful of administrative agents of Rhodes's Company. They came seeking gold; and the Shona appear to have thought that as soon as they had taken all the gold they could find, a matter of no great moment to the Shona themselves, these little groups of white men would go away again. But no: the gold-seekers turned into farmers, and the farmers, needing land and labour, took both with a free hand. The Shona found they had become a subject people by virtue of promulgations in a distant country, and then by force of European guns.

White attempts at administration were at first quite mimimal. So as to get it on the cheap, the exercise of law and order was handed by the Company to the settlers themselves. Regarding the Shona as 'cowardly and miserable niggers', the settlers behaved as one would expect. Backed by mercenary police, they behaved so badly that even the Company felt obliged to do something about it. Special Commissioners were appointed. They met with a difficult task. 'I found that I had to try and gain the confidence of natives that they might not run away on the sight of a white man,' wrote one of these Commissioners: 'They were very timid, especially the women. The reason for this appeared to be on account of some of the police formerly stationed there making a practice of assaulting and raping any native woman they found in the veld alone.'

Punitive expeditions became the order of the day. 'We then proceeded down the valley', recalled this same Commissioner, 'in search of something to destroy.' Chiefs had refused to pay the new hut tax, had taken back cattle already made in payment of it, and had fired on a Native Commissioner's messengers. Chief Native Commissioner Brabant thought he should teach them a lesson. 'The police boys and messengers and camp followers scattered over the hills and burnt down all the kraals they came across until the whole atmosphere was dense with smoke of burning rapoko and other corn and grass', while the whites passed the time in 'a pig-sticking match on foot and horseback'.

Flogging became a matter of course, forced labour a familiar routine. Even the missionaries, whose writings reveal a fairly general thought that God would welcome a 'strong hand' in aid against heathen who stubbornly preferred their own religion to the blessings of Christianity, were moved to protest. 'We hold', some of them wrote in early 1896, 'that the plan of sending native constables through the country collecting the natives by armed force, compelling them to labour here and there, wherever their services happen to be required ... their wives being seized as hostages in case they attempt to escape, is unjust and government has no right thus to arrest and impress natives.'

But the settlers and their Company government saw nothing particularly wrong with this 'plan'. After all, it was only a projection of the South African system within which they had formed their ideas of right and wrong. Besides, no other 'plan' seemed feasible if settlement was going to be made to pay; and what was feasible, in their view, could not be misconceived. In any case the natives deserved no better: by now they were a broken lot, or at least a beaten one.

Or so it was believed. The awakening to reality proved harsh. In March 1896 the Ndebele rose with their spears and guns, and cleared the greater part of their country. Within a week of their rising, 'not a white man was left alive in the outlying districts of Matabeleland whilst the survivors were confined to the laagers of Bulawayo, Gwelo, Belingwe, and Tuli'. Only after nine months of warfare could the Company again win the upper hand. Then the Ndebele chiefs accepted peace on conditions which left them and their people somewhat less badly off than before.

But another surprise had already occurred. In June 1896, to the shattered disbelief of Europeans who were sure that this 'down-trodden' people would never again lift a hand in anger, the Shona joined the Ndebele in driving out the settlers and restoring an independence which, in fact, they had never admitted to having lost. And the Shona continued fighting long after the Ndebele accepted peace. Not until April 1898, or nearly two years after they had begun, was their rising finally quenched. The quenching was ruthless: what followed after Miss Schreiner's book was published proved even sorrier than what had gone before.

This old and famous story yields two points that should concern us here. The first is on the nature of these wars of resistance; the second on their place in the broader spectrum of African self-defence during the past hundred years.

These wars were of the 'delayed primary' type in that their inspiration and ideology fell within the traditional framework. As some of the more perceptive Europeans began to see in the course of the risings, they could be described as wars not only of self-defence but also of religion. They drew their strength from spiritual loyalties attached to ancestral charters. They called men to action in answer to the commands of God, whether through the ancient cult of Mwari in the western area or through oracles long venerated in the eastern area.

Not only that. Though the cults were Shona in origin, they found a hearing among the Ndebele as well. Exceedingly old, they were the cults of the Rozwi chiefs of the fifteenth century, and no doubt much earlier. They rested on the political achievements of Shona statehood in the past. Moving in from the south in recent times, the Ndebele had taken Shona land and cattle but had made their peace with these strong ancestral spirits. So it came about that the priestly leaders of the risings, men such as Mkwati in the west and the Nehanda medium in the east, could speak in terms of Shona religion that Ndebele as well as Shona would respect and many would heed. What they said, essentially, was that the evil under which the land now suffered by the hand of Europeans was the fruit of maleficent interruption of God's natural order. Restoration would be possible only when the instruments of that interruption, the Europeans, were driven out or reduced to impotence: such was the message of the ancestral spirits. The wars might be fought with guns on either side as well as African spears. They might be conducted by methods of warfare that were sometimes decidedly new. They might be addressed to the righting of wrongs unknown a few years earlier. But they remained traditional in their inner drive and conception.

These matters were not understood by Europeans. Then and later, the priestly strategists of the risings were generally written off as 'fraudulent agitators', or, alternatively, as crazy wizards of the Rider Haggard school of romantic fiction. Only with Ranger's work in the 1960s does the fuller picture come clearly through. Now it can be seen that these exotic mystics were men of unusual political gifts who worked within a framework of belief and action which had long proved their worth.

Though primary, their resistance also had an 'intermediate' aspect. At least some of the leaders of the risings appear to have glimpsed the outline of new forms of society. They were not blind to what was going on around them. God had given them the land by virtue of their ancestors; but God had also brought other things – all those other things that the Europeans possessed: new kinds of useful goods, new kinds of useful knowledge. These new things had fallen into the hands of their oppressors. Only by remedial action could they be re-directed into African hands. Through the story of the risings there winds a stubbornly millennial theme, somewhat reminiscent of the 'cargo cults' of Melanesia and elsewhere: men were urged to reject all these European goods so that, in God's own time, they could and would become the goods of the Africans as well. Mkwati and his fellow-strategists were firm that their warriors should kill Europeans but never take European things for themselves: all captured goods were to be delivered – and large quantities were so delivered – to the shrines where God or the ancestral spirits spoke through their intermediaries on Earth.

There is likewise evidence that some of the leading mediums were already thinking, by the end of 1896, in terms of restoring the old Rozwi confederacy in ways such as could take account of these new things. Their programme, Ranger thinks, 'was in some ways revolutionary in its vision of society'. There was repudiation of white mastery but also 'a longing for African control of modern sources of wealth and power in an African environment'. The Ndebele-Shona risings may thus be said to have displayed an effort at containment and resistance within the old frameworks, but also, and more emphatically as the months passed by, an attempt at accommodation to a different world.

Complex and various in form, this evolution from primary to intermediate resistance also occurred elsewhere.

During the 1890s imperial Germany began to establish a colony in the far south-western lands of the Herero and Nama. Again the initial encroachments were accompanied by the tricks and evasions which had distinguished some of the more important 'treaties' signed by Rhodes's agents north of the Limpopo and Zambezi. Here again missionaries played the same part as men like Coillard among the Lozi in helping to open the road to the businessmen, who in turn opened it to the soldiers. It was a member of the Rhenish Mission who persuaded the Nama chief Joseph Fredericks to sign the two initial treaties with the businessman Lüderitz. These made over possession of the land round the bay of Angra Pequena, and, secondly, of a coastal strip about 200 miles long.

This coastal strip was defined in the second of these treaties as being 'twenty miles in breadth'. But what was 'twenty miles'? The Nama thought it meant twenty English miles, the only kind they knew of, while the Germans were determined to make it mean twenty German miles, this German mile being equal to 4⅘ English miles. 'But let Joseph Fredericks go on thinking for the time being,' Lüderitz wrote in 1884, 'that we mean English miles.' Later on, as Imperial Commissioner Goering (father of the Nazi leader Hermann Goering) reported to Berlin, this Nama group 'heard with horror that according to the text of the treaty they had sold almost their whole country ...' Which did not prevent Commissioner Goering from trying to make the treaty stick.

North of the Nama, the Herero chiefs likewise 'sold' huge tracts of land to German companies and settlers. Badly hit by rinderpest in the early 1890s, they needed a helping hand and barely glanced at where it might be coming from. Perhaps they should have known better, and yet fraud on this scale was something they had not met before. They sold their land mostly for a song. It appears from the imperial German records that settlers were able to acquire it, by juggling with the price of goods they gave in exchange, for half a mark or even less per hectare (2·2 acres). By 1903 the Germans had obtained formal ownership of a total of 336,000 square kilometres, including much of the best farming land in South-West Africa.

Like the Ndebele, the Herero also lost most of their cattle by strong-arm seizure, fraudulent trade or other dubious means. Before the coming of these Germans the Herero as a whole may have grazed about 100,000 head of cattle. By 1902 the situation was such that about 80,000 Herero possessed about 46,000 head, while a few hundred German settlers, having arrived ten years earlier with empty hands, had got hold of about 45,000 head. Another estimate made early in 1904 showed the value of settler property as being worth around twenty million marks, of which some fourteen million were in cattle.

On 12 January 1904 the Herero took to arms, uniting their lineage groups under Samuel Maherero, and fought battles with the German army and settler volunteers until their power of resistance was finally overwhelmed about a year later. Few colonial wars have deserved the name of genocide: this one does. General von Trotha drove the surviving Herero regiments and their women and children, the remnants of a whole people, deliberately into the waterless sands of the Omaheke. Only a tiny number survived. About 1,200 got away into British Bechuanaland next door, while a larger but still very small number broke back westward through the German blockade into eventual captivity.

Like the Shona a few years earlier, the Nama bided their time while the Herero fought. They took to arms only towards the end of 1904, thus missing the chance of united action. But once they had begun they proved, again like the Shona, a hard enemy to beat. They were broken only three years later, and were handled grimly. Estimates based on official statistics indicate that 'by 1911 only 15,130 Herero remained alive of their former total of about 80,000 and only 9,781 Nama out of about 20,000'. All in all, four-fifths of the Herero and half of the Nama had died. 'Even the Bergdama, who had taken no part at all in these wars, lost almost a third of their total, German troops being unable to distinguish between them and the Herero.'

Too little work has been done on these events to enable any sociological analysis of methods of organization on the African side. They appear to fall within the terms of delayed-primary resistance, but show some evidence of being intermediate as well. The Herero were able to realize an unaccustomed unity of action in face of an entirely new kind of peril; and so to a lesser degree were the Nama. On the Nama side the guerrilla leader Jacob Morenga emerges very much as a modernizing figure. His tactical skills came to be greatly respected.

Even the German army was forced to applaud Morenga's tactical ability. Captain Bayer of the General Staff, for example, thought that Morenga had 'by means of criss-cross moves, clever surprise attacks, and, above all, through the influences on his followers or his outstanding personality, prolonged the war and done us incalculable damage . . . His conduct of the war had something grand about it and in its form was far superior to that of all the other native leaders. Altogether he was an outstanding soldier to whom we as the enemy do not wish to deny our respect.'

Perhaps we may yet see his memory renewed by a 'Morenga Battalion' in the coming wars of southern Africa.

Another clear example of 'delayed primary-intermediate' reaction to the beginning of the colonial period was the Maji Maji war, also against the Germans, in the Tanganyika of 1905–7. Before it was over a large number of ethnic groups, living in the area of about a million people, were drawn into common action under a more or less unified leadership. Few of these groups had shown any previous resistance to European infiltration: like others, no doubt, they had misunderstood the nature of the process. None of them appears ever to have achieved, or seen any point in trying to achieve, an effective unity of action during earlier times.

What these segmentaries – the Pogoro, Mbunga and others – now did was to forge a unity for defensive war through spirit mediums, notably of a cult called Kolelo. This cult appears to have been perfectly within the structure of pre-colonial society in that its chief object was to safeguard the ideal and ancestral equilibrium by hunting out witches, and thus expelling evil. According to one account, it was believed that 'the creator, Mungo, had sent Kolelo [a great snake] "to restore order to all that is corrupted here on earth" '.

Yet the context, and what came out of the Kolelo cult, were new. For what was 'corrupted here on earth' was the doing of the Europeans, who caused hardship, extracted taxes never known before, and dispossessed people. So Kolelo forbade the paying of taxes, and foretold that a great flood would soon destroy the whites and all their works. Thus empowered, the revolt spread from one people to the next, and much fighting was needed before the Germans could overcome it. Nothing like this had occurred before. Yet the Maji Maji alliance – so named after Kolelo's 'water medicine' carried by his priests or spokesmen from village to village, binding men to action – was still locked within its traditional ideology. It might point to a future alliance of many peoples against colonial rule. Its cultural ground lay in the past.

This was the ambivalence in thought and action whose range of possibilities was to be exploited by many peoples as the realities of colonial rule became apparent. Some of them, such as the Nandi and Masai, were able to evolve new forms of inter-lineage unity by means of priestly leaders whose influence rested partly in religion and partly in the pressure of new grievances.

Others acquired new leaders. In 1913, for example, the Kenya Luo gave birth to a cult of Mumbo whose aims were manifestly political in a sense that was new. It enjoyed considerable success, and its leaders were eventually exiled by the British in 1919. With Mumbo, moving into forms of resistance intermediate between past and future, there came also the first faint fore-shadowings of modern nationalism: of the ideas linked to the slogan, coined in the 1890s by non-conformist missionaries in Nyasaland, of 'Africa for the Africans'.

Go and tell all Africans ...' the serpent god Mumbo commanded his medium, a Luo named Onyango Dunde, 'that from henceforth I am their God. Those whom I choose personally and also those who acknowledge me, will live forever in plenty ... The Christian religion is rotten and so is its practice of making its believers wear clothes. My followers must let their hair grow – never cutting it. Their clothes shall be the skins of goats and cattle and they must never wash. All Europeans are your enemies, but the time is shortly coming when they will all disappear from our country.

Mumbo's leaders 'preached a complete rejection of everything European and a return to the African way of life. They promised a new "golden age" of plenty that was to be attained as a result of the complete transformation of society.' The themes of Mumbo may thus relate, if indirectly, to what happened in the 1950s in the forests of the Aberdares and Mount Kenya, during a much greater movement of resistance. The serpent god's mediums might speak the millennarian language of the prophets, of the Shona priests of Mwari and Nehanda, and of countless others in other African lands: but they looked forward, however confusedly, to the nationalist inheritance of half a century later.

As the colonial years passed by, there came a shifting of the ideological ground. At least among those who made the running, ideas of Christianity partly displaced those of traditional religion. Within the context of European rule, however, these Christian ideas acquired a tone and accent that were very different from their European projection. They became emphatically political, and persistently millennial. They preached the coming of the Millennium, of a time of happiness and benign government 'on

Earth as it is in Heaven'. They spoke and hoped in terms that other dispossessed Christians had used or nourished in other times and places, promising a New Jerusalem free of the yoke of oppressors who had 'spoiled the land'.

And so the twilight of the old gods merged with a new illumination. This was to light the way through strange and sometimes desperate paths. Yet it did light the way. Even where the essential springs of protest remained as before – in the belief that Good must actively be helped to expel Evil – the framework ever more consciously acquired a modern context, language and deployment of ideas. There came the birth of separatist Christian churches where the Christian God became African: a God more potent than Mumbo and his kind because he was a modern deity acknowledged by power-wielding Europeans, but none the less a God who would give Africa back to the Africans.

With this ideological shift the intense – and intensely activist – religiosity of these peoples found new beliefs. These stood rooted in the old, and yet were no longer the same as the old. For the new churches looked to a different future: they became, in territory after territory, the foster-parents of the politics of later years. Nothing if not complex, this was a process little studied until very recent times and even less understood.

## 29   New Redeemers

The directly political implications of African Christianity were generally deplored by European Christians. Taking their own possession of the temple for granted, Jesus having long become an honorary European, they were pained by this unruly clamour in the back rows of the congregation. One can understand their feelings. They had opened the doors, after all, and now the flock was making trouble. Had these natives no sense of gratitude?

Yet the political emphasis of African Christianity was of a piece with all African attitudes to religion. The pact with the ancestors might be conceived in suprasensible terms; its *practical* character as a guide to the affairs of everyday life, whether moral, social or political, had never been in doubt. With the spread of Christian ideas, religion and politics continued to march hand in hand. They nourished each other as before. But now they marched towards ever more serious clashes with authority.

Some of these became notorious. There was the case of Pastor Enoch Mgijima's Children of Israel in South Africa soon after the first world war. South Africa in those days was not yet ruled by any system of legalized *apartheid*, of 'separate development'. But a great deal of legal discrimination against Africans, especially in the matter of land disposal, was already on the statute book. In 1921 the Children of Israel built a settlement on the Bulhoek commonage in the Ciskei area of Cape Province, a good country where the foothills of the Drakensberg pile in blue enchantment to a far horizon. This was now land forbidden to African settlement. The Israelites were ordered to move on. They refused. They were ordered again, and still refused. On 5 May 1921 the government of General Smuts sent in troops to clear the Bulhoek commonage, and the troops opened fire, killing 163 and wounding 129 of these perversely stubborn Christians. A few of the remainder were moved on into prison; most were sent to the newly created Native Reserves.

For those days it was not a particularly rare incident. Africa knew many upheavals against colonial law; and many little massacres were quietly conducted in repressing them. South Africa perhaps had more of these than most, even under the reputedly liberal regime of General Smuts. Much has been said in praise of General Smuts. Not everyone saw him in that light. There were others who preferred the mordant judgement of the white South African poet Roy Campbell, who greeted the appearance of Smuts's book of philosophy with four scathing lines in memory of the shootings of the Israelites and of a South-West African people called the Bondelswaart:

> The love of Nature burning in his heart,
> Our new Saint Francis offers us his book –
> The Saint who fed the birds at Bondelswaart
> And fattened up the vultures at Bulhoek.

By 1921, the Israelites had a long heritage of African resistance. Through most of the nineteenth century the peoples of the Cape Province, such as the Xhosa and their neighbours, had fought repeatedly in defence of the lands where their ancestors had settled. Like others who were gradually overcome by superior fire-power and military organization, they had also looked for spiritual explanations of a long disaster. They had asked themselves why their appointed ancestors, their intermediaries with God, should have thus withheld a saving arm. Like others, they had found the answer in their own failings of devotion. Evil had triumphed because they had neglected the service of Good.

The Xhosa of the 1850s provide a startling example. Prolonged drought and cattle sickness, coupled with military pressure by Europeans, saw the rise among them of a new prophet, Mhlakaza. This intermediary with God had visions of royal ancestors. They told him they had seen the misery of Xhosa subjection, and would come to save their people. But the people must first of all turn away from bad things. More, they should make a supreme sacrifice in expiation of their sins. Not only must witchcraft be hunted out, but the Xhosa should also slaughter their cattle, destroy the corn in their granaries, and stop working their fields. To those who obeyed there were promised new stocks of grain and cattle, the restoration of the power of the ancestors, and the eviction of the Europeans whose goods the Xhosa would then enjoy as well. In slightly different guise, it was essentially the message of the Shona mediums of forty years later, of Mumbo among the Luo later still, and of many others of the same kind: the recognition of new times and of a need for new masteries over nature, but couched firmly within the ancestral framework.

Characteristically for such movements, a Day of Judgement was fixed: 18 February 1857. Then the sun would break in pieces and the ancestors, carried in a mighty whirlwind but armed only with spears, would sweep away the Europeans and punish those who had served them. Awaiting this salvation, the Xhosa obeyed. In a desperate effort at self-regeneration they slaughtered between 150,000 and 200,000 head of stock. Thousands of people on the Day of Salvation found only the prospect of death by famine. But the failure of the ancestors carried off more than their hopes or their health. It killed for a long time their means of further resistance.

The European triumph was apparently complete. And in the wake of this calamity, as in the wake of other if less ruinous ancestral failures in other African lands, Christian missionaries began to find a wider audience. New mission stations were founded, especially by churches favourable to the training of a native priesthood. This pushed things a step further, for with this, if hesitantly, there came the ideological shift from one form of religion to another, and a consequent readjustment in political thought. There arose the idea of a Christianity which could be independent of European pastors who seemed hand in glove with European policemen and soldiers. It was significant of this new thinking that thousands of African Christians, during the last 'kaffir war', should have joined the ranks of their non-Christian fellow countrymen in armed defence of their pastures as their fathers and grandfathers had done. And being to some extent 'detribalized' – a term now becoming popular with Europeans when referring to Africans who could see beyond the limits of tradition – these African Christians were able sometimes to promote a new unity among threatened peoples.

From there it was only a step to separate African churches whose implications were far more clearly political. There emerged what Theal, the white South African historian, called 'the beginning of that pernicious revolt against European guidance, now known as the Ethiopian movement'. With its ideological roots in the biblical prophecy that 'Ethiopia shall soon stretch forth its hands to God' – equating 'Ethiopia' with Africa – Ethiopianism developed what Shepperson has called 'a general process of African reaction to European culture'.

This took shape in many separatist Christian movements. Early among these was the Tembu Church of South Africa, founded in 1884 by the Reverend Nehemia Tile under the aegis of the Tembu paramount chief Ngangelizwe. Eight years later James Mata Dwane founded his Ethiopian Church. A third South African breakaway was that of the Reverend P. Nzimba and his Bantu Presbyterian Church among the Fingo. Others followed, Enoch Mgijima's Bulhoek Israelites among them.

With the Israelites and their contemporaries, the clash became sharper. They were faced with the gathering attrition of white South African government after withdrawal of British imperial control in 1910. Enoch Mgijima began his mission at a moment when the Land Act of 1913 had barred nine-tenths of all South Africa to African settlement, an expropriation which proved catalytic in its consequences. There followed 'an effervescence of new and apocalyptic Messianic Separatist Churches in the fateful years when the Bantu population woke up to find what had happened to them'. Now the clash became immediate and direct, and a bitter price was exacted from the Israelites for defiance of the law which had dispossessed them. From then onward the gulf between white and black, carefully excavated by one legalized discrimination after another, has continued to widen almost year by year.

The line which leads from ancestral oracles to African churches – what has been called 'the passage from prophets to leaders of sects' – may at times be hard to see. Yet it runs unbroken through these harassing years, moving by many half-hidden or un-acknowledged paths through the pain of defeat, the misery of expropriation, the gradual dismantlement of village life that followed on the continual pumping out of migrant labour, the chaos of peri-urban settlement in 'native locations' piled at the entry of the white men's towns, and much else beside. The answers previously sought at ancestral shrines were increasingly asked at Christian altars, and were increasingly political in content. And steadily, whether through Ethiopianism or other forms of new response, there came a new identification of Christian and non-Christian belief in the possibility of acting to obtain divine succour and protection.

This Christian-'pagan' identification of fundamental belief seems particularly clear in the British protectorate of Nyasaland, which is now Malawi. Here there were developments which deeply influenced the whole of central southern Africa and perhaps territories still further afield. For it was in Nyasaland that two great streams of millennial belief, African and Christian, first flowed openly together, reinforced each other, and impelled a synthesis whose persuasive power was able to win multitudes of village people. The central movement embodied by this synthesis, though afterwards elaborated in derivative forms, was the African Watch Tower under the apocalyptic guidance of Kenan Kam-wana. This too has a history of its own, and a strange one.

In 1852, almost exactly when Mhlakaza of the Xhosa was getting ready to proclaim 1857 as the Year of Judgement when the ancestors would sweep Evil from the land and initiate a new Golden Age, there was born to Scots-Irish parents in Pittsburg, Pennsylvania, a child named Charles Taze Russell. With Russell there opened a remarkable interplay between the New World and the Old.

Russell was raised in a stern tradition of pessimistic noncon-formism. Humanity being what it lamentably was, nothing could be expected but a future of everlasting divine punishment for all who stood outside the ranks of the saved. The saved, it appeared, were depressingly few. As a young man, Russell found un-bearable the prospect of this wholesale and helpless damnation. He turned to the Scriptures for something less forbidding, and duly found it. He decided that Christ had actually returned to Earth in 1874 in order to sow the seeds of a new age. In a strange prediction he forecast that 'the buds will thrive but will bear no perfect fruit before October 1914 – the full end of "Gentile Times" ... The time of trouble or "day of wrath" which began October 1874 ... will cease about 1915.'

What would happen then was familiar in the millennial thought of northern Europe and northern America, but this time with a new twist for the unconverted. There would come the 'Battle of Armageddon, the Millennium, the Final Judgement, and the ultimate and everlasting reign of God's Kingdom, when the forces of Evil would be defeated, mankind purified and fitted for the Kingdom, and those unrepentant souls who had not taken advantage of [this] second chance would be consigned to final, irrevocable death'.

One may note in passing that the same 'revised tradition' has continued. It was renewed during the 1950s, this time in Islamic guise, by Elijah Muhammad and the Black Moslems of the United States. They prophesied world destruction between 1970 and 2000, but Allah would give eight to ten days' advance notice so that 'people will be given a chance to decide'. The Day of Judgement was to be sounded by 'a siren coming from a plane in the sky. It will be heard everywhere and it will be so loud that it will shake the earth. The plane will drop pamphlets written in Arabic and English and everyone will have between eight and ten days during which they may decide to get out of this hell. There will be people posted at strategic points to tell us where to go. These people will ask everyone which side they are on.'

A hundred years ago, however, there was a second new element in these teachings: they were carried into the work of a number of missionaries in central and southern Africa. These missionaries found comfort in Russell's message. They too had been discouraged by the thought that Africa's unconverted millions were bound to burn in hellfire for all eternity, simply because there were not enough missionaries to reach them in time. Among those who came to feel like this was an English nonconformist called Joseph Booth, a man of stubborn persistence in 'dangerous thoughts'. He was one of several who saw the need to establish an African Christianity in its own right, not merely as a kind of second-class antechamber to the European church; and his religion had accordingly taken a political turn. As early as 1897, with an African called John Chilembwe who was later to become famous, Booth set up a society dedicated:

> ... to pursue steadily and unswervingly the policy:
> 'AFRICA FOR THE AFRICANS'
> and look for and hasten by prayer and united effort
> the forming of a united
> AFRICAN CHRISTIAN NATION
> By God's power and blessing and in His own time and way.

Yet converts were hard to come by, and Booth grew saddened 'by the thought that all who were not brought to a knowledge and love of the Saviour were going to eternal torment ...; he felt sure that something was radically wrong with his message'. In this discouragement he was introduced to the teachings of Russell's Watch Tower Bible and Tract Society, and at once took fresh hope from the belief that even unconverted Africans could have a chance to escape the flames. He set to work in Nyasaland as an evangelist for Watch Tower teachings. In 1909 he claimed seventy-six followers.

Much flowed from Booth's work, though indirectly. One of those who came under his influence as early as 1900 was a man of the Lake Tonga people of Malawi, Kenan Kamwana.

Kamwana was among several outstanding African preachers in those years of trial and questioning who found it very possible to fit the ancestral principles of good and evil, and the millennial ideas they easily promoted, into a Christian framework; and, in so doing, to give these ideas new force and meaning in response to colonial pressures. What he preached with wide success was certainly apocalyptic, foreshadowing as it did the coming of a new age in 1914; but it was also revolutionary. 'Pointing to the [colonial governor's] Residency, he would say: "These people you soon will see no more ... We shall build our own ships, make our own powder, and make or import our own guns."' Understandably, the British authorities disliked this kind of talk. They arrested Kamwana in 1909 and sentenced him to deportation from Nyasaland until 1914: until, that is, 'the danger period of his prophecy had passed'.

But the seed had taken root. For long after 1914 the teachings of Watch Tower, whether directly or through other sects, could be heard in fulmination against authority, denying the payment of taxes and preaching the millennium for some later date. 'Look here Government', the founder of the Ana a Mulungu Church, or Church of the Children of God, is reported in the colonial police files as telling his followers in 1938, 'I and my Christian followers, starting from today we shall never pay tax for the British Kingdom.'

Released from exile only in 1937 but still true to his mission, Kenan Kamwana founded the Watchman's Society. According to the police files (and other illumination is not to hand), its message declared that 'We are the children of God and must therefore pay no attention to the laws of the *boma* [that is, of the colonial government] ... Be of courage for the time of trouble is near. People must not be afraid to break government laws.' Kamwana's message went on to add, echoing a resentment of European contempt that was to become powerful in the nationalism then about to come to birth, that: 'Nobody should remove his hat to the Provincial Commissioner or the District Commissioner. These gentlemen ... are pretenders.'

Many years earlier another pioneer, the African missionary Charles Domingo in Nyasaland, had said it still more frankly.

Poor Resident, he thinks too much of his skin and not of his heart. What is the difference between a white man and a black man? Are we not of the same blood and all from Adam? ... If we had power to communicate ourselves to Europe we would advise them not to call themselves 'Christendom' but 'Europeandom'.

Later on, the nationalist movements would acquire the necessary 'power of communication', and find their own ways of giving this advice.

In those years there were to be many movements which combined the beliefs of the past with those of a world where Christianity seemed to hold the key, and thereby married the ideology of anti-witchcraft with the promise of a new salvation. Another Malawi, Tomo Nyirenda, was prominent in one of them. With him the fundamental Christian-'pagan' identification of belief becomes extraordinarily clear. Wandering about in search of wage-labour, like countless other Africans set moving by colonial demands, Nyirenda came under Watch Tower influence in Northern Rhodesia during 1925.

Nyirenda accepted baptism and began to preach the Watch Tower message. But he gave it a traditional turn. He linked it with other ideas more or less explicit in the atmosphere of the time. 'Like others of similar belief, he foretold the arrival of Americans who would divide a great wealth among the baptized African elect. These Americans, he said, would drive away the white men and would help the Africans to enslave the remaining white women, all of whom would thereafter serve as porters ...': the rôles of black houseboy and white mistress-of-the-house were to be reversed. His followers would 'end taxation and welcome supplies of food that would fall from heaven'. At the Second Coming, which he advised his believers to await with patience, 'God would come through the trees in the middle of a shining light'.

Proclaiming himself Mwana Lesa, the Son of God, Nyirenda was soon in trouble with the authorities. One can blame the British in Northern Rhodesia no more than the Romans in Jerusalem: to them, with a somewhat slender hold on a territory always liable to give trouble, this kind of teaching was bound to be a nuisance. They watched with apprehension, and moved only when he brought in the second wing of his teaching. This was an anti-witchcraft campaign which he developed among the Lala of Chief Shaiwala's local jurisdiction. But the Son of God added a twist of his own. He turned baptism into a witchcraft test.

Not being modern Christians, or even Christians of any sort, the Lala were always open to belief that their troubles – and these were many in the 1920s – came from maleficent witchcraft. Chief Shaiwala and his people certainly thought so. But who were the witches? How track them down? Nyirenda came to their aid. He explained that the witches could be identified by their failure to achieve full immersion during baptism: if they 'floated' they were guilty and should be dealt with as such. This was tried, and with sad results.

'At first, those who remained "on top of the water" were merely ostracized by their fellow villagers.' But the number of witches grew alarmingly, 'and Chief Shaiwala urged the Mwana Lesa to remove them permanently from Lala society.' This he proceeded to do, and many unfortunates were killed. Yet Nyirenda's view of the matter was that he had done no more than he should. 'I killed those witches', he is reported to have said, 'because God is coming, and before God comes the witches must be killed to keep the villages clean.' No pious African could have disagreed with him on the principle of the thing.

But could Nyirenda have really thought himself the Son of God? There will have been no lack of charlatans. In Northern Rhodesia, afterwards Zambia, 'Luvale men' acquired a widespread reputation for their skills in the conjuror's art, not always exercised for fun. The following case, of a humble kind familiar in many parts of Africa, suggests at least a venerable pedigree of fraud. It happened that a Native Treasury clerk was 'down' in his accounts by about £70 of tax money. He could save his job only by applying for help to hard-pressed relatives. But at this point along comes a 'Luvale man' who claims a skill which can triple any quantity of money, provided the money be suitably 'treated'. Much relieved, the clerk agrees to put £500 of Native Treasury money in a closed box under his bed. In three weeks' time, says the Luvale man who helps him to stow away the money in the box, the clerk can open the lid and find £1,500: it simply cannot fail. But there is one condition. The clerk must not open the box before the three weeks are up. If he does, the money will 'fly away' and he will lose it all.

In this sad but true little story, you will guess what happens next. Anxiously impatient, the clerk opens the box almost at once. Sure enough, the money is gone. But it also happens that the Luvale man is still in town, perhaps expecting his victim to show a more respectful patience. Overtaken by a now frantic clerk, he replies: 'You opened it? Then of course the money has flown away. I told you it would.' Still deceived, the clerk is desperate. 'Well,' counsels the Luvale man, 'if I were you I would just go and get more money out of the Treasury. Then I will make the spells all over again – only this time you won't open the box for three weeks.' The clerk goes back to his office and lifts all the remaining money in the till, a little more than £600; and, with the assistance of the light-fingered Luvale man, the duly re-enchanted box is again put beneath his bed, this time until it can produce £1,800. The case against the clerk was heard in the courts not long afterwards.

It may be that the Mwana Lesa was another such Luvale man on a grander scale; but the records suggest otherwise. What the records suggest is that he and his believers were a product of ideological confusion, in a period of painful change, of the kind that is similarly suggested by the witchcraft records of Europe. So long as they remained intact, the ancestral structures had been able to control the use of anti-witchcraft movements: whenever these threatened to get out of hand, to the point of disintegrating a whole community, there were counter-techniques which could be exercised as a check. Medieval Christianity had given a large place to belief in witches, but the Church had similarly seen to it that violent action against witchcraft should remain a minor feature of society. In something of the same way a people such as the Nuer, whose structure has remained largely intact, seem not to have suffered from anything approaching 'witchcraft hysteria'.

Yet once the structures are seriously undermined, the situation evidently changes. Then it is that the controlling mechanisms begin to fail in face of more profound anxieties; and these open the way to strange psychological phenomena. Not only do witch-fearers clamour for protective action, but the action becomes ever more compulsive, while the 'witches' themselves hasten forward and accept their fate. Many of Mwana Lesa's victims, Rotberg tells us, 'appear to have accepted their failure to immerse, and the judgement of Mwana Lesa, as evidence of their own guilt'. One thinks of those Ga women who made so free of having 'killed' so many children. Wherever the Devil goeth about like a roaring lion, anyone may get devoured irrespective of their merits or their wishes. The question of charlatanry is really not in issue.

Other examples point the same way. The Christian-'pagan' synthesis became in many territories a means of self-defence which promised renewal as well as restoration, and, little by little, gave rise to ideological syntheses which were as much political as religious.

The Congo is another large territory where prophets became leaders of sects, and sects took to action. Their teaching varied in content. Some were strong on the anti-witchcraft side, such as the Mabwa and other 'anti-*ndoki*' movements. Others nourished millennial hopes of 'divine revolution'. Of them all the most influential was no doubt the church of Simon Kimbangu, founded among the Kongo of the western Congo basin and northern Angola in that same troubled year of 1921 which saw the Bulhoek shootings in South Africa and, in Kenya, the first 'disturbances' of a decidedly political sort.

Kimbangu began his mission in the district of Nkamba, which

Star symbol on a hillside near Shembe's African Christian Church not far from Johannesburg

he named Jerusalem. His 'witness' became the inspirer of a numerous and sometimes turbulent politico-religious progeny. Heavily repressed by the Belgian authorities for their anti-colonial implications, these Congo sects continued to enjoy a vivid life beneath the surface. With persecution and the passing of the years, their influence grew ever more political; they were undoubtedly a source of popular support for the Congolese nationalism which emerged in the late 1950s. Several years before 1960, when the Congo became at least in name an independent state, little tracts were circulating in Congolese townships. They showed a picture of Christ handing the keys of power, at the request of Simon Kimbangu, to an African political leader.

Other examples in British territories, where the use of English opened direct channels to the United States, emphasize the often seminal rôle played by black American thought and action. Watch Tower was by no means the only Afro-American movement whose call for human equality through God-inspired action found a response among colonized Africans. The history of East African protest, for instance, is deeply marked by the influence of Marcus Garvey, a Jamaican who lived in the United States. In 1914, leading a black American movement away from the 'respectable' acceptance of a permanent second-class citizenship, Garvey 'founded the Universal Negro Improvement Association, described himself as "Provisional President of Africa", created African orders of nobility, established an African Orthodox Church, published *The Negro World*, and organized international conventions for Africans and non-African Negroes' as well as greatly helping to spread 'the idea of independent African churches as an instrument of African liberation'. He had wide influence. It was from such ideas that a Ugandan called Reuben Mukasa, better known as Reuben Spartas, developed an attitude which combined 'a genuine intellectual search for theological truth' with 'a feeling for African nationalism which was hardly yet conscious' in the East Africa of the 1920s. It was in this atmosphere of striving for new mastery of a world in chaos that Kenya's early rebels, men such as Harry Thuku, shaped their ideas and actions.

That Christianity should lead to politics, and specifically anti-

European politics, remained a matter of surprise to many European clerics, officials and farmers. They had forgotten the history of their own countries, where national politics had for centuries marched with national religion. Making this point in relation to Kenya nationalism, Welbourn remarks that an official description of the Kikuyu Independent Schools Association, another founding influence in modern Kenya, could just as well describe the English church in Tudor times, changing only one word: 'A Church (of the English, governed by the English, and for the English) to make daily supplications to Almighty God by priests who have the welfare of Englishmen at heart.' Parish prayers on patriotic occasions have continued to make the same point.

Onward from the 1850s, in sum, there came a steady though uneven displacement of the old charters in favour of new forms of explanation and of hope. This ideological shift had particular importance for the European-educated few, and their response holds a special place in the sequence of African adjustment. Experience in schools where teachers appeared so seldom to distinguish between what Domingo called Christendom and Europeandom led to a new *prise de conscience*. These men acquired a better understanding of the colonial condition: having it, they sought to conceptualize Africa's problems in non-colonial terms and then in anti-colonial terms. Out of their initial orthodoxy, their 'collaboration' in the processes of assimilation to European cultural values, there emerged a new non-orthodoxy, a new dissatisfaction with European teachings, a new resistance. Again the trans-Atlantic influence was often strong, while the pioneers came chiefly from those territories where a measure of new-style education was possible for Africans. Notable among these were the British and French territories in West Africa.

Africans had been going to Europe since distant times of European contact. Soon after 1500 the king of Portugal welcomed an ambassador from the king of Benin, and found him 'a man of good speech and natural wisdom'. A son of the king of Kongo, studying at Rome, was made a bishop in 1518. 'There are two black princes of Anomabu here,' Horace Walpole was noting in his London diary for 1749, 'who are in fashion at all assemblies', being received at Covent Garden with a 'loud clap of applause'. At about the same moment another young man from the Gold Coast, Anthony William Amo, was awarded a doctorate of laws by the University of Wittenberg, and appointed counsellor of state by the Court of Berlin.

These were exceptions. Until late in the nineteenth century few Africans were able to travel abroad except as slaves, and only a handful acquired a modern education. By the 1870s, however, the potentially positive aspect of European presence – the opening of channels to new learning – had begun to take effect in a few places, especially in British-influenced West Africa and in French-influenced Senegal.

On the Gold Coast, moreover, the British acquired their supremacy in no small part thanks to an alliance with coastal peoples, notably the Fanti, against the Asante empire. Long before that empire was finally defeated, Fanti leaders had begun to think about a qualified independence within the British sphere. They made some small progress towards this. As early as 1870 one of their spokesmen could claim that 'the whole of the Fanti race, numbering some 400,000 souls, can now, for the first time, boast of a national assembly'. Although the ultimate history of the Fanti Confederation, duly formed in 1871, became little more than a diary of unavailing protest against British hegemony, there remained some encouragement for independent thought about the future.

A majority of the educated few tended to see themselves as Europeans by adoption and, as such, to reject and even despise the cultures from which they sprang. The same reaction was for a long while common to black thought in the United States after the Civil War. Yet others saw their position differently, and began to preach the regeneration of Africa's civilization. They turned their energies to a revaluation of traditional cultures. They applied the judgements of history, and found invigorating answers. 'Origen, Tertullian, Augustin, Clemens, Alexandrinus and Cyril', wrote the Sierra Leonean 'Ethiopian', J. Africanus Horton, in his *Vindication of the African Race* of 1868, 'were fathers and writers of the Primitive Church, were tawny African bishops of Apostolic renown. Many eminent writers and historians agree that these ancient Ethiopians were Negroes.'

Such Ethiopianist attitudes – today we might call them Africanist – became a force in many countries. They are easily apparent in the work of the Yoruba Baptist pastor, Mojola Agbebi, in Nigeria. Having broken away from his European parent church and formed his own community, Agbebi exhorted his congregation to take pride in their past. 'Do not be alarmed at the hideousness or grotesqueness of some forms of heathenism', he preached in 1902. 'Somewhere beyond the ugly exterior there lies a fine interior.' There was even, Shepperson thinks, 'something of an informal Ethiopianist International at the turn of the twentieth century and for its first decade and a half'.

Its teachings urged a new respect for local cultures, but increasingly, now, with a terminology and ideological framework having a strongly European echo. As early as the 1890s *The Gold Coast Methodist Times* under the editorship of the Reverend Attoh Ahuma was writing against the immixture of English words in Fanti, and defending the 'wonderful vitality' of Fanti in language which the spokesmen of the 'submerged nationalities' of Habsburg Europe, battling for their own new nation-states, might have taken for their own. In 1914 another African-controlled newspaper, significantly named *The Gold Coast Nation*, attacked the Churches for 'dragging poor souls along the path

of a strange tongue to do homage to the Great King without the
heart and mind in tow with the lips'. A little while back, it went
on,

the majority of our scholars thought it most detractory for their training to be heard speaking their mother tongue in public. Some went to
the extreme of thinking it a 'grand' thing to affect gross ignorance of
the vernacular and would not so much as listen when accosted in it ...
Now there is no scholar but holds the vernacular to be as good as the
most elegant foreign language.

This was no doubt an exaggeration; but the trend towards a new
self-respect, now with a nation-state accent, was clearly there.

Its intellectual revolt against European paternalism made head-
way. People began to talk about an African history that should
be more than an appendix to European enterprise. 'The study
of their own ancient as well as modern history', affirmed J.
Mensah Sarbah, another nationalist pioneer, in a book of 1906,
'has been shamefully neglected by the educated inhabitants of
the Gold Coast.' He went on to sketch a programme of work on
Fanti history that should demonstrate 'the existence of an African State, to trace the broad outlines of Akan-Fanti communities, and to explain the principles controlling and regulating
the government thereof'. These intentions may seem altogether
normal and moderate today. To most non-Africans of that generation, they appeared perverse if not positively absurd.

These trends ripened into politics in 1919. The National Congress of British West Africa was founded under the energetic
leadership of a Gold Coast lawyer, J. E. Casely Hayford. Its first
conference, in Accra a year later, saw the attendance of six
Nigerians, three Sierra Leoneans, one Gambian, and forty
Ghanaians, with the support of almost the whole English-lan-
guage press of West Africa. The influence of this African
journalism in English – or in French – has been generally under-
estimated. It was almost certainly a great influence, and spoke its
mind in forceful if sometimes florid prose.

Yet modern politics remained for a long while with intellectuals who, no matter what they might think about the cultures of
Africa, had few links with the village masses, and even fewer

with the growing numbers of workers and petty traders in the towns. This was largely because educated Africans found it relatively easy to find a place in West African colonial society, where Europeans were few and European settlers almost non-existent. British rule may not have welcomed the ideas of political reformism, but it seldom repressed them and sometimes, now and then, saw advantage in them. As with similar ventures elsewhere, the National Congress became increasingly moderate with age: content to agitate politely inside legal limits, it accepted an indefinite future of steady but slow advance towards self-rule. Even when its 'young Turks' formed a directly political party, the United Gold Coast Convention, after the Second World War, they leaned heavily to the conservative side of things. Mostly, they were lawyer-politicians linked to traditional ruling groups. Whatever savoured to them of sweat and vulgarity appeared undesirable, if not positively dangerous, because it could be subversive not only of colonial rule but also of their own positions in society.

Much of the same became true of French-speaking West Africa, but with a different accent drawn from the ideas of 1789 and the ideals of 'French civilization' as guaranteeing a supranational brotherhood of man. Pioneers of African equality such as Blaise Diagne in Senegal and Louis Hunkanrin in Dahomey spoke for the Rights of Man as applied to Africans in French colonies; and those, like Hunkanrin, who held firm against administrative pressure paid a bitter price for their resistance.

After 1945 there came new opportunities for freedom of thought and action. Dozens of gifted young men were able to acquire higher education in France. But of those who went home again there were few whose notions about the future included anything like the building of barricades or the scaling of colonial bastions. When it came to the pinch it was to be a minority amongst them, or else men such as Sékou Touré who had passed through a different school, especially of trade unionism, who were to make the running under the egalitarian banners of the Rassemblement Démocratique Africain – just as, in Ghana, it was Kwame Nkrumah and his despised 'verandah boys' who were to outpass the lawyers with a mass political organization, the Con-

# 31 The Masses React

The Mumboites, followers of a serpent god whose medium had promised the removal of Europeans, were duly smitten by an indignant colonial authority and were themselves removed, with their leaders exiled to the offshore Kenya island of Lamu and their ranks dispersed. But their ideas were not so easily banished. They stayed in the consciousness of the 1920s and 30s. After the gruelling enlightenment on world realities provided by the First World War, other Africans began to give these ideas a more practical turn. There came a second ideological shift from the ideologies of the past. Having achieved, with Christianity, an African interpretation of European things-spiritual, men began to form an African interpretation of European things-temporal. They moved their dissidence from the sphere of religion to more secular ground. There emerged among ordinary people, by no means necessarily attached to any élite, what may be called proto-nationalism.

One of its early manifestations, this time, in East Africa, was the Young Kikuyu Association founded in 1921 by Harry Thuku, then a telephone operator in the Nairobi treasury department. Like Mumbo's prophet, Thuku had no use for European moral teachings. 'Because the European missionaries did not come here to preach the word of God but of the devil only,' he said in a speech of 1921, 'I do not want them here.' Yet what he founded was not a dissident church but a dissident political organization; and his advice to his audience was not to await the millennium but to organize against the Europeans.

There followed a pattern of events that was to become familiar in many colonies. 'A crowd collected in front of the Police Lines [i.e. barracks] where [Thuku] was detained, and a shot fired by a nervous and over-tired policeman started a volley' – in the colonial records one is constantly finding these 'nervous and over-tired policemen' – 'ending in the death of twenty-one Africans. Thuku was deported and the Young Kikuyu Association banned.' Years of increasingly political agitation, sometimes open, often clandestine, followed upon this. They were difficult pre-

*Anyanwu* – The Awakening – in Ben Enwonwu's symbolic bronze of the renewal of independence: outside the Nigerian National Museum in Lagos

paratory years. After the Second World War, with another large helping of enlightenment about the world, the ideas of Kenya nationalism could at last grow to maturity in a fully political movement of mass dimensions.

This transition from religious to secular politics was nowhere simple or immediate. The educated few might come easily to think in reformist terms of votes and constitutional advances: the masses in villages and peri-urban slums had to fight their way to clarity through more familiar categories of thought. Two sets of factors, respectively, external and internal to Africa, helped them in this.

Of the external factors Shepperson has listed six of major importance. The first of these was the shaping influence of the culture of the colonial power in question. This greatly varied. To be an African in 'British Africa' was to face a different 'occupying phenomenon' than in 'French Africa', while it was different again to be an African in a 'settler territory' than in one where land was barred to European settlement. These differences led to different responses. But they were all productive of new thought.

A second external factor lay in the influence of vigorous individuals from outside Africa who identified themselves in one degree or other with the cause of African advancement. Booth was one of these. Another, with other ideas, was the Liberian of West Indian origin Edward Blyden, whose writings and speeches did so much to lay the theoretical foundations for the concepts of 'African personality' and *'négritude'*. Another West Indian, George Padmore, was a third whose influence proved more modern and directly political.

Residence overseas made a third formative factor, though chiefly of importance to the educated few. They could forge links with political movements in the imperialist countries, and also with movements in other countries which were not imperialist. Some of the pioneering 'tribunes of the people' were influenced in this way. A fourth factor, of especial importance to ordinary people who went on migrant labour, was residence outside one's own territory. Such was the case with the Malawian Clements Kadalie, who became an outstanding trade union leader in South Africa.

The two world wars composed a fifth external factor, helping to bring about a 'deep and fundamental' change, in the words of a former British Governor of Kenya, 'in the relations of the African people with the great unknown world which suddenly fell upon them and insisted that they must become a part of it'. These wars affected not only the tens of thousands who were drawn into the fighting in one way or another, but also the multitudes who suffered from wartime hardships at home. In 1945 it was from returned ex-servicemen that many of the new mass movements drew an important part of their strength.

External ideological influences were a sixth factor which grew in force. High on their list, aside from rebellious Christianity in the teachings of men like Booth, were all those ideas which sprang into Africa from liberation movements elsewhere, whether social in Europe or national in Asia. The example of the Indian National Congress had deep effect in South Africa, where it helped to promote the African National Congress and a numerous progeny in other territories. The very nature of the Second World War, anti-racialist in its opposition to Nazi-Fascist doctrines, anti-colonialist in many of its implications, opened the way for a questioning of white supremacy. The victories of the Soviet Union gave the ideas of revolutionary socialism an impetus and volume they had never had before in Africa. Even the cautious claims of the British Labour Party, sharing power with the Conservative Party in a wartime coalition, thrust a toe in the door. Trade unions were legalized. The rights of Africans were discussed. So was the notion of African independence in the relatively near future.

Yet one may doubt whether all these influences, even in their cumulative effect, could have successfully tackled the colonial dragon in the middle of the twentieth century, had it not been for the sickness of the beast itself. When comprehensive and objective detailed histories of the colonial period at last appear – and several territorial studies of this kind were already to hand in the late 1960s – it will be seen that the colonial condition by 1945 had become acutely deplorable for a large and growing number of Africans, and perhaps for a majority. This is not, of course, what orthodox opinion has generally believed; but orthodox opinion has rather seldom cared to look beneath the surface. On the surface there might be progress towards modern education, some growth of social services, the beginnings of a new culture; beneath it, the picture was a different one. If the colonial condition was alleviated by fringe benefits, including higher education in Europe for several thousands of West Africans, these scarcely touched the masses.

What did touch the masses were colonial factors – factors internal to the colonial process – of another kind. And it was these internal factors which completed the transition from élite protest to popular nationalism; which urged great crowds to political meetings for the first time; which drove and powered the machinery of constitutional change.

Twenty-five years earlier, in the wake of the 'pacification' that had followed invasion or infiltration, most tropical African peoples had accepted their defeat and had striven only to defend the continued efficacy of their traditional ways of life. In those days it had been by no means so clear that these ways must decay and die. Even when undermined by foreign rule, the structures could still appear sufficiently intact. But by 1945 no such optimism was any longer possible for all but rare exceptions.

The best and boldest saw this clearly, and responded with a new militancy. All that they had learned and experienced abroad, whether during the Second World War or immediately after, may have helped to form their hopes and actions. Yet as one of them from 'Portuguese Africa' commented in 1965, 'it must be said frankly that it was also, and even more, the actual conditions of life that moved us: it was the poverty, ignorance, sufferings of every kind, complete deprivation of the most elementary rights, that dictated our position in the fight against Portuguese colonialism'.

And this was the more so because the colonial condition proved not to be a static one. At least during the later colonial years the processes of change acquired what Verhaegen has perceptively called an autonomy of their own. They moved now from their own volition. And it was this autonomous movement, soon accelerating out of all control even when colonial administrations tried hard to halt it, that finally transformed the colonial condition into a major social and economic crisis, and brought the masses into action.

These processes of change were both direct and indirect. But they added up to continued dismantlement of the traditional structures. This went on even though such dismantlement was in general no part of colonial policy, and often sharply against it.

Like Lord Salisbury and the movement for colonies a century earlier, the administrators found themselves involved in another 'revolution' which they distrusted and deplored, but could not prevent. However hard they might try to prop traditional structures in place, by supporting chiefs or by appointing chiefs where none had previously existed, the very fact of colonial presence ate deeply into the structure and the fabric of ancestral charters. Even where this presence reinforced the power of rulers, as in the emirates of northern Nigeria, it did so at the cost of weakening those checks and balances by which the old systems had controlled the abuse of power, and so in turn prepared the way for change.

It is evident from such colonial archives as are now available that the constant wish of most administrations was to conserve 'village Africa'. They listened eagerly to all those elders who argued against change, and concluded that they were acting as good trustees. Unhappily for them, they were in growing contradiction with themselves. Their settlers and concession companies called even more imperatively for land, cattle and forced or very cheap labour. In the nature of things, these were the demands that generally carried the day.

Expropriation of cattle and land in the settler territories, the forcing out of migrant labour into wage employment far from home in very many territories and on a massive scale, the gruelling *corvées* of the Second World War, the deepening solitude and misery of villages bereft of their active menfolk for long periods of time: these and other such factors all hastened the work of dismantlement. And then, as Verhaegen says, the process acquired a dynamic of its own. Things began to happen which no one had foreseen, or no one likely to be listened to. The very decay of village life proved a spur to getting out of it. Men tramped away to the white man's towns and mines, and there they glimpsed, if only from the gutters, a different world, dangerous but challenging, harsh yet immeasurably exciting when compared with the old slow life in the bush. Young men began making it a point of manhood to accept this difficult challenge; young women began to prefer young men who had 'passed their test' in these hostile and yet beckoning cities. Those who could began to take their families, or to form new families in the 'native townships'.

These townships swelled enormously after 1945, spawning huge conurbations of rootless folk, assaulting the old beliefs and patterns of social interdependence in a tide of frantic individualism. Verhaegen is speaking for many territories when he writes of the Belgian Congo that 'towards the end of the colonial period an irresistible social pressure burst through the administrative and police barriers designed to protect the towns and their peripheries from the tide of rural emigration'. In 1930 only five per cent of the Congolese population had lived outside the rural areas; by 1957 it was twenty-two per cent, and shooting skywards.

At Léopoldville [Kinshasa] the creation of 'squatting' zones doubled the size of the town and its number of inhabitants in only three years. From 380,000 people the total rose to more than 800,000. The same thing happened on a smaller scale in all the provincial capitals of the Congo.

All this reflected another colonial contradiction. A general rise in the size of populations, still to be explained but due no doubt to a variety of factors including a certain amount of preventive medicine in the towns, clashed with an entirely insufficient expansion of food production. Africa, for the first time, began to be faced with widespread 'over-population' – with a generalized human growth in critical excess of growth in the material means of livelihood.

In this vast welter of confusion the values of village life could no more survive than any ordinary man or woman who tried to live by them. No matter how much conscientious people might try to remember the rules they had learned at home, the new 'urban values' of 'free enterprise' swept all before them. The *gravitas* of family life went by the board, old respectabilities thrown over the rail together with old servitudes. Quantities of socially-subjected women took the advice that Bernard Shaw had put into Mrs Warren's mouth in another time and place of transitional stress and strain: that 'the only way for a woman to provide for herself decently is for her to be good to some man that can afford to be good to her'. Early in the 1950s it was guessed by an intelligent Belgian administrator that a quarter of the women in the African townships of Elisabethville [Lubumbashi] were *femmes libres* who got their living in this way, and the case was evidently far from unique.

These *femmes libres* were also part of the great transition, however obscurely, for they often represented a deliberate act of feminine emancipation. 'More or less brilliantly dressed and made up, with bold eyes and lacquered finger nails, audacious, determined, frivolous, fickle, seizing life with both hands', as I remember seeing them in these towns of the early 1950s, 'they dominate the city life of Congo Africans: on that everyone agrees. They flock to the bars' – to La Délicatesse, La Joie Kinoise, and scores of others gay with bare electric-light bulbs and blaring jazz – 'laugh the innocents out of their fears, initiate the village boys new to the city, corrupt the stolidly married husband, organize in their own defence, fleece the lascivious European, and generally carry on in gross defiance of Morality and Family Order.' Over the river in Brazzaville, Balandier had found just the same. Dozens of women's associations – the Dollar, the Diamond, Lolita, even Jeunesse Malade-Monnaie – 'curiously mingle mutual aid [to each other and to their parents] with amusement and with prostitution'.

Here was one aspect of dismantlement. It was watched with lamentation by colonial officials already beginning to feel that the time had come for them to go. Another if different aspect appeared with the steady growth of primary education in all except the Portuguese colonies, and even of some secondary education as well. In 1934 the proportion of school-age children in Belgian Congo primary schools had been twelve per cent: by 1957 it had climbed to fifty-six per cent. Much the same was true of certain other colonies, especially in West Africa. Literate education became the touchstone of progress. Private and public schools proliferated. Yet this was education which had turned abruptly from the teachings of the past. A new world called to ordinary people, and the road to it went through school doors. Soon it was the primary-school leavers who powered the mass movements of the 1950s, and carried modern political ideas into every corner of the continent.

This picture of the long-term undermining of traditional charters, initiated by colonial subjection but completed by processes of reaction to colonial rule, needs balancing against the 'village situation' where a majority of Africans, though a rapidly dwindling one, continued to live and have their being.

Though sorely afflicted, the old charters still had power to command respect and evoke remedial action. Here, often enough, what I have called the first ideological shift from primary resistance – the shift from traditional religion to Christianity – had taken only partial effect and sometimes none at all. Even in the towns where Christianity had a stronger hold, the old beliefs were not forgotten. As the 1966 report on the Owegbe Cult opined, 'most Binis [citizens of Benin], Christians or not, worship their juju'. While sorely troubled peoples sought to understand and control the new problems and dilemmas of their colonial situation, beliefs about witches and witchcraft spread and proliferated.

There are two obvious explanations. In the measure that the old order of the 'right and natural' slipped beyond social control, so too did the nature of witchcraft belief and its manifestations: as, for example, with those Africans who were found guilty of digging up a dead baby in Fort Victoria, Rhodesia, a country where the 'right and natural' of tradition had long been turned upon its head.

Secondly, colonial rule forbade the persecution of witches: forebade, that is, the use of traditional sanctions against the incidence of evil. Consequently, as troubles multiplied, so did the belief and the elaboration of belief in witchcraft. As long as forty years ago a Pondo defined the resultant situation as it appears to have been widely apprehended in Africa. 'Times long ago were good,' he told Monica Wilson. 'Everything is bad now ... The killing of witches was a very good thing. They were few then. They are many now.'

All observers seem to agree on this. Apart from examples I have already mentioned – those of the Zande, Amba and others – LeVine reports a similar efflorescence of witchcraft belief among the Gusii of Kenya. In Uganda Gisu told La Fontaine that the use of witchcraft had grown since the arrival of the Europeans. Among the Kaguru of Tanzania Beidelman found the same, linked interestingly to Christian teachings. Beidelman explains,

The Kaguru whom the missionaries have the best chance of shaking from their traditional beliefs are those who are literate. But in the Swahili Bible they read: 'Thou shalt not suffer a witch to live' (Exodus xxii, 18); 'Regard not them that have familiar spirits, neither seek after wizards, to be defiled by them ...' (Leviticus xix, 31); 'A man also or woman that hath a familiar spirit, or that is a wizard shall surely be put to death ...' (Leviticus xx, 27).

And so it has come about that traditional beliefs, whether or not linked with Christian teachings or millennial ideas, have continued as a muted note off-stage, yet bursting violently into the drama from time to time with reminders, more or less intense, of fears and aspirations couched in the language and attachments of the past.

Such outbreaks may be disconcerting to those who would like to think that Africans should have left 'all that' behind them. But do peoples ever pass so neatly from one great stage of culture to another? It is long since Europe quit the Middle Ages. Yet otherwise reputable European houses are still being exorcized for ghosts. Only the other day a canon of Southwark cathedral was noting that he had 'cleared' ten houses in the previous eighteen months of ghosts who included 'two arrogant Tudor monks, an Irish maid the monks had poisoned, and a tramp' as well as a couple of defunct vicars of the Church of England. 'They are all people', explained the canon, 'who have got stuck here ... They knock about to draw attention to themselves.' Clearly this could still be upsetting. In 1966 a British chairman of magistrates found it right to withhold a prison sentence from a man whose case had the extenuating circumstance that his house was haunted. His wife had met the ghost several times, and was able to describe him as 'an old man dressed in rusty black clothes, Victorian clothes, with a gold stud in his collar'. Even more recently an Italian professor of philosophy has had to stand charges of binding malevolent spells on two of his students. Now I am not implying here that suprasensible phenomona necessarily do not 'exist'; it depends, no doubt, on what you mean by existence. The point is that black beliefs in ghosts should be no more surprising than white beliefs: indeed, given the context of cultural stress, far less surprising.

In September 1953, in such a time of stress, a village woman of north-eastern Northern Rhodesia (now Zambia), Alice Lenshina Milenga Lubusha, then aged about twenty-nine, 'fell sick and died, and while dead she was brought into the presence of God who, giving her two books, told her to return to earth and preach against evil'.

Before proceeding on her way, Alice took care to consult local missionaries about the meaning of her resurrection. Two months later they baptized her, and she at once set forth on village preaching which led to the formation of her own community, the Lumpa Church. She was greatly successful. So strong was her appeal that 60,000 pilgrims flocked to her 'New Zion' of Kasomo village two years later. By 1956 there were Lumpa branches in other parts of the country, as well as in the copper-mining towns which drew semi-migrant labour from Alice's region.

This was Mwana Lesa in a revised context. Alice preached against witchcraft and all its manifestations because God had told her to preach against evil. The Lumpa Church became an agent of the Principle of Good in a moment when its contrary seemed, with social change and upheaval, to be eating deeply into the securities of traditional life. Gaining followers precisely because she promised remedial action, Alice was able to evoke in them a powerful morale. 'A strong fatalistic feeling ran through the Church from the earlier days,' notes an official report, 'and this belief no doubt conditioned the minds of its followers to believing that persecution was bound to come and that they must be prepared to welcome this persecution in the furtherance of their faith.'

But was it a 'fatalistic feeling' that moved them? To act for Good meant to act against the agents of Evil. It would be hard to do this effectively without acting against authority. Persecution must therefore be accepted as a part of salvation: the unforgotten case of Mwana Lesa had proved as much. Belief in coming persecution was perfectly rational.

Alice's followers did not act directly against witches as Mwana Lesa had done. Instead, they took evasive action. Firmly linking Evil with the Authority under whose aegis evil forces were conceived to be at work, they tried to withdraw from the control of government-appointed chiefs and missionaries into 'witch free' villages of their own. Soon the resultant tensions led to a direct clash with Authority of one kind or another.

Late in 1956 a Lumpa churchman called an African Roman Catholic priest a witch, and was sentenced to a month's imprisonment. Lumpa demonstrations against authority followed, and were punished by the law. 'One of those arrested,' says the official report, 'was Petros Chintankwa, Alice's husband, who was later convicted and sentenced to two years' imprisonment with hard labour for proposing violence to an assembly.' Fresh incidents developed from meetings unauthorized by the police. Yet government pressure failed to overawe Alice's deacons and congregations. They continued to win new members. Significantly for the retentive power of its own millennial appeal, the Watch Tower movement was 'perhaps the only church which did not lose any of its followers to the Lenshina movement'.

So far, the Lumpa church might have become assimilated into the nationalist movement growing in those years. Early relations with the nationalists were good. Understandably so: though in different ways, both were hostile to colonial authority. The break between them occurred, and just as understandably, when the nationalist movement during 1962 became the obvious heir to colonial authority. When that happened – even though the colonial government was still in control – the Lumpa church and the nationalists soon fell into bitter violence. 'Lenshina supporters increasingly withdrew themselves into separate settlements, aggravating the tensions and fear that existed on both sides', and returning an angry negative to nationalist appeals for political unity. Official figures for the period of June 1963 to July 1964 show the nationalists as having killed fourteen Lumpa members, destroyed 121 Lumpa houses, and burned down twenty-eight Lumpa churches, while Lumpa members killed seven nationalists and destroyed two houses. Large-scale security operations in 1964 brought another 710 killed, including seven soldiers and policemen, and 601 wounded of whom soldiers and policemen numbered nineteen.

Nothing more aptly if painfully illustrates the complexity of these years. If many people made the second ideological shift from religious politics to secular politics, others did not; and the heritage of this stubborn 'staying with the past' was at times to weigh heavily on the new national parties and movements.

The complexities continued. As they continued, however, it became possible during the middle 1960s to detect the outline of a third ideological shift, and even several distinctive variants of it. This was a shift away from the politics of reform towards the politics of revolution.

Dissident politics during the 1950s had led to the emergence of nation-states under the guidance of the educated few. These took a variety of forms and policies, reflecting the vigour with which the educated few had grasped their opportunities. After 1945 many intellectuals in British and French colonies had mastered difficult disciplines, campaigned for nationalist ideas, considered an array of ideological alternatives, travelled widely overseas. All this experience they applied to the shaping of self-rule, asserting the right of Africans to find their own ways into the future. The times were filled with new kinds of hope.

Yet the cleft between intellectuals and masses continued, and grew wider. Often, to the intellectuals, the reality of village Africa – of 'mass Africa' – seemed far away. The political and social models upon which most of them concentrated their efforts were understandably those which appeared most readily applicable to relieving the colonial condition. But these were models of the nation-state that could mean little to rural Africans steeped in the memory and practice of their own structures. The educated few proved very capable of working the machinery of national and parliamentary protocol, of adapting the procedures of Westminster and the Palais Bourbon, of managing the whole portentous symbolism of flag and anthem. But to make all this popularly meaningful was another matter.

Most of the immediate pre- and post-independence structures enjoyed wide popular support: Africans manifestly wanted to be free. Yet at the same time, both because of their nature and this manner of their taking shape, many of these new structures remained shallow at the roots, unfertilized by any strong sense of social or even national unity, open to grave abuse by individuals or pressure groups, and consequently liable to quick decay. Implanted from above rather than cultivated from below, they soon withered under the trials of self-rule. In doing so they opened still more widely the gulf between the mass of ordinary citizens and the 'beneficiaries' of decolonization: between the urban or rural poor and those now known as the WaBenzi (or an equivalent) from their addiction to expensive cars such as the Mercedes Benz, and other luxurious forms of privilege. After 1965 not a few of the new regimes were forced to retreat behind the shelter of army rule. Other regimes bravely wrestled with their problems in a democratic way, working to close the gulf between leaders and led. Aside from these few, however, the question was increasingly posed as to what should come next? Hesitantly and often obscurely, even before 1965, there began to be heard a series of new answers.

Pierre Mulele's revolt was one of these.

It burst forth in the forests of the Kwilu, far south-eastward of the Congo capital where reformist politicians argued and went through seemingly fruitless antics. The time was 1964, three years after Lumumba's murder and at a moment when the cause of genuine independence seemed menaced with extinction. Pierre Mulele launched a rebellion for a 'second independence' – an independence, this time, that was intended to be as real as the first one of 1960 had proved manifestly false.

In his social origins, formation, and reliance on traditional as well as modern ideas Mulele may be defined, it seems to me, as the harbinger of a 'new élite'. This was to be closer to the African milieu, less detached by European education from the village masses, and 'petty-bourgeois' rather than 'middle-class' in social formation.

There had been others of this type in the recent past, Lumumba among them, and there were to be others again in the near future. Mulele cut away from the Belgian or American models of the 'middle-class' reformism which had led, in his view, only to a new if indirect colonial dependence. Seeking for alternatives, he tried to marry revolutionary models to those of the past. So that with him and his rebellion there came a strange symbiosis of old and new ideologies which remains of extraordinary historical interest, as anyone may see from the documents in Benoît Verhaegen's invaluable book. Mulele's fighters in the Kwilu forests were asked to read, when they were able, moral and military maxims copied from the revolutionary writings of Mao Tsetung. But the real power behind the revolt appears to have derived from perfectly traditional developments.

These were evidently the fruit of another millennial movement, this time among the Pende of the Kwilu a few years earlier. In the late 1950s this Pende movement, called Mpeve, had taught hostility to Europeans as the necessary prelude to an entirely new life which was to begin on the day of independence.

The ancestors and principally the former chiefs whom the whites had ignored or suppressed, would return on the day of independence and expel bad chiefs and all who had collaborated with the whites ... With this return on the day of independence the people would become rich like the whites, and the whites would vanish from the scene.

It was a message almost identical with the one received by the Pondo of South Africa a hundred years earlier, and by many others since.

Independence duly came on 30 June 1960, and nothing changed. The people did not become rich. The old chiefs did not return. Some whites went away; most remained. On this occasion, however, disappointment did not end the matter. Instead, Mulele arrived to preach a second independence – as it were, another chance for the millennium – and found willing listeners among the Pende. They took to arms with Mulele as their leader. How far their disappointment of 1960 was in fact linked with Mulele's success remains unclear, and Mulele himself will not be able to tell us. Taking advantage of an amnesty extended to him by the Congolese Foreign Minister, Justin Bomboko, he returned to Kinshasa late in September 1968, only to be sentenced to death by a military court and summarily executed.

He was defeated in 1964, but not easily. He won many followers, and it was months before his revolt fell away in failure, while other Congolese revolts flared at much the same time and perhaps in much the same way. They were all aimed at the reformist élites, now far gone in helpless or detested abdication, and were also powered by a certain ethnic separatism. To some extent they were all marked by revolutionary ideas, but even more strongly by a courage which came from magical beliefs in bullet-liquefying charms and spells of venerable heritage. Mulele himself grew celebrated as more than a man, ubiquitous, capable of becoming invisible, beyond the danger of defeat. In this strange halfway house of revolution, where the teachings of Chairman Mao went hand in hand with the comfort of magicians, the old and the new became inextricably mingled. Yet whatever was gained from the old in the way of individual self-assurance was lost in the way of political incapacity. As the fate of these risings showed, they were unable to evolve a political strategy which could exploit their initial military success.

But other developments now began to suggest that the possibilities inherent in this third ideological shift were only just beginning. Whether in the Congo or elsewhere, political independence had arrived to a scene of profound economic dislocation, deep social disturbance, a wild confusion of hopes and fears. The people at the top might claim to be operating in a modern world of parliamentary power, national politics, technical development, programmes of unfolding progress. To the people at the bottom, all too often, this claim became increasingly a lie. Looking back, it is easy to perceive the weakness of the élites who had assumed the mantle of government. They had forgotten the lesson of the old Asante proverb, *Worebɛforu dua a, wofi n'ase, na womfi soro*, Anyone who wants to climb a tree begins at the bottom and not at the top. As it was, these reformist élites had been lifted to the top by a colonial policy which had argued, whether in English or French, for the building of an 'indigenous middle class' which should inherit colonial power. Duly installed at the top, most of them were content to survey the lofty scene, caring all too seldom for whatever might go on below.

This is being wise after the event. Perhaps the reformist élites could have done no other than they did. Perhaps there was bound to be a period of marking time while realities became clear. These realities were not so easy to see at the time. For the educated few the colonial period rarely appeared as only the latest in the great 'mechanisms of change' which had helped to shape and reshape African civilization through the centuries. On the contrary: so profound was the colonial impact, so traumatic in its consequences for those who most nearly felt it, that it often appeared to have 'changed everything'. Ensnared in this delusion, trapped in its implications for their own status, the educated few found it sensible to turn their backs on historical Africa, village Africa, as though this were a world which had passed away, or, if still surviving, one that need no longer much concern them.

Yet the masses of the people were still 'at the bottom', looking up that tall tree of privilege, and less and less liking what they saw. As the gap between them and the educated few grew rapidly clear, they tended to echo the words of a Tanzanian official document of 1967. Deploring how a lucky or unscrupulous few could interpret independence merely as a gate to self-enrichment, this document trounced privileged people who 'say "the poor are black, and we are black, therefore it is alright for us to exploit them" ... pretending that there is something more evil in a brown or white Tanzanian doing the exploiting than there is in a black Tanzanian doing it'.

With the independence of 1960 so glaringly a fraud, as many now thought with good reason or with bad, the 'new élites' who spoke for this point of view began to turn their minds increasingly away from reform. This implied revolt, if not necessarily revolution, and was the context of Mulele's rising. But Mulele's rising foundered in the tides of traditional belief. There was clearly needed a more consequential line of action, moving out entirely and consciously from traditional belief and its magical suppositions. As it happened, this was the moment when groups of rebels in the Portuguese colonies – their road in any case barred to reformism by Portuguese intransigence – had begun moving into an ideology of revolution on modern lines. By the late 1960s, with some of these anti-Portuguese revolts, it became possible to trace a far more rational and coherent development of the onward shift from reformist politics; and one that might now, it seemed, increasingly command the future wherever reformism proved incapable of achieving any general progress, whether towards lesser poverty or greater independence.

This new variant of thought and action could be seen, for example, in the microcosmic territory of Guinea-Bissau, as well as in Angola and Mozambique. The men and women who had launched these armed struggles for new structures of society were also 'petty bourgeois'. Except for two or three who had acquired a university training in Lisbon, they were mechanics, clerks, medical assistants or urban semi-employed of little or no formal education.

Portuguese reformism might still have led them in the same direction as the older élites of the British and French colonies. But there was no Portuguese reformism, no parliamentary model: they had once existed but had died in the clubs and cafés of the Portuguese Republic thirty years earlier. For these men and women, now and long since, the only possible choice lay crudely between insurrection and continued surrender. Having decided for insurrection, they discovered no simple road ahead of them. When they began their agitation in the late 1950s they found nothing to work with but a deep if confused and uncertain sense of grievance among a people almost entirely rural and pre-literate. Often this sense of grievance was blurred by a despair of things ever being able to be different. Ethnic rivalries made unity of action still more difficult.

These pioneers had accordingly to begin at the beginning. They had to climb their tree, hand over hand, from the bottom. They had to study a country of which they knew little. They had to learn exactly what divided or might unify the many ethnic groups in each of these territories. They had to understand at what points the old systems still held firm, and where these systems had degenerated into mere agencies of colonial rule: they had to get inside, and be accepted inside, extremely *local* situations. And then, when they had done all this as best they could, they had to show that nothing was to be hoped of the old remedies, whether magical or not.

In Guinea-Bissau, for example, they worked in the villages for three years after 1959, talking no longer in big words about freedom and independence but in small ones about colonial prices and taxes and *corvées*. Not until 1963 did they feel strong enough in popular support to open guerrilla warfare. But then they reaped their harvest. By 1966, ten years after they had formed their independence party as a mere handful of men and women in Bissau, they had cleared the Portuguese army and administration out of more than half the countryside except for isolated garrisons.

Yet they had still solved only the first part of their problem. They had still to fix their long-term political strategy, their enduring social objectives, and prepare to offer a better alternative to Portuguese rule. In 1963–4, testing themselves along these lines, they began shaping their movement into an organization of village committees, peasant committees, each with its own field of local responsibilities, each with a new school as teachers trained abroad became available, each with a clinic and perhaps a nurse, and each, above all, with its task of working slowly through the ideological problem, *local and native*, of *socio-economic* reconstruction. They began, in short, to transform revolt into revolution, and in ways which made a strong contrast with what was happening, or about to happen, in the Congo.

They were not, of course, typical of the wider scene. They were even most exceptional. Yet perhaps they were typical of a certain crucial trend in these years. How far this trend would now strengthen and crystallize – how far the search for new structures of society would now impose new objectives – remained obscure. Meanwhile these revolutionaries hold their place in the record. For in ways that were original and repeatedly effective, conducted by often exceptional leaders, they have dramatized and demonstrated the whole arduous and testing challenge of transition from the world of the past to the world of the future.

# Epilogue: African Destinies

What kind of Africa may now emerge, what modern variant of an old civilization? Happily it is no part of an historian's duty to be wise before the event. If this book has any value, however, it must raise certain practical questions. Perhaps I may end by discussing briefly what these are.

The upheavals of the late 1960s were not the fruit of accident, bad luck or human incapacity, but of a crisis long in the making, a crisis of institutions on a continental scale. Its early signs may be found in some regions soon after 1800; in others, perhaps, as far back as the massive export of captives after 1650. Masked or delayed in pre-colonial times by the repeated adaptation of traditional institutions, this is also a crisis that was often deepened by the dismantlement of the colonial period.

It is furthermore a crisis whose ideological confusion has been again enlarged by various illusions. Many people outside Africa, and some within, have mistakenly believed that the colonial period not only swept away the old but also, like the English industrial revolution, laid foundations for the new. Any balanced survey of the evidence will now reveal that it achieved the first but not the second. All that emerged from the colonial period, in a structural sense, was an institutional void concealed for a while behind a political safety-curtain painted with parliamentary symbols of European provenance, a mere façade of order on lines drawn by alien cultures.

To most of those behind this curtain it might be distressingly clear that the old structures were in collapse, and that no new ones of enduring value had arrived to take their place. Most of those in front of the curtain were content to think otherwise. They learned better after the curtain had gone up, on the day of independence, and the élites of western European and American training were duly embarked on their allocated roles. Soon a growing tumult could be heard in the wings. Soon this tumult rushed on stage.

This is not, I know, how a majority of colonial observers have understood the drama. For them the colonial period was constructive because it was thought to have conducted Africans into the modern world, and deliberately laid down the road to African equality with the rest of mankind. I do not myself belong to this 'cheerful school' of colonial historians. The parallel, it seems to me, is once again with Britain. There too we have had a 'cheerful school' of thought about the industrial revolution. The labouring poor may have continually rebelled against the poverty and squalor of industrialism: in truth, we are told, their sufferings were less than the blessings they received. Their average standard of living, on this view, went on rising all through the industrial revolution. And so it should follow, *sous-entendu*, that the case for capitalism has been comfortably made.

Others have questioned these reassuring wage statistics. They have seen greater meaning in all those desperate acts of self-defence – the machine smashing and the workers' combinations, a myriad riots and upheavals. They have believed that the consequences of the industrial revolution were typical of 'the first impact of new economic patterns, [which] threaten or disrupt the previous social relationships, while not immediately supplying new security devices in their place'; and that the industrial revolution really did produce 'a catastrophic dislocation of the lives of the common people'.

We have had the same division of opinion about what happened in Africa. Here too the 'cheerful school' has greatly flourished. Their belief that civilization – whether as law, order, morality, or even history itself – essentially began with European rule may be found in great raftloads of books written in the last fifty years, and still being written. These views may now be seen to have ignored the evidence of history, and their interpretations to have been factitious. All those wars of self-defence, bitter rebellions, anti-witchcraft movements, millennial uprisings and a million individual acts of protest were set airily aside as the mere product of benighted savagery, perverted superstition or natural foolishness. All those new urban slums, miseries, moral squalors were explained, when they were explained at all, as the outcome of African fecklessness, incompetence or worse. And so with the post-independence upheavals: excellent institutions, it was said, had been provided – whose fault but African incapacity if they now failed to work?

In face of this kind of handling of the evidence one might perhaps argue polemically if impolitely the force of another Asante proverb: *Nkura dodowa bɔre tu a, endɔ*, When many mice dig a hole, it does not become deep. The fact remains that the hole dug by the 'cheerful school' has proved a pretty wide pit for educated Africans. No few of them have tumbled into it, and come to think that colonialism was institutionally a positive as well as a negative force, and that it really marked the beginning of civilization in Africa.

Not all such Africans have fallen into the pit: here too the 'cheerful school' has had its critics. 'From whichever angle you look at the first year of independence,' commented a Nigerian headmaster in 1960, 'you are faced with the stark reality of the fact that we were never, ideologically, prepared for independence.' In many cases, remarked a qualified engineer somewhat later, 'methods of winning independence and plans for the future have had no kind of theoretical basis, and, what is more, have been more or less detached from actual realities'. And the weight of evidence seems mightily to support them.

From another standpoint, this is also a crisis of growth. In several senses: most strikingly, perhaps, in that of population. For reasons not yet explained but which can be only in some part due to preventive medicine, the rate of natural increase has gone steeply upward for several decades. Few reliable statistics are to hand, yet they all point this way. Sample statistics put the rate of natural increase in the Belgian Congo, for example, at as low as 0·6 per cent a year in 1932, and 1 per cent in 1945: by 1957, however, it had reached 2·3 per cent. Careful reviews have argued that by the middle 1960s the rate had risen to about 2·4 per cent a year for the whole continent. At the same time other evidence suggests that the rate of expansion in food supply cannot now maintain the average standard of living even at its present low general level.

With the pressing likelihood of a total population again re-doubled by the year 2000 or so, Africa for the first time confronts the prospect of chronic famine. The rich countries' aid seems unlikely to do anything serious about this: as commentators were noting in 1968, the rich countries appear no longer capable of rescuing the Third World reformism they have sponsored and at least verbally cherished. Perhaps, in a certain harsh way, it may prove to be as well. Most authorities agree that nothing can avert disaster in Africa except an accelerating rise in African produc-tivity. But no such rise is possible without a great change in rural attitudes; and any such change must call in turn for radical shifts in socio-economic structure, both within Africa and within the relationship between African economies and the rest of the world.

Other fields also display the growth aspects of this crisis. In all of them the answer seems to be the same: nothing but major structural change can now complete the work of transition.

By the late 1960s, for example, the concept of the sovereign and separate nation-state inherited from Europe was already in trouble. The building and maintaining of some forty such states had begun to wreck itself on two great reefs: first, that it could take far too little account of the ethnic particularities of many of these states; secondly, that many of them were in any case too small or too poor to be viable as sovereign and separate entities. The one great attempt at federation – in Nigeria – had gone far towards ruin through the rivalry of its constituent élites. Mani-festly federation still held the key: just as clearly it would have to be federation on a structural basis far more popular than élitist rule could apparently provide.

Again one may cite the small but so instructive case of Guinea-Bissau. To build an independent state out of five or more ethnic groups in the same colony can obviously make good sense. Yet these total fewer than a million people. Can it make good sense to try to build them into a *nation*-state? Obviously not, accord-ing to the experience of others, by proceeding on the élitist assumptions of European example. But, if not, then how marry their group independence, vital to any progress, to a due regard on one hand for the needs of their separate cultures and, on the other, for the needs of a wider unity with neighbours? Such questions began to be asked with a new urgency as the problems of re-organization became increasingly acute. Generalizing in some words of Julius Nyerere's in 1968, how build 'a union of African states – a transfer of some sovereignty from our national units to a single unit of which we are all part ... [and so, among other things,] coordinate and facilitate the economic development of Africa as a whole, in such a manner as to ensure the well-being of every part of the continent', conserving the many-coloured fabric of African civilization while greatly strengthening and enlarging it? Or how transform, at other levels, the old methods of repre-sentation into new methods capable of integrating the rural mil-lions into everyday political life? How devise structures of economic participation such as can enthuse and energize these rural millions, and so call forth work and sacrifice intense enough to change the future? How protect the chances of African eco-nomic expansion from world 'terms of trade' – especially, the falling value of African exports in terms of African imports – which have worked, and still work, so harshly against the interests of the Third World?

In the end it will be a matter of knowing how the civilization of the past can be remade by a new and bold vision. The Africans sorely need their modern revolution: profound and far-reaching in creative stimulus, unleashing fresh energies, opening new free-doms. The world's experience may help. But the structures that are needed will have to stand on their own soil. Perhaps this is only another way of saying that these new structures, as and when they emerge, will be nourished by the vigour and resilience of native genius, by all the inheritance of self-respect and inno-vating confidence that has carried these peoples through past centuries of change and cultural expansion.

# Notes and References

*Prologue   A Scattered Wisdom*

15. This Ananse story was first recorded, so far as I know, by J. G. Christaller in *Tschi Mmebusem*, 1879, where he prints 3,600 Akan proverbs and tales. R. S. Rattray translates 800 of these, including this one, in *Ashanti Proverbs*, Oxford U.P., 1916.

16. H. and H. A. Frankfort, J. A. Wilson, T. Jacobsen, *Before Philosophy*, Penguin, 1959; *The Intellectual Adventure of Ancient Man*, University of Chicago Press (repr.).

## I   *'Just plain nonsense. . . .' and after*

21. *Transactions of Ethnogr. Soc.*, new series, vol. i, 1867, p. 316. One should note, of course, the steady influence of a quite significant liberal school of thought among Victorian ethnographers who took a different view from that of Burton and his like.

22. H. A. C. Cairns, *Prelude to Imperialism*, Routledge, 1965, esp. p. 85, offers a rich collection of Burtoniana. See also *Trans. Ethnogr. Soc.* 1867, p. 115. There are plenty of non-European parallels. As early as A.D. 1060 a Chinese writer opined that the Africans 'are the worst kind of Barbarians'. Yu-Yang Hsio, quoted by J. J. L. Duyvendak, *China's Discovery of Africa*, 1945, p. 15. For Muslim Arab prejudices, Ibn Khaldun I. pp. 175–6.

23. Comment on Jevons by Evans-Pritchard 1965, p. 5. Dean Farrar was famous for his moralising school story, *Eric, or Little by Little*. The wretched Eric's fate, declining from uncharitable thoughts to deeds without a name, was positively 'African'. He fell beyond recall. For modern Farrarisms of the 'frontal lobe' variety, see espec. J. C. Carothers, *The Psychology of Mau Mau*, Nairobi, 1954, and other of his works.

23. Lothrop Stoddard: I was introduced to this racist writer, who published his work nearly fifty years ago, by receiving through the post a new rehearsal of his views by C. Putnam, *Race and Reality*, Public Affairs Press, Washington, D.C., 1967.

24. St Clair Drake, 'Africa seen by American Negroes', *Présence Africaine*, 1958, p. 27.

## Notes and References

The Brazilian is quoted from *L'Anthropologie*, xlix, by G. Freyre *The Mansions and the Shanties*, New York, Knopf, 1963, p. 383. For anthropological a-historicism and anti-historicism see A. I. Richards, 'Social mechanisms for the transfer of political rights in some African tribes', *Jnl Roy. Anthrop. Inst.*, xc, 2, 1960; Radcliffe-Brown, p. 2; and, for critical discussion, Evans-Pritchard 1962, pp. 13–65, and Gluckman 1963, p. 208.

25. V. L. Grottanelli, 'Sul Significato della Scultura Africana', Lugard Memorial Lecture 1961, (repr.) *Africa*, xxxi, October 1961.

## 2 Formative Origins

27. L. S. B. Leakey, 'The Evolution of Man in the African Continent', *Tarikh*, 1966, no. 3.

27. M. Posnansky, ed, *Prelude to East African History*, Oxford U.P. 1966, p. 34; also for review of population estimates.
For recent conclusions on blood-group analysis: C. Gabel 'Prehistoric populations of Africa', in *Boston University Papers on Africa*, vol. ii, 1966, p. 11. For Bushman populations, Gabel, p. 13, referring to Tobias and Singer.
For Bantu migrations: M. Guthrie, 'Some developments in the pre-history of the Bantu languages', *Jnl African Hist.*, iii. 2, 1962; and R. Oliver, 'Bantu genesis', *Jnl Roy. Soc. Arts*, September 1966; and M. Posnansky, 'Bantu genesis – Archaelogical reflexions' in *Jnl African Hist.*, ix, 1, 1968.

28. Greenberg, 1963.

29. Lozi proverb: *Ya butali u yema ko len yemi babanata; kapa ya butali u ya koku ya babanata.*
Luo: Ogot 1967. Luyia proverb in J. Osogo, *The Baluyia*, Oxford U.P. 1965, pp. 7–8.

## 3 The Physical Problem

31. Work on population densities is among the more pressing problems of African historical research. But 150 million was probably the *order* of magnitude around 1850.
Julian: account by John of Ephesus, quoted in P. L. Shinnie, *Medieval Nubia*, Sudan Antiquities Service, Khartoum, 1954.

34–5. Grahame Clark, 'The Economic Approach to Prehistory', *Proceedings of British Academy*, xxxix, 1953.

## 4 Unity and Variation

36. M. J. Finley, *The Ancient Greeks*, Chatto & Windus, 1963, p. 20. Herodotus, *Histories*, trans. A. de Selincourt, Penguin 1954, p. 103. For a glimpse of modern research into the diffusion of Egyp-

tian ideas, see J. Leclant, 'Histoire de la diffusion des cultes Egyptiens', *Annuaire 1967–68* of 5th Section of École Pratique des Hautes Études, Paris, 1967, p. 112.

37. Dinka, Lienhardt 1961, p. 33; Ashanti, Rattray 1916, p. 20.

37–8. See Brentjes for an interesting summary of African 'common fund' ideas. For pythons, see Merlo and Vidaud.

38–9. Babylonian ideology, Thompson, p. 82; Dogon, Griaule in Forde 1954, p. 84; Bambara, Dieterlen; Mossi, Zahan in Forde and Kaberry, p. 152; Mesopotamian ideology, Jacobsen in Frankfort, *et al, Before Philosophy supra* p. 138; Aztecs, G. C. Vaillant, *The Aztecs of Mexico*, Penguin, 1950, p. 175.

39. For useful summaries of African religious tenets see E. W. Smith 1952, with suggestive 'common fund' examples, e.g. p. 30: 'As in Greek mythology Ouranos and Gaia were husband and wife, and in Egyptian mythology Geb and Nut were wife and husband, so the Africans Earth-Mother is widely known as the spouse of the Sky, whose seminal showers fructify her, so that she gives birth to gods and men and all things.' Again for summaries, E. W. Smith 1950; Parrinder 1961.

39–40. Goody on Griaule: review in *American Anthropologist*, lxix, 2, 1967, pp. 240–41.

## 5  Founding Ancestors

43. I use the term 'social charter' in a more than Malinowskian sense, and as the network of rights and duties – sanctioned necessarily, in the Iron Age context, by ancestral legitimation – within which a people identified itself and lived.

45. *Trans. Ethnogr. Soc.*, 1867, p. 115.

45–6. Shona tradition; D. P. Abraham, 'The Monomotapa Dynasty' in *Southern Rhodesia Native Affairs Department Annual*, 1959, p. 71; *Ibid.*, 'The early political history of the Kingdom of the Mwene Mutapa (850–1589)', *Proceedings* of Leverhulme Inter-Collegiate History Conference, Salisbury (Rhodesia) 1960, p. 61.

48. Sangree, p. 44.

49. *Mhondoro*: Gelfand 1959, p. 30; also Crawford, p. 77.

50. I. M. Kimambo, *The Political History of the Pare People of Tanzania*, forthcoming.

51. Padhola Luo: Ogot 1966.

51–2. Orishanla-Oduduwa conflation: Idowu, p. 27.

51. Oduduwa's offspring: J. F. A. Ajayi and R. Smith, *Yoruba Warfare in the Nineteenth Century*, Cambridge U.P. 1964, p. 1.

53. Kongo: Vansini 1966, p. 38. The process of installation and its attendant mythology are discussed in Balandier 1965, p. 22.

53–4. Palmarès: R. K. Kent, 'An African State in Brazil', *Jnl of*

*Afr. Hist.*, vi, 2 of 1965; and for 'Bush Negroes', Herskovits 1966, p. 267.

## 6   *The Balance with Nature*

55. Lineage and citizenship: Peristiany, 'Law' in Evans-Pritchard *et al.* 1961, p. 44. Kongo saying: Balandier 1965. p. 178. Gluckman 1965, p. 239.

Fortes 1959

56. Middleton and Tait, p. 8.

58. Amba: E. H. Winter, 'The aboriginal political structure of Bwamba', in Middleton and Tait, p. 136.

59. Lugbara: Middleton 1960, p. 25.

60ff. Dinka; Lienhardt 1961; and *ibid.*, 'The Western Dinka' in Middleton and Tait, p. 97.

What Baker told the Ethnographical Society (*Transactions* 1867, p. 231) may still be worth a footnote. Of 'the races of the Nile Basin' he reported that 'without any exception, they are without a belief in a Supreme Being, neither have they any form of worship or idolatry; nor is the darkness of their minds enlightened by even a ray of super-stition. The mind is as stagnant as the morass which forms its puny world.' Many opinions were to flow from 'pioneering' statements such as this. Baker's object, however, was to question the credentials of the evolutionists: 'upon what evidence can we claim the co-relationship with the wild savage of the Nile Basin? Can we venture to date from one common origin, and claim him as a "man and a brother"?' Baker's answers proved reassuring.

63ff. Karimojong: Dyson-Hudson 1966.

For discussion of colonial policy towards the Karimojong, and the vain attempt to impose upon them chiefs who would conform to it, see J. P. Barber, 'The Karamoja District of Uganda' in *Jnl Afr. Hist.* iii, 1, 1962.

65–6. Bemba farming: C. M. N. White, 'Factors determining the content of African land-tenure systems in Northern Rhodesia', Lusaka n.d.; Allan, pp. 66–76.

P. Hill: 'A plea for indigenous economics,' *Economic Development and Cultural Change*, University of Chicago, October 1966.

66. Bishop Mackenzie: D. and C. Livingstone, *The Zambesi and Its Tributaries*, 1966, p. 524.

66. P. H. Nye and D. J. Greenland, *The Soil under Shifting Culti-vation*, Commonwealth Agricultural Bureaux 1960, p. 134.

'Conformity': reference here is to Shona, Gelfand 1962, p. 172.

67. Gluckman 1963, p. 96.

## 7   *A Moral Order*

68. G. M. Carstairs, *This Island Now* (Reith Lectures 1962)

Hogarth Press 1963, p. 55. See also E. Leach, *A Runaway World?* Reith Lectures, BBC 1967, and many others.

69. Wilson 1936, p. 317. How much can be achieved by study of the oral traditions of 'segmentary' societies is shown in Ogot 1966. This kind of information is now becoming more available. For a useful example see Goody, 'The Akan and the North', *Ghana Notes and Queries*, ix, 18–23.

70ff. Amba: Winter, in Middleton and Tait, loc. cit.

71. Kongo self-confidence: G. A. Cavazzi da Montecuccolo. *Istorica Descrizione de' Tre Regni Congo, Matamba et Angola*, Bologna 1687, p. 63.

71–2. Tallensi: Fortes 1949, p. 343.

72–3. Venda: Van Warmelo, p. 47.

73. Zulu: E. J. Krige, 'Girls' puberty songs . . .', *Africa*, ix, April 1968. See also T. O. Beidelman, 'Some Nuer notions of nakedness . . .' loc. cit.

73. Nyakyusa: M. Wilson 1951, p. 77.

74. Fortes 1949, p. 4; also Fortes and Evans-Pritchard 1940, p. 243n.

75. Fortes and Evans-Pritchard 1940, pp. 244–5; pp. 241–3.

75–6. Lozi: Gluckman 1952, p. 65.

77. Fortes in Gluckman 1962, p. 65.

77–8. Zande: Evans-Pritchard 1965, p. 65.

78–9. Konkomba: Tait 1961, p. 39.

80. Evans-Pritchard 1965, p. 88.

## 8 *Elaborations I: Age Sets*

82. Distinction discussed by Radcliffe-Brown in Fortes and Evans-Pritchard 1940. Introduction. See also Horton in 1969(b) for useful definitions and summaries.

83. T. Bowdich, *Mission from Cape Coast to Ashantee*, 1819. See Wilks for the changing position of Asante chiefs in the nineteenth century.

83–4. Asante/Ashanti: Fortes in Gluckman 1962, p. 58.

84. The point about the continuum is well made by Fortes in Radcliffe-Brown and Forde 1950, p. 283: 'Kinship plays an important part in Ashanti social life. It is not only the source of the critical norms governing the jural and personal relations of individuals in many fields of social life, but it also determines the structure of the corporate groups on which the political organization is based and influences political relations at all levels.' This situation was modified during the nineteenth century by reforms which followed Osei Kojo's earlier initiative in breaking the ascriptive rule for accession to office; but the kinship structure appears to have remained paramount even then. See also Horton 1969(b).

86ff. Tiriki: Sangree espec. p. 48 and p. 67. For contrasting details about a neighbouring Kenya people, Peristiany 1939, e.g. p. 32.

87–8. Sangree, p. 71.

88–9. Karimojong: Dyson-Hudson, p. 153.

90. *ibid.*, pp. 181–2.

91. Nyakyusa: M. Wilson 1949.

92. *ibid.*, 1951, p. 66.

92. God and the Devil: expressed in a multitude of ways. For an interesting discussion see Merlo and Vidaud.

## 9   *Elaborations II: Secret Societies*

93. African writers have compared Ibo systems and attitudes with those of ancient Greece. Dike says that the Aro colonies were like those of 'the Greeks, the course of whose colonizing expeditions was largely directed by the priests of the Delphic Oracle', as those of the Aro men were by the oracle at Arochuku. K. O. Dike, *Trade and Politics in the Niger Delta*, Oxford U.P. 1956, p. 38, Writing of Ibo institutions, K. N. Nzimiro ('Political Ideas and Institutions of an African People: A Case Study of Ibo Politics and Government', seminar paper, Nsukka 1963) argues that 'in discovering the political philosophy of the Ibos, my inspiration should ... come from the words of Plato and Aristotle'.

93. Ibo: Webster *et al.*, p. 177.

94–5. Ibo marketing network: U. I. Ukwu, 'The development of trade and marketing in Iboland'. in *Jnl Hist. Soc. Nigeria*, 1967, 4.

95. O. Equiano, *The Interesting Narrative of the Life of* ... 1789, esp. pp. 3–25.

96. Igbo-Ukwu dates: T. Shaw, 'Radiocarbon dates from Nigeria' in *Jnl Hist. Soc. Nigeria*, 1967, 4; and ibid 'Spectrographic Analyses ...', *Archaeometry*, vol. 8, 1965.

97–8. For Delta states and Ekpe: Dike, op. cit.; G. I. Jones, *The Trading States of the Oil Rivers*, Oxford U.P. 1963; and Nzimiro, *supra*. For comparison with Kalabari Ekine, see Horton 1969(a).

99. Antera Duke: diary reproduced with translation in D. Forde, ed, *Efik Traders of Old Calabar*, Oxford U.P. 1956. For discussioin see also Davidson 1961, p. 179.

100–101. Arochuku system: Ukwu op. cit.

101–2. Fernandes: quoted in C. Fyfe 1964, p. 24. Other interesting if confused observations were made by an early Swedish ethnographer at the end of the eighteenth century: *Adam Afzelius: Sierra Leone Journals 1705–96*, Uppsala 1967, e.g. p. 29.

102ff. Poro: Little 1965–6, and bibliography. For a general discussion on 'secret societies', Horton 1969(b).

105. Ogboni: P. M. Morton-Williams, 'The Yoruba Ogboni cult in Oyo', *Africa* 4 of 1960; 'An outline of the cosmology and cult

organization of the Oyo Yoruba', *Africa*, xxxiv, 3, 1964; 'Two studies of Ifa divination', *Africa*, xxxvi, 4, 1966.

105ff. *Report of the Commission Appointed to Enquire into the Owegbe Cult*, Benin 1966. For background, esp. of specific nature of Ogboni in Benin, see Bradbury in Lewis 1968, p. 243.

## 10  A Science of Social Control

111. The separation of scientific thought from theology was of course a long and hardfought process; battles and victims are strewn across the history of the Middle Ages and after, even down to this day. Commenting on Vatican II of the 1960s and its 'present crisis', a prominent Catholic theologian, Bishop Christopher Butler of Westminster, has noted that 'the Church's protest against the Reformation became a protest against the whole great stream of human development in the European West. We stood apart from progress and from democracy, and looked with suspicion on natural science, and with grave suspicion on historical science' (*Sunday Times*, 6 October 1968).

Evans-Pritchard 1965, at various points.

'Axiomatic values': Fortes 1969, p. 53.

113. 'Awareness of alternatives': Horton 1967, part 11, 'The "closed" and "open" predicaments'.

Lévi-Strauss 1966, ch. 1.

114. Karimojong: Dyson-Hudson, p. 16n. and p. 97.

Lévi-Strauss 1962 (b), p. 43.

Horton 1964.

115ff. Kalabari: Horton 1967.

116. The notion of 'freelance spirits' was probably widespread. cf. the *mashave* of the Shona, Crawford, p. 82.

117. Lozi origins: oral tradition told me by the Lozi historian, Ndembu of Itufa near Senanga, in 1966.

J.P. Lebeuf, 'L'Histoire de la région Tchadienne' in Vansina 1964, p. 249.

118. M. d'Hertefelt, 'Mythes et idéologies dans le Rwanda ancien et contemporain', in Vansina 1964, p. 228.

For a discussion of the selective nature and meaning of taboos, see Horton 1967, esp. p. 167; and Lévi-Strauss 1962 (a). On Islamic defences against predictive failure, Ibn Khaldun I. p. 190.

119–20. Ndembu: Turner 1957, 1962, and in Fortes and Dieterlen, p. 79.

120. 'Tangible substance to moral obligations': Fortes in Gluckman 1962, p. 82.

'Conviction of moral order': E. W. Smith 1952, p. 29.

120–21. Dinka: Lienhardt 1961, p. 298.

121. Oyo: P. Morton-Williams, 'The Kingdom of Oyo' in Forde and Kaberry, p. 53.

## 11  Of Witches and Sorcerers

121. These Fort Victoria Africans were prosecuted under a Witch-craft Suppression Act (Rhodesia: 1899) which provides sanctions against all persons 'proved' by trial 'to be by habit and repute a witch doctor or witch finder' – a legal formulation which in itself says much about the nature of the evidence and the preconceptions of the courts. For the general nature of witchcraft confession see following pages of text and especially ch. 16; Field 1960; and Crawford, p. 45.
Kenyatta: *The Times*, 17 January 1968.

124. Harald and Gregory: Janssen, vol. xvi, 1910, pp. 226–7. Synod of Treves: ibid., p. 229.

125. Janssen, op. cit. p. 269. Two key dates for a new repressive attitude by the Church were 1484, when the papal bull *Summis Desiderantes Affectibus* was promulgated, and 1486, when the great witch-hunting book, *Malleus Maleficarum*, was published.

126. ibid., p. 420.

127. Fortes in Evans-Pritchard 1961, p. 88.

128–9ff. Ga and Fanti: Field 1937, esp. ch. IV. See also *Field 1960*, p. 280.

130–31. For a discussion of the witchcraft–sorcery distinction that is characteristic of modern approaches, see introduction by Middleton and Winter to the essays edited in their book of 1963. Some peoples have united the two under one name: e.g. Shona *uroyi*, (wizardry).

## 12  Upside-Down People

132–3. Douglas 1966, p. 171.

133. Evans-Pritchard 1937, p. 107.

133–4. Middleton 1960, p. 236, and, for discussion, the whole of his chapter 5. pp. 230–70.

134–5. Middleton 1960, p. 36, and 'Witchcraft and sorcery in Lugbara', in Middleton and Winter 1963, p. 258.

135. Nadel 1952.

136. Practical distinctions between religion and magic are ancient, and were argued as long ago as Pliny the Elder. See discussion by R. Schilling, 'Religion et magie à Rome', in *Annuaire 1967–8* of 5th Section of École Pratiques des Hautes Études, pp. 31–55.

136–7. G. C. Brown and A. McD. B. Hutt, *Anthropology in Action*, Oxford U.P. 1935, p. 182.

137ff. Marwick 1965, p. 15, and esp. ch. 8, 'Sorcery as a moral force', p. 221.

138–44. Attitudes to death have to be seen in their whole context. Most African belief has strongly held that he dead continue to live in suiritual terms. 'Men enjoy eternal life in the sense that their vital spiritual energy is not lost to the tribal community, but returns to it again and again in a recognizable way, a way which is commonly recognized in African naming ceremonies.' So death is not a fearful ending.

Such beliefs must be of great antiquity. 'The Pygmies of Equatorial Africa sing to the newly-dead body how the spirits of the dead swirl and flutter in the wind of the underworld like mosquitoes or dead leaves; but they do so only to await the visit of God, who will tell them when and how to return to he world' (G. Moore, 'The Meaning of Rebirth in the Pagan and Islamic Literature of Africa', seminar paper, School of Oriental and African Studies, London 1968.)

A 'sociology of death' might show that the fear of death has advanced together with universal religions which have themselves reflected a deepening isolation of the individual from the community, and a corresponding growth of the idea of survival in another world, not this one.

138–9. Marwick's conclusions, Marwick 1965, pp. 245–6.
For the scope for selection among alternatives – for 'optation' – see van Velsen and Frankenburg.

## 13  *Explanation and Prediction*

140–41. Fortes 1959, p. 51.
141. Horton 1967, pp. 162 and 69.
142. Beattie, 'Sorcery in Bunyoro', in Middleton and Winter, p. 50.
143. Marwick, p. 14.
Lele: Douglas, 'Techniques of sorcery control in Central Africa' in Middleton and Winter, p. 128.
Kaguru: T. O. Beidelman, 'Witchcraft in Ukaguru', in Middleton and Winter, p. 63.
Tallensi: Fortes 1959, p. 57.
144. Marwick, p. 243. See also note for pp. 136–42.
Beattie loc. cit., p. 52.
Evans-Pritchard 1937, p. 64.

## 14  *The Danger Within*

146. Marwick, p. 235.
147. ibid., p. 95.
147–8. ibid., pp. 1 and 95.
148. Evans-Pritchard 1937, p. 110.
Lugbara: Middleton, 'Witchcraft and sorcery in Lugbara', in Middleton and Winter, p. 272.
Last paragraph: A. R. Radcliffe-Brown, *Structure and Function in Primitive Society*, Cohen 1952, p. 154.
149. Amba: Winter, 'The enemy within: Amba witchcraft and sociological theory', in Middleton and Winter, p. 277.

## 15   Useful Magic

150. Kalabari: Horton 1962.
Mbugwe: R. F. Gray, 'Some structural aspects of Mbugwe witch-craft', in Middleton and Winter, p. 148.

151. Mitchell, J. Clyde, 'The meaning in Misfortune for Urban Africans', in Fortes and Dieterlen, p. 192.
Cavazzi op. cit., p. 237.

152-3. Kaguru: Beidelman, p. 93.
Nandi: G. W. B. Huntingford 'Nandi Witchcraft' in Middleton and Winter, p. 180.

## 16   Answers to Anxiety

154. Case discussed by E. F. B. Forster, 'Treatment of the African mental patient', in Lambo n.d., p. 277.

154-5. Interview in the *Listener*, 8 July 1965.
Limitations: Forster loc. cit.
A. H. Leighton and J. M. Hughes, 'Yoruba concepts of psychiatric disorder', in Lambo n.d., p. 138. The whole of this statement is of great interest.
A. Lewis in Lambo n.d., p. 23.

157. R. Prince, 'Some notes on Yoruba native doctors and their management of mental illness', in Lambo n.d., p. 280.

157. R. S. Rattray describes training of priest doctors in *Religion and Art among the Ashanti*, Oxford U.P. 1927, esp., p. 39.
Gluckman 1962, p. 31.

159-60. Field 1960, p. 38.

160. ibid., p. 107.

161. ibid., p. 126.

161-2. 'Over 60 per cent of the patient population of a large general hospital in Western Nigeria received treatment from native practitioners in one form or another during the time they were being treated in the hospital.' Quoted by Lewis in Lambo n.d., p. 23.
In a Zambian inquiry, 'nearly two-thirds of all *n'angas* (tradi-tional healers') patients had previously consulted "western" medical advisers. This applied to more than half of every diagnostic category except for mental disorder, i.e. madness and spirit possession, for which 55 per cent and 80 per cent respectively had consulted a *n'ganga* first.' Another 156 *n'ganga* patients were excluded from this analysis, because they had sought divination of the cause of death, protection from evil spirits, and treatment of bad dreams, rather than treatment of a disease: J. Leeson, '*Paths to Medical Care*', Lusaka 1967.

162. Fortes in Evans-Pritchard 1961, p. 90.

V. W. Turner, 'An Ndembu doctor on practice,' in Kiev 1964. Douglas 1966, p. 70, has useful discussion.

### 17   Art for Life's Sake

164. Douglas, 1966, p. 58.
166. Dinka: Lienhardt 1961, p. 280.
166. Bushmen: quoted in Douglas, p. 58.
Lienhardt in Evans-Pritchard 1961, p. 104.
167–70. Kalabari: Horton 1963.
171. Worringer: quoted by E. R. Leach in Evans-Pritchard 1961, p. 30. This essay offers other gems of the same sort. Thus Eric Newton of African sculpture in 1946: 'The spirit behind it is always the same. It is that of a trapped animal trying to escape by means of magic.'

### 18   The Dynamics of Reality

173–6. Dogon: Griaule 1965, introduction by G. Dieterlen, and esp. pp. 30–46.
176–7. Bambara: Dieterlen 1951, esp. chs 1 and 2.
177. Diola: L. V. Thomas 'Brève esquisse sur la pensée cosmologique du Diola', in Fortes and Dieterlen, p. 374.
Lienhardt 1964, p. 176.
178ff. Horton 1967 at various points; Fortes 1959, ch. V.
178. Lévi-Strauss 1962 (b): Eng. trans. 1966, p. 269.
179–80. Evans-Pritchard 1936, p. 194.
181. Horton 1967, p. 156.
A. Lebeuf, 'Le système classificatoire des Fali', in Fortes and Dieterlen, p. 330.
182. A. Adesanya, 'Yoruba metaphysical thinking', *Odu* 5 of 1958 (Ibadan), quoted from J. Jahn, *Muntu* 1961, p. 96.
182–3. Brass chiefs: '*Report by Sir John Kirk on the Disturbances at Brass*'. H.M.S.O., Africa, no. 3 of 1896.
183. Swahili poet: Saiyid Abdallah, *Utendi wa Inkishafi*: trans. L. Harries, *Swahili Poetry*, Oxford U.P. 1962, pp. 95–6.

### 19   From Elders to Kings

188–9. Speculation on the origins of central government is not new. For Africa, however, I rather doubt if we are much advanced beyond Ibn Khaldun I, p. 380, and II, p. 3.
192. Luo: Ogot 1967, pp. 41–7.
193. ibid., pp. 123–4.

194. B. A. Ogot, 'Kingship and statelessness among the Nilotes' in Vansina 1964, p. 298.

195. Jukun: M. W. Young, 'The divine kingship of the Jukun: a re-evaluation of some theories', *Africa*, xxxvi, 2, 1966, p. 146.

195. M. Bloch, *La Société féodale: les classes et le gouvernement des hommes* (Paris) (repr.) 1949, p. 195.

al-Mas'udi, *Les Prairies d'Or ...* , trans. Paris 1864, vol. 3, p. 29.

199–200. That the Golden Stool was in the nature of a national shrine, and no more to be sat upon than an altar, was something the British invaders had to learn the hard way. The error has nonetheless persisted: e.g. S. and P. Ottenberg, *Cultures and Societies of Africa*, 1960, 'the kingdom of Ashanti ... was ... ruled by the *Asante Hene*, who sat upon the famed Golden Stool'. For the most recent description, see A. Kyerematen, 'The Royal Stools of Ashanti,' *Africa*, xxxix, 1, 1969.

200. See esp. Goody 1966 for succession customs.

200–201. Mossi: D. Zahan, 'The Mossi Kingdoms', in Forde and Kaberry, p. 152.

202. Gonja: 'The Over-Kingdom of Gonja,' in ibid., p. 179.

Dahomey: J. Lombard, '*The Kingdom of Dahomey*' ibid., p. 70.

202ff. Barotse: Gluckman 1965, pp. 40 and 45.

203ff. Afro-European parallels: I stress these here for the light they can throw on European as well as African history. Other factors conditioning the growth of society in Africa and Europe were becoming very divergent even by European medieval times: mainly, as Goody has emphasized, through certain differences in productive systems, notably in land rights, means of cultivation, transport. cf. Goody, 1968.

204. Gluckman 1965, p. 57ff.

205–6. Jukun: Young loc. cit., p. 140.

206. K. H. Kantorowicz, *The King's Two Bodies*, Princeton U.P. 1957, pp. 395, 418–30; and Young loc. cit., pp. 147–50.

e.g. Evans-Pritchard 1948, p. 17: 'The Kingship is the common symbol of the Shilluk people and Nyikang [cf. English *dignitas*; Jukun *juwe*; etc.] being immortal, an abiding institution which binds past and present and future generations ... The correspondence of political structure with religious cult can be seen at every point in the structure.'

207. Gluckman, 1965, pp. 243 and 269.

Legal parallels remain a field to be explored. But something can be done even with elementary texts: e.g. F. L. Ganshof, *Feudalism*, Longmans (repr.) 1964, p. 83.

### 21 Conquest and Clientage

208ff. Institutions: see, e.g. A. Kagame, 'Le code des institutions politiques du Rwanda precolonial', *Inst. Roy. Col. Belge*, 1952; ibid. 'L'Histoire des armées-bovines dans l'ancien Rwanda', 1961; and, for further elaboration of religion, L. de Heusch in *Annuaire 1968* of 5th Secn. of École Pratigne des Hautes Études, pp. 71–4.

209ff. Maquet in Forde 1954, p. 169. Parallels: Goody 1966.

211. Blackstone, *Commentaries* 1765, vol I, p. 246.

213–14. K. Oberg in Fortes and Evans-Pritchard, p. 148.

214–15. H. F. Morris, *The Heroic Recitations of the Bahima of Ankole*, Oxford U.P. 1964, p. 60.

### 22 Trade and Islam

216. About 250,000 folios of business documents, mainly of the eleventh and twelfth centuries, have survived from the storerooms – *genizas* – of a synagogue and cemetery of Old Cairo. See Goitein 1966, pp. 239, 298, 337; as well as Goitein 1967 for extensive discussion.

218. For early Muslim trans-Saharan trade, T. Lewicki, 'Quelques extraits inédits relatifs aux voyages des commerçants ibadites ...', *Folia Orientalis*, Krakow 1961, pp. 1–27; ibid. 'Traits d'Histoire du Commerce Transsaharien. Marchands et Missionaires Ibadites ...', *Etnografia Polska*, vii, 1964; ibid., 'Tahert et ses relations ...', *Cahiers d'Etudes Africaines*, Paris, 8 of 1962.

218–20. *Minhadj*, Cahen, Muslim-Spanish slaves, E. Lévi-Provençal, *Histoire de l'Espagne Musulmane*, vol. 3, Paris 1967, pp. 177, 206–9, 259, 314; Goitein on cost of slaves, 1967 pp. 130; Iraq exception, Cahen 1968, pp. 137; see also '*Abd* in *Ency. of Islam* 1960, vol. 1.

219. Goitein 1967, p. 132; and, foot of page, Goitein 1966, p. 303.

222–3. For recent light on Almoravids, P. Semonin in *Trans. Hist. Soc. of Ghana*, 1965, pp. 42–59; P. Farias, 'The Almoravids ...' in *Bull. Franç. de l'Afrique Noire*, Dakar, nos. 3–4 of 1967.

227. Tudor govt.: C. Wilson, *England's Apprenticeship*, Longmans 1965, pp. 89–90.

228. On king's appointment of officials outside his own lineage, 'not of his own skin,' cf. Ibn Khaldun, vol. 1, p. 372.

228–9. Zaria: M. G. Smith 1960, p. 40, and *in extenso*; also ibid. 1964.

### 23 Power, Rank and Privilege

231. Dahomey: for a recent survey of evidence for economic con-

centration, K. Polanyi, *Dahomey and the Slave Trade*, Univ. of Washington Press 1966, chs. 3–6.

231. For examples and discussion of deliberate 'accruing of royal authority', see Wilks (Asante) in Forde and, Kaberry; Lloyd (Yoruba), Southwold (Baganda), and Bradbury (Benin) in Lewis 1968; also Horton 1969(b).

233ff. Oyo: Webster et al., pp. 92–101. I am grateful to Prof. Webster for a number of points made in private correspondence.

239. Fall of Songhay, J. Rouch, *Contributions à l'Histoire des Songhay*, Dakar 1953, esp. in this context p. 219. On Hausaland see esp. M. G. Smith, The Hague 1964; and M. Last, *The Sokoto Caliphate*, Longmans 1967.

## 24  The Crisis Opens

241. Salisbury: in Robinson et al., pp. 17, 30.

243. D. F. Ellenberger, *History of the Basuto* 1912, p. 117. The classic sources are those of Fynn, a contemporary of Shaka's, and later Bryant. For a recent appraisal of the evidence for Nguni (Ngoni) expansion see S. Marks in *Jnl of African Hist.*, viii, 3, 1967, pp. 529–40; and ibid. in R. Oliver, *The Middle Age of African History*, Oxford U.P. 1967, pp. 85–91.

244. Swazi: Kuper, p. 123.
Ganda: A. Kaggwa, *Basakabaka be Buganda*, trans. and ed. by M. S. Kiwanuka (thesis in Senate House, London University) 1965, p. 332.

245–6. Fire-arms: B. Davidson, *East and Central Africa to the Nineteenth Century*, Longmans 1967, p. 199; R. W. Beachey, 'The arms trade in East Africa in the late nineteenth century', in *Jnl African Hist.*, iii, 3, 1962.

## 25  From a Guerrilla Diary

253. F. Fanon, *Towards the African Revolution*, Monthly Review Press, New York, 1967, p. 102.
Nationalist resistance in the Portuguese territory of Guinea-Bissau, a west African wedge of forest and savannah about the size of Switzerland, is the work of Partido Africano de Independência de Guiné e Cabo Verde (P.A.I.G.C.), See Davidson 1969.

## 26  The Great Transition

260. H. Arendt, *The Burden of Our Times*, Secker 1951, p. 227.
262. For the Shona text of this oath, and its translation I am grateful to Mr Chenhamo Chimutengwende, who swore it himself.

## 27  The Kings Resist

263–5. Asante: Webster p. 126, I. Wilks in Forde and Kaberry, p. 213.

266–7. Hargreaves, ch. 3; Webster, p. 28; Suret-Canale, 1964, pp. 241–3.

267. Samori; J. Holden, 'The Empire of Samory', seminar paper, University of Ghana 1964; also M. Legassick on Samorian organization in *Jnl African Hist.*, 1 of 1966.

269–70. al-Hajj Umar of Kete Krachi: B. G. Martin in J. A. Braimah and J. R. Goody, *Salaga: The Struggle for Power*, Longmans 1967, pp. 189–209. See also T. Hodgkin, 'The Islamic literary tradition in Ghana' in Lewis 1966, pp. 453–4.

## 28  Twilight of the Old Gods

272ff. Ndebele and Shona: Ranger for this and following quotes, pp.59–60, 67ff., 127, 352ff.

275. 'Cargo cults', see Worsley.

276ff. Herero and Nama: Dreschler 1966 for this and following quotes, e.g. pp. 32, 180–84, 197, 252

277–8. von Trotha's methods: Dreschler, p. 180; Davidson 1968, p. 251.

278. Morenga: Dreschler 1967.

278–9. Maji Maji: the key interpretation here is J. Iliffe, 'The Organization of the Maji Maji Rebellion' in *Jnl African Hist.*, viii, 3, 1967, p. 495. See also G. C. K. Gwassa and J. Iliffe, *Records of the Maji Maji Rising*, Dar-es-Salaam 1968, and J. Iliffe, *Tanganyika under German Rule 1905–1912*, Cambridge U.P. 1969, chs. 2 and 3. For Mumbo, see Ogot 1963.

## 29  New Redeemers

283. Roy Campbell, *Collected Poems*, Lane 1949, vol. 1, p. 197.

285. Theal: quoted by Shepperson in Baëta, p. 250.

286. Millennial expectations were also encouraged by Islam, though not in Central Africa. A 'central point of Muslim eschatology' has been that 'a deliverer, or a saviour, will appear to restore the true religion and "fill the world with equity and justice after it has been filled with tyranny and oppression" ...' A. A. Al-Hajj, 'Mahdist Expectations ...' *Bulletin of Centre of Arabic Documentation*, Ibadan, July 1967, p. 100.

286. Russell: Shepperson and Price, p. 150.

287. Black Muslims: E. U. Essien-Udom, *Black Nationalism: The*

*Rise of the Black Muslims in the USA*, Penguin 1966, pp. 84, 120, 129.

288. Booth and Chilembwe: Shepperson and Price, p. 533.

288–9. Kamwana: Shepperson and Price, pp. 153 etc; Rotberg 1966, pp. 150.

289. Ana a Mulungu: Rotberg 1966, pp. 151, 150.
Domingo: Shepperson and Price, pp. 163–4.

289ff. Nyirenda: Rotberg 1966, pp. 143–4. See also H. J. Greschat, 'Witchcraft und Kirchlicher Separatismus in Zentral Afrika', in Benz, pp. 96–7; and O. F. Raum, 'Von Stammespropheten zu Sektenfuehrer', loc. cit.

291–2. 'Luvale man': I am grateful to Attorney-General James Skinner of Zambia for this account. Crawford (p. 7) says that selling medicine to multiply money is a fairly common crime in Rhodesia.

293–4. Kimbangu: P. Raymaekers, 'L'Eglise de Jésus-Christ sur la terre par le prophète Simon Kimbangu: Contribution à l'étude des mouvements messianiques dans le Bas-Kongo', *Zaire*, xiii, 7, 1959.
The case of Simão Toco in neighbouring Angola is closely relevant.
Garvey: Hodgkin 1956, p. 101.

294. Spartas: Welbourn, p. 77. Tudor comparison, ibid., p. 176.

## 30 The Modern Context

297. Agbebi. Shepperson in Baëta, pp. 258–9.

298. Newspaper quotes in Kimble, pp. 512–13 etc.

298. J. Mensah Sarbah, *Fanti National Constitution*, London 1906, p. 71.
For West African journalism, see July, Kimble, Spiegler.

299. Louis Hunkanrin: J. Suret-Canale 'Un pionnier méconnu du mouvement democratique et national en Afrique', *Études Daho-méennes*, December 1964; and, generally for nationalism in French-speaking territories, Spiegler.
Elsewhere, nationalist development showed basically similar trends, even in the Portuguese colonies, where reformist opportunities remained minimal.

## 31 The Masses React

301–2. Thuku: Welborn, pp. 129–30.

303. Shepperson 1961.

304–5. All judgements on the colonial condition are bound to be controversial at this stage. For my own more extensive arguments and evidence, see Davidson 1967, chs. 6 and 7.

305. A. Cabral, 'L'Unité politique et morale: force principale de notre Lutte commune': speech, Dar-es-Salaam, October 1965.
Verhaegen, p. 18.

307. ibid., pp. 19–20.

307–8. B. Davidson, *The African Awakening*, Cape, 1955, p. 132.

308. Balandier in ibid., ref. 96.

Congolese schools: Verhaegen, p. 21.

309. Wilson 1936, p. 555.

309. Le Vine, La Fontaine, Beidelman, in Middleton and Winter respectively, pp. 255, 218, 95.

For recent years the literature describes a wide range of anti-witch-craft movements of the same basic type as those considered here; e.g. R. G. Willis, 'Kamcape: an anti-sorcery movement in South West Tanzania', *Africa*, xxxviii, 1, 1968. Of this movement, active in 1963, Willis comments: 'It may be assumed ... that the accusations made during a Kamcape ("cleansing") operation relate primarily to general and social ... conflicts within a village community.'

Southwark exorcism, *The Times*, 3 April 1968; 'Victorian ghost', *The Sun* 19 May 1966; Italian spells, *The Guardian* 7 Dec. 1967.

311ff. Lumpa Church: *Report on the Commission of Inquiry into the ...* Govt. Printer, Lusaka 1965. Though in a revised context, Alice was centrally concerned with opposing witchcraft. Rule 4 of the Lumpa Church laid down that 'a Christian must avoid covetous-ness, witchcraft, stealing, adultery, witch-hunting, sorcery, discrimi-nation, drunkenness, bewitching and immoral songs dancing and other pagan things': or, in short, all those sins, those interruptions of the 'right and natural', which traditional thought refers to witchcraft or its consequences. And while men might no longer punish witches, God certainly would. Rule 12 concluded: 'Any one who does not obey the rules is not liked by our Lord, the Almighty God, and that is why our Lord said, "Stop practising witchcraft and live in my love". Any one who is found practising witchcraft will suffer more when his time comes to an end because he or she will be heavily punished' (ibid. p. 17).

314ff. Mulelist revolt: Verhaegen.

315. Killing of Mulele: *The Times*, 9 October 1968; *Time*, 18 October 1968.

317. Tanzanian official document: *Answers to Questions on the Arusha Declaration*, Govt Printers, Dar-es-Salaam, 1967.

318–19. See Davidson 1969 for detailed description and discussion of origins and policies of P.A.I.G.C. in Guinea-Bissau; and cf. E. Mondlane, *The Struggle for Mozambique*, Penguin 1969. In Angola the M.P.L.A. shows a parallel development.

*Epilogue   African Destinies*

321–2. I have argued the partial parallel with the industrial revolu-tion in Davidson 1968, pp. 261–75.

322. For discussion on conditions in the English industrial revolu-

tion, see E. J. Hobsbawm, 'The British standard of living 1790–1850', and 'History of the dark satanic mills', in *Labouring Men*, Weidenfeld & Nicolson 1964, pp. 64 and 105; and E. Thompson, *The Making of the English Working Class*, Gollancz 1963. The two quotations are respectively from W. E. Moore, *Industrialization and Labor*, Cornell U.P. 1951, p. 21, and K. Polanyi, *Origins of Our Time*, Gollancz 1945, p. 41.

323. Critics quoted: T. Solarin in *African Independence*, ed. P. Judd, Dell, N.Y. 1963, p. 248; A. Cabral, 'Une Crise de Conscience', paper delivered Cairo 1961.
Congo population, Verhaegen 1966.

324. General rate of increase: Economic Commission for Africa in W. A. Hance, 'The race between population and resources', *Africa Report*, January 1968. Outlook for foreign aid reviewed by T. J. Mboya at 8th Sessn of E.C.A., Lagos, February 1967. See also A. F. Ewing, 'Self-Reliance in Africa', *Jnl of Mod. Afr. Studies*, Dar-es-Salaam, vi, 3, 1968.
That the famine prospect for Africa, as for other Third World regions, is now extremely menacing is argued in detail in R. Dumont and B. Rosier, *Nous Allons à la Famine*, Le Seuil, Paris 1966 (Eng. edn: *The Hungry Future*, André Deutsch, 1969).
'The failure of the rich nations to offer new hope to the poor' at the 2nd U.N. Conf. on Trade and Development (New Delhi, February–March 1968), '. . . may be seen as marking the end of the hopes of the world's poor for an easier road ahead than the way of revolutionary war' (M. Barratt-Brown in *New Society*, 11 April 1968, p. 526).
At this vast conference 'practically nothing was achieved . . . (It) must have been a nightmare to anybody who cared at all about what happens to the . . . poor countries . . . (and) it must also have increased the attractiveness of other policies. Self-reliance à la Tanzania, for instance; or revolution' (T. Hayter, in loc. cit., pp. 528–9).

325. Nyerere: quoted in *West Africa*, 16 March 1968.

# Select Bibliography

ALLAN, W., *The African Husbandman*, Oliver & Boyd, 1965.

BABALOLA, S. A., *The Content and Form of Yoruba Ijalo*, Oxford U.P., 1966.

BAETA, C. G., ed., *Christianity in Tropical Africa*, Oxford U.P., 1968.

BALANDIER, G., 'Le Travail non-salarié dans les "Brazzavilles Noires"', *Zaire*, July–August 1952.

*Sociologie actuelle de l'Afrique Noire*, Presses Univ. de France, Paris, 1963.

*La Vie quotidienne au royaume de Kongo*, Paris, 1965: trans. H. Weaver, as *Daily Life in the Kingdom of the Kongo*, Allen & Unwin, 1968.

BAUMANN, H. and WESTERMANN, D., *Les Peuples et Civilisations de l'Afrique*, Payot, Paris, 1948.

BEATTIE, J., *Bunyoro, an African Kingdom*, New York, Holt, 1960.

BENIN: MINISTRY OF INTERNAL AFFAIRS AND INFORMATION, *Report of the Commission Appointed to Enquire into the Owegbe Cult*, Benin, 1966.

BENZ, E., ed., *Messianische Kirchen, Sekten und Bewegungen im Heutigen Afrika*, Leiden, 1965.

BIRMINGHAM, D., *Trade and Conflict in Angola, 1483–1790*, Oxford U.P., 1966.

BOHANNAN, P. J., *Justice and Judgment among the Tiv*, Oxford U.P., 1957.

BRENTJES, B., 'Orientalisch-mediterrane Kulturmonumente Altwestafrikas', in *Wissensch. Zeitschr. der Martin-Luther-Universität*, Halle-Wittenberg, Sept. 1962.

CAHEN, C., 'Douanes et commerce dans les ports mediterranéens de l'Egypte mediévale d'après le Minhadj d'al-Makhzumi', *Jnl of the Econ. and Soc. Hist of the Orient*, Leiden, Nov. 1964.

*Der Islam: Vom Ursprung bis zu den Anfängen des Osmanenreiches*, Fischer Weltgeschichte, Frankfurt, 1968.

COHEN, R., 'The Dynamics of Feudalism in Bornu', *Boston Univ. Papers: African Hist.*, ed. J. Butler, 1966.

COLSON, E. and GLUCKMAN, M., ed., *Seven Tribes of British Central Africa*, Oxford U.P., 1951.

CRAWFORD, J. R., *Witchcraft and Sorcery in Rhodesia*, Oxford U.P., 1967.

CUNNISON, I. G., *The Luapula Peoples of Northern Rhodesia: Custom and history in tribal politics*, Oxford U.P., 1959.

CURTIN, P. D., *The Image of Africa, British Ideas and Action 1780–1850*, Macmillan, 1963.

DAVIDSON, B., *Old Africa Rediscovered*, Gollancz, 1959.

*Black Mother: The African Slave Trade*, Gollancz, 1961.

*Which Way Africa? The Search for a New Society*, Penguin, third revised edn, 1971.

*Africa in History: Themes and Outlines*, Weidenfeld & Nicolson, 1968.

*The Liberation of Guiné: Aspects of an African Revolution*, Penguin, 1969.

DESCHAMPS, H., *Traditions orales et archives au Gabon*, Berger-Levrault, Paris, 1962.

DIETERLEN, G., *Essai sur la Réligion Bambara*, Presses Univ. de France, Paris, 1951.

DOUGLAS, M., *Purity and Danger: An Analysis of Concepts of Pollution and Taboo*, Routledge, 1966; also Penguin, 1970.

Ed. with Kaberry, P. M., *Man in Africa*, Tavistock, 1969.

DRESCHLER, H., *Suedwestafrika unter deutscher Kolonialherrschaft: der Kampf der Herero und Nama*, Berlin, 1966.

'Jacob Morenga: a New Kind of South-West African Leader' *African Studies*, Leipzig, 1967.

DYSON-HUDSON, N., *Karimojong Politics*, Oxford U.P., 1966.

EINZIG, P., *Primitive Money*, Eyre & Spottiswoode, 1949.

ELIAS, T. O., *The Nature of African Customary Law*, Manchester U.P., 1956.

*Government and Politics in Africa*, rev. edn, Asia Publishing House, London, 1963.

EVANS-PRITCHARD, E. E., *Witchcraft, Oracles and Magic among the Azande*, Oxford U.P., 1937.

*The Political System of the Anuak of the Anglo-Egyptian Sudan*, Lund Humphries, 1940.

*The Divine Kingship of the Shilluk of the Nilotic Sudan*, Cambridge U.P. (Frazer Lecture), 1948.

*Nuer Religion*, Oxford U.P., 1956.

'Zande Kings and Princes', *Anthropol. Qly*, July 1957.

*Essays in Social Anthropology*, Faber, 1962.

*Theories of Primitive Religion*, Oxford U.P., 1965.

With seven others, *The Institutions of Primitive Society*, Oxford U.P., 1961.

FALLERS, L. A., *Bantu Bureaucracy: A Century of Evolution among the Basoga of Uganda*, University of Chicago Press (repr.), 1966.

FIELD, M., *Religion and Medicine of the Ga People*, Oxford U.P., 1937.

*Search for Security: an Ethno-psychiatric Study of Rural Ghana*, Faber, 1960.

FORDE, D., ed., *African Worlds: Studies in the Cosmological Ideas and Social Values of African Peoples*, Oxford U.P., 1954.

*Yakö Studies*, Oxford U.P., 1964.

With KABERRY, P. M., ed., *West African Kingdoms in the Nineteenth Century*, Oxford U.P., 1967.

FORTES, M., *The Dynamics of Clanship among the Tallensi*, Oxford U.P., 1945.

*The Web of Kinship among the Tallensi*, Oxford U.P., 1949.

*Oedipus and Job in West African Religion*, Cambridge U.P., 1959.

With EVANS-PRITCHARD, E. E., ed., *African Political Systems*, Oxford U.P., 1940.

With DIETERLEN, G., ed., *African Systems of Thought*, Oxford U.P., 1965.

FRANKENBURG, R., 'The Challenge of the New Africa to the Sociological Study of Small-scale Social Process', seminar paper, Lusaka, 1967.

FYFE, C., *A History of Sierra Leone*, Oxford U.P., 1962.

GELFAND, M., *Shona Ritual*, London, 1959.

*Shona Religion*, London, 1962.

GINSBERG, M., 'On the Diversity of Morals', *Jnl of Roy. Anthrop. Inst.*, lxxxiii, 2, 1953.

GLUCKMAN, M., ed., *Essays on the Ritual of Social Relations, Custom and Conflict in Tribal Africa*, Manchester U.P., 1962.

*Order and Rebellion in Tribal Africa*, Cohen, 1963.

*The Ideas in Barotse Jurisprudence*, Yale U.P., 1965.

*Politics, Law and Ritual in Tribal Society*, Blackwell, 1965.

GOITEIN, S. D., *Studies in Islamic History and Institutions*, Brill, 1966.

*A Mediterranean Society*, vol. I: *Economic Foundations*, Univ. of California and Cambridge U.P., 1967.

GOODY, J. A., *Death, Property and the Ancestors*, Cambridge U.P., 1962.

Ed., *Succession to High Office*, Cambridge U.P., 1966.

'Economy and Feudalism in Africa', seminar paper, Institute of Commonwealth Studies, 1968.

GRAY, R. F., *see* MBEE.

GREENBERG, J. H., *The Languages of Africa*, Indiana University Press, 1963.

GRIAULE, M., *Masques Dogon*, Inst. d'Ethnologie, Paris, 1938.

*Dieu d'Eau*, Paris, 1948; Eng. trans., *Conversations with Ogotêmmeli, An Introduction to Dogon Religious Ideas*, Oxford U.P., 1965.

GROTTANELLI, V. L., 'Asonu Worship among the Nzema: a Study in Akan art and religion', *Africa*, xxxi, 1, 1961.

GUTHRIE, M., 'Some Developments in the Prehistory of the Bantu Languages', *Jnl. of Afr. Hist.*, iii, 2, 1962.

HARGREAVES, J. D., *Prelude to the Partition of West Africa*, Macmillan, 1963.

HERSKOVITS, M. J., *Dahomey, an Ancient West African Kingdom*, 2 vols., London, 1938.

*The Human Factor in Changing Africa*, Routledge, 1962.

Ed. F. S. Herskovits, *The New World Negro*, Indiana U.P., 1966.

HIERNAUX, J., *La Diversité humaine en Afrique Subsaharienne*, Inst. de Sociologie, Université Libre de Bruxelles, 1968.

HODGKIN, T. L., *Nationalism in Colonial Africa*, Muller, 1956.

HOLAS, B., *Les Masques Kono: leur rôle dans le vie religieuse et politique*, Paris, 1952.

HORTON, R., 'The Kalabari World View: An Outline and Interpretation', *Africa*, xxxii, 2, 1962.

'The Kalabari *Ekine* Society', *Africa*, xxxiii, 2, 1963.

'Ritual Man in Africa', *Africa*, xxxiv, 2, 1964.

'A Definition of Religion and its Uses', *Jnl of Roy. Anthrop. Inst.*, xc, 2, 1960.

'African Traditional Thought and Western Science', *Africa*, xxxvii, 2, 1967.

'From Fishing Village to City-state', in Douglas and Kaberry, 1969(a).

'Stateless Societies in the History of West Africa', in J. A. Ajayi and M. Crowder, *History of West Africa*, Longman, 1972, vol. 1.

IBN KHALDUN, *The Muqaddimah*, trans. F. Rosenthal, New York and London, Routledge, 3 vols., 1967.

IDOWU, E. B., *Olódùmarè: God in Yoruba Belief*, Longman, 1962.

JANSSEN, J., *History of the German People at the Close of the Middle Ages*, 16 vols., Kegan Paul, London, 1896–1910.

JULY, R. W., *The Origins of Modern African Thought*, Faber, 1968.

KAGAME, A., *Le Code des institutions politiques du Rwanda précolonial*, Inst. Roy. Col. Belge, Brussels, 1952.

*La Philosophie bantu-rwandaise de l'être*, Brussels, 1955.

KIEV, A., ed., *Magic, Faith and Healing*, Collier-Macmillan, 1964.

KIMBLE, D., *A Political History of Ghana: The Rise of Gold Coast Nationalism (1850–1928)*, Oxford U.P., 1963.

KUPER, H., *An African Aristocracy: Rank among the Swazi*, Oxford U.P. (repr.), 1961.

LAMBO, T. A., ed., *Report of First Pan-African Psychiatric Conference*, n.d., Abeokuta.

'Important Areas of Ignorance and Doubt in the Psychology of the African', in *Proceedings of First Internat. Congress of Africanists*, Accra, 1964.

LÉVI-STRAUSS, C., *Le Totémisme aujourd'hui*, Paris, 1962(a).
*La Pensée sauvage*, Plon, Paris, 1962(b); Eng. trans. *The Savage Mind*, Weidenfeld & Nicolson, 1966.

LEWIS, I. M., ed., *Islam in Tropical Africa*, Oxford U.P., 1966.
Ed., *History and Social Anthropology*, Tavistock, 1968.

LIENHARDT, G., *Divinity and Experience: The Religion of the Dinka*, Oxford U.P., 1961.

*Social Anthropology*, Oxford U.P., 1964.

LITTLE, K., 'The Political Function of the Poro', two parts, *Africa*, xxxv, 4, 1965 and xxxvi, 1, 1966.

LLOYD, P. C., *Yoruba Land Law*, Oxford U.P., 1962.

LOWRIE, R. H., *Primitive Religion*, New York, Liveright, 1948.

MALINOWSKI, B., *The Dynamics of Culture Change*, ed. P. M. Kaberry, Yale U.P., 1945.

MAQUET, J. J., *Le système des relations sociales dans le Ruanda ancien*, Tervuren, 1954.

*The Premise of Inequality in Ruanda*, Oxford U.P., 1961.

MARWICK, M. G., *Sorcery in its Social Setting: a Study of the Northern Rhodesian Cewa*, Manchester U.P., 1965.

MBEE, G., ed. R. F. Gray, 'Letter from Mbugwe, Tanganyika', *Africa*, xxxv, 2, 1965.

MBEKI, G., *South Africa: The Peasants' Revolt*, Penguin, 1964.

MERLO, C. and VIDAUD, P., 'The Black Serpent Who Opened the Eyes of Man', in *Diogenes*, 55, 1966.

349

MEYEROWITZ, E. L. R., *The Akan of Ghana: Their Ancient Beliefs*, Faber, 1958.

MIDDLETON, J., *Lugbara Religion*, Oxford U.P., 1960.

With TAIT, D., ed., *Tribes Without Rulers: Studies in African Segmentary Systems*, Routledge, 1958.

With WINTER, E. H., ed., *Witchcraft and Sorcery in East Africa*, Routledge, 1963.

MURRAY, M. A., *The Witch-Cult in Western Europe*, Oxford U.P., (repr.) 1962.

NADEL, S. F., *A Black Byzantium*, Oxford U.P., 1942.

Witchcraft in Four African Societies: an Essay in Comparison', *American Anthropologist*, liv, 1952.

NIANE, D. T., 'Recherches sur l'Empire du Mali au Moyen Age', Inst. Nat. de Recherches, Conakry, 1962.

OGOT, B. A., 'British Administration in the Central Nyanza District of Kenya, 1900–60', *Jnl of Afr. Hist.*, iv, 2, 1963.

'Naturreligion und vorkoloniale Geschichte in Afrika', *Afrika Heute*, 1 July 1966.

*History of the Southern Luo:* vol. I, *Migration and Settlement 1500–1900*, East African Publishing House, Nairobi, 1967.

OJO, G. J. A., *Yoruba Culture*, University of London Press, 1966.

OLIVER, R. A., *The Missionary Factor in East Africa*, Longman, 1952.

PARRINDER, G., *Witchcraft*, Penguin, 1958.

*West African Religion*, Epworth Press, 1961.

PERISTIANY, J. G., *The Social Institutions of the Kipsigis*, Routledge, 1939.

RADCLIFFE-BROWN, A. R. and FORDE, D., ed., *African Systems of Kinship and Marriage*, Oxford U.P., 1950.

RANGER, T. O., *Revolt in South Rhodesia: A Study in African Resistance*, Heinemann Educational, 1967.

RAPONDA-WALKER, A. and SILLANS, R., *Rites et croyances des peuples du Gabon*, Présence Africaine, Paris, 1962.

RATTRAY, R. S., *Ashanti Proverbs*, Oxford U.P., 1916.

*Ashanti*, Oxford U.P., 1923.

*Religion and Art in Ashanti*, Oxford U.P., 1927.

RICHARDS, A. I., 'Social Mechanisms for the Transfer of Political rights in some African tribes', *Jnl Roy. Anthrop. Inst.*, xc, 2, 1960.

*East African Chiefs*, 1963.

ROBINSON, R., GALLAGHER, J. and DENNY, A., *Africa and the Victorians*, Macmillan, 1961.

ROSCOE, J., *The Northern Bantu*, London, 1915.

ROTBERG, R. L., *Christian Missionaries and the Creation of Northern Rhodesia 1800–1924*, Princeton U.P. and Oxford U.P., 1965.

*The Rise of Nationalism in Central Africa: The Making of Malawi and Zambia 1873–1964*, Oxford U.P., 1966.

RYDER, A. F. C., *Benin and the Europeans 1485–1897*, Longman, 1969.

SANGREE, W. H., *Age, Prayer and Politics in Tiriki, Kenya*, Oxford U.P., 1966.

SCHAPERA, I., *The Khoisan Peoples of South Africa*, Routledge, 1937.

SHAREVSKAYA, T. I., *Star'e i Nov'e Religii Tropicheskoi i Yuzhnoi Afriki*, Nauka, Moscow, 1964.

SHEPPERSON, G., 'Ethiopianism and African Nationalism', in *Phylon*, 1, 1953.

'The Politics of African Church Separatist Movements in British Central Africa, 1892–1916', *Africa*, xxiv, 1954.

'External factors in the development of African nationalism', in *Phylon*, no. 3 of 1961.

'Ethiopianism: Past and Present' in *Baëta*, 1968, p. 249.

SHEPPERSON, G., with PRICE, T., *Independent African: John Chilembwe and . . . the Nyasaland Native Rising of 1915*, Edinburgh U.P., 1958.

SMITH, E. W., ed., *African Ideas of God*, Edinburgh, 1950.

'African Symbolism', *Jnl Roy. Anthrop. Inst.*, lxxxii, 1, 1952.

SMITH, M. G., *Government in Zazzau*, Oxford U.P., 1960.

'History and Social Anthropology', *Jnl Roy. Anthrop. Inst.*, xcii, 1, 1962.

'The Beginnings of Hausa Society', in Vansina *et al.*, 1964.

'Historical and Cultural Conditions of Political Corruption among the Hausa', *Comparative Studies in Society and History*, iv, 2, 1964.

SPIEGLER, J. S., 'Aspects of Nationalist Thought among French-speaking West Africans, 1921–39', doctoral thesis, Oxford, 1968.

SUNDKLER, B. G. M., *Bantu Prophets in South Africa*, 2nd edn, Oxford U.P., 1961.

SURET-CANALE, J., *Afrique Noire occidentale et centrale: l'ère coloniale (1900–45)*, Éditions Sociales, 1964.

'La Fin de la chefferie en Guinée, *Jnl Afr. Hist.*, vii, 3, 1966.

TAIT, D., *The Konkomba of Northern Ghana*, Oxford U.P., 1961.

TEMPELS, P., *La Philosophie bantoue*, Présence Africaine, Paris, 1949.

THOMSON, G. D., *Studies in Ancient Greek Society:* vol. 2, *The First Philosophers*, Lawrence & Wishart, 1955; new edn, 1961.

TURNBULL, C. M., *The Forest People*, Chatto & Windus, 1961.

TURNER, V. W., *Schism and Continuity in an African Society: a Study of Ndembu Village Life*, Manchester U.P., 1957.

'Three Symbols of Passage in Ndembu Circumcision ritual', in Gluckman, 1962, p. 126.

'Ritual Symbolism, Morality and Social Structure among the Ndembu', in Fortes and Dieterlen, 1965, p. 79.

VAN VELSEN, J., *The Politics of Kinship: a Study in Social Manipulation among the Lakeside Tonga of Nyasaland*, Manchester U.P., 1964.

VANSINA, J., *De la Tradition orale*, Brussels, 1961: Eng. trans. *Oral Tradition*, Routledge, 1965.

*Kingdoms of the Savanna*, Wisconsin, 1966.

With MAUNY, R., and THOMAS, L. V., ed, *The Historian in Tropical Africa*, Oxford U.P., 1964.

VAN WARMELO, N. J., *Contributions towards Venda History, Religion and Tribal Ritual*, Dept of Native Affairs, Pretoria, 1960.

VAN WING, J., *Études Bakongo*, Brussels (repr.), 1959.

'La Situation actuelle des populations congolaises', *Bull. des Séances, Inst. Roy. Col. Belge*, 3, 1945.

VIEILLARD, G., 'Notes sur les Peuls du Fouta-Djallon', in *Bull. Inst. Fr. d'Afrique Noire*, ii, 12, January–April 1940.

VERHAEGEN, B., *Rébellions au Congo*, I, C.R.I.S.P., Brussels, 1966.

WEBSTER, J. B., BOAHEN, A. A. and IDOWU, H. O., *The Revolutionary Years. West Africa since 1800*, Longman, 1967.

WELBOURN, F. B., *East African Rebels*, S.C.M. Press, 1961.

WILKS, I., 'Ashanti Government', in Forde and Kaberry, 1967.

WILSON, M., *Reaction to Conquest*, Oxford U.P., 1936.

'Nyakusa Age-villages', *Jnl Roy. Anthrop. Inst.*, lxxxix, 1949.

*Good Company: Nyakyusa Age-Group Villages*, Oxford U.P., 1951.

WINTER, E. H., see Middleton and Winter.

WORSLEY, P., *The Trumpet Shall Sound: A Study of 'Cargo' Cults in Melanesia*, MacGibbon & Kee, 1957.

YOUNG, M. W., 'The Divine Kingship of the Jukun: a Re-evaluation of Some Theories', *Africa*, xxxvi, 2, 1966.

# Index

References to illustrations, maps, statistical tables and diagrams are in *italic* figures.

199, 216–29 *passim*, 230, 233
(*see also* oceanic *and* trans-
Saharan *below*); oceanic
(Atlantic and Indian Ocean),
97, 99, 100 *bis*, 102, 104, 208,
237–8; societies for, 100 (*see
also* Ekpe); trans-Saharan,
191, 208, 216, 218, 219, 220,
222; and the development of
kingdoms in Africa, 191; and
Islam, 216–29; commodities
of, 218; local or short-distance,
230, 233
transition from traditional to
modern political ideas and
institutions, 257–62;
resistance to, *see* resistance;
and continuity of
past beliefs, 261–2;
accommodation, 263, 276
treaties of protection, 268
trees, sacred, 119–20
Turay, Muhammad (ruler of
Songhay empire), 225
Tutsi, *12*, 118, 194, 209–13
*passim*
Tutu, Osei, 199 *bis*
Twa Pygmies, 209, 212

Uganda, 51, 58, 86, 133, 191,
192, 209
*ukwangela* (enjoyment of good
company), 91–2
Umar bin Said, al-Hajj, 247,
268, 269
Umar of Kete Krachi, al-Hajj
(poet and pedagogue), 269;
*quoted*, 269–70
Union of African States, how to
form a (?), 325
United Gold Coast Convention,
299
United States of America:
ethnology of citizens of, 49,
297; and Black Moslems,
287; influences in Africa, 287,
294

Universal Negro Improvement
Association, 294
Ununio tomb (near Dar es-
Salaam), *248*
urban economy (regulated and
monopolistic), 190–1
Uthman dan Fodio (Fulani
leader), 226, 239 *bis*

Venda, *12*, 72–3
venereal disease, 142, 162
village life in Africa,
disappearing but persisting,
306, 307, 313, 317
'vital force', *see* 'Life Force'

Warfare (*see also* guerrilla
warfare): discouraged by
Tallensi, 76; purposes of, and
justification for, 76; in
central-eastern Africa, 215;
for aggrandisement, 230, 231;
Yoruba, 237; *jihads* (holy
wars), 239; in southern Africa,
243; in south-eastern Africa,
244; for, and against,
slave-taking, 245; for survival,
245; *versus* Portuguese rule in
Africa today, 253
Watch Tower Bible and Tract
Society, 288
Watch Tower movement, 286–9,
290 *bis*, 294, 312
Watchman's Society, 289
'water-medicine', 279
water-people (spirits), Kalabari,
116, 169; mask of, *168*
West Africa, 67, 159, 218, 220,
295, 296, 298, 299 *bis*
'Will of God', 143 *bis*
'will of legality', 143
wisdom (knowledge): the World's
collected by Ananse, 15; about
Africa's past, 15–16
witchcraft (and sorcery) in Africa
(*see also* anti-witchcraft), 16,
67, 73, 92, 102, 122–5 *passim*,

## More About Penguins
## and Pelicans

*Penguinews*, which appears every month, contains
details of all the new books issued by Penguins as
they are published. From time to time it is
supplemented by *Penguins in Print*, which is a
complete list of all available books published by
Penguins. (There are well over four thousand of
these.)

A specimen copy of *Penguinews* will be sent to you
free on request. For a year's issues (including the
complete lists) please send 30p if you live in the
United Kingdom, or 60p if you live elsewhere.
Just write to Dept EP, Penguin Books Ltd,
Harmondsworth, Middlesex, enclosing a cheque or
postal order, and your name will be added to the
mailing list.

Note: *Penguinews* and *Penguins in Print* are not
available in the U.S.A. or Canada

*Also by Basil Davidson in the Penguin African Library*

# Which Way Africa?

*The Search for a New Society*

### Revised Edition

A man would have to be very brave or very foolhardy to try to forecast precisely the pattern of Africa's future. Where events outrun the printing-presses, discretion is the better part of omniscience.

In *Which Way Africa?* Basil Davidson, the well-known writer on African affairs, has steered clear of political ju-ju. Instead – and infinitely more to the purpose – he has made what is the only up-to-date and comprehensive analysis in English – and probably in any language – of the social, economic, and political motives, myths, ideas, and beliefs which underlie modern African nationalism.

Events in almost every corner of the continent have shown the world an Africa poised on the threshold of new ventures, an Africa in flux. Only such an analysis as the author has successfully achieved in this volume can help to delineate the kind of societies which will now tend to emerge there.

### Also Available

THE LIBERATION OF GUINÉ
Aspects of an African Revolution